Books by MAURICE SAMUEL

THE SECOND CRUCIFIXION
(1960)

THE PROFESSOR AND THE FOSSIL
(1956)

CERTAIN PEOPLE OF THE BOOK
(1955)

LEVEL SUNLIGHT
(1953)

THE DEVIL THAT FAILED
(1952)

THE GENTLEMAN AND THE JEW
(1950)

PRINCE OF THE GHETTO
(1948)

WEB OF LUCIFER
(1947)

HARVEST IN THE DESERT
(1944, 1945)

THE WORLD OF SHOLOM ALEICHEM
(1943)

The World of Sholom Aleichem

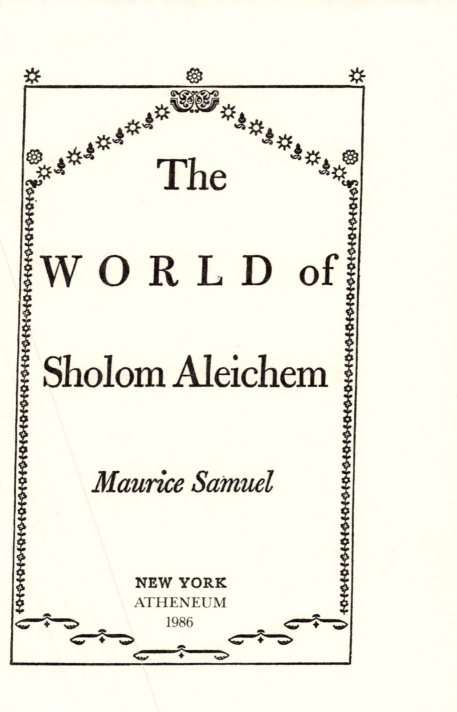

The

W O R L D of

Sholom Aleichem

Maurice Samuel

NEW YORK
ATHENEUM
1986

Library of Congress Cataloging-in-Publication Data
Samuel, Maurice, 1895-1972.
The world of Sholom Aleichem.
1. Sholom Aleichem, 1859-1916. 2. Authors, Yiddish—
Biography. 3. Jews—Ukraine—Social life and customs.
I. Title
PJ5129.R2Z8   1986   839′.098309   [B]   86-47697
ISBN 0-689-70709-6 (pbk.)

Published simultaneously in Canada by Collier Macmillan Canada, Inc.
Manufactured by Fairfield Graphics, Fairfield, Pennsylvania
First Atheneum Paperback Edition

v

Contents

CHAPTER I

Of Certain Grandfathers

❊

THIS book is a sort of pilgrimage among the cities and inhabitants of a world which only yesterday — as history goes — harboured the grandfathers and grandmothers of some millions of American citizens. As a pilgrimage it is an act of piety; on the other hand it is an exercise in necromancy, or calling up of the dead, which was the sin of Saul. For that world is no more. The fiery harrows of two world wars have passed closely across its soil within the lifetime of a generation; and in between it was a participant in one of the world's great revolutions. Fragments of it remain *in situ;* other fragments, still recognizable but slowly losing their shape in the wastage of time, are lodged in America. From these fragments alone, were there no records in memory or writing, we should be as hard put to it to reconstruct the warm, breathing original creation as to recapture the proto-Indo-European language from the syllables embedded in a score of modern languages.

The world of Sholom Aleichem is mostly — not wholly — the internal world of Russian Jewry forty, fifty, sixty, and seventy years ago. It is — again mostly — the world of the Jewish Pale of Settlement, with special emphasis on a section south and west and east of Kiev. Hereabouts Jews had lived their separate life from very ancient times. There were synagogues in the Crimea long before there were churches, and Jewish pedlars long before there were pogroms. Hereabouts, too, there was once — eleven and twelve centuries ago — a Jewish kingdom of converted Tatars. Kiev boasted its first pogrom in the twelfth century; we have the names of rabbis of that period; and we know that Jews of that period went west for their education. But the world of Sholom Aleichem had no connection except by collateral descent with the original communities of southeastern Russia. Khazar kings and Hebrew merchants were absorbed by masses of Jewish immigrants who came eastward under the pressure of the Crusades, bringing with them the language which developed into Yiddish, and a way of life which retained its identity for a score of generations.

In the innocent childhood of our century the Russian-Jewish Pale of Settlement was the disgrace of Western humanity, the last word in reaction and brutality. We have travelled far since then. Just as our world wars may look back on the piddling squabbles of our first decade — our Boer wars, our Russo-Japanese and Balkan wars — and ask contemptuously: " Do you call *that* a war? " so Hitlerian anti-Semitism can look back on the discomfort of Jews under the Romanovs and ask: " Do you call that persecution and oppression? " Perhaps the Jews of a generation or two ago owe history an apology for having set up such a clamour about the occasional slaughters — they never amounted to more than a few hundred men, women, and children at a time — the wholesale robberies, the expulsions, discriminations, and humiliations. It was a principle of Russian law that everything was for-

4

bidden to Jews unless specifically permitted. But by an oversight which Germany has since corrected, the right to remain alive was not challenged. Within the vast semi-ghetto which was the Pale and outside of which the Jews could not settle, Jewish life grew and unfolded. Russia acquired her Jews reluctantly, through the partitions of Poland; having acquired them, she fastened them down where they were, deprived them of land, instituted for them, in the high schools and universities, the *numerus clausus* or system of educational rationing, and did her best generally to discourage in them the appetite for life. But Russia lacked — as we shall see in the course of the pilgrimage — the high ideal of wickedness. Perhaps, then, the clamour of the Jews was justified only as a warning to the world. They managed to survive and even to flourish; but the world which failed to understand the possibilities behind the persecutions was to pay a heavy price for its callousness or sloth.

They managed to survive and even to flourish. But their prosperity was spiritual rather than material. They maintained a remarkable civilization, with values which the world cannot spare. Simply as a demonstration of character in adversity, that civilization should not be forgotten. If it was inevitable that the good perish with the bad, we must perhaps shrug our shoulders and repeat the Occidental equivalent of the Arab's " Kismet " — " That's history." But it is not inevitable or desirable that the memory of that world should wholly perish.

One man became the mirror of Russian Jewry. His name was Sholom Rabinovitch, and he adopted the pen-name " Sholom Aleichem," the common daily greeting of Jews, which originally meant " Peace be unto you," but which usage has whittled down to something like " How

5

do you do? " We shall get glimpses of him throughout this book, for he is, in himself, part of the object of our pilgrimage. He was a part of Russian Jewry; he was Russian Jewry itself. It is hard to think of him as a " writer." He was the common people in utterance. He was in a way the " anonymous " of Jewish self-expression, achieving the stature of a legendary figure even in his own lifetime.

Many other writers have left us records of Russian-Jewish life, and some of them compare well with the best-known in the Western world. None of them had this natural gift for complete self-identification with a people which makes Sholom Aleichem unique. He wrote no great panoramic novels in the manner of a Balzac or a Tolstoy. He did not set out with the conscious and self-conscious purpose of " putting it down for posterity." He wrote because of a simple communicative impulse, as men chat in a tavern or in a waiting crowd with their like. He never tried his hand at solemn passages and mighty themes, any more than people do in a casual, friendly conversation. But his language had an incomparable authenticity, and his humour — he is the greatest of Jewish humorists, and in the world's front rank — was that of a folk, not of an individual.

Thus it comes about that the phrase " the world of Sholom Aleichem " has two meanings in one. It is the world in which Sholom Aleichem lived, with which he suffered and laughed, himself its focus or miniature. It is also the world which appears in his books. We pass without a break from his descriptions, his men, women, children, cities, and townlets, to historic Russian Jewry, as we might reconstruct it (though not so well) from other sources. We pass back again, fusing external and internal material in a natural whole. We could write a

Middletown of the Russian-Jewish Pale basing ourselves solely on the novels and stories and sketches of Sholom Aleichem, and it would be as reliable a scientific document as any " factual " study; more so, indeed, for we should get, in addition to the material of a straightforward social inquiry, the intangible spirit which informs the material and gives it its living significance.

Sholom Aleichem is almost unknown to millions of Americans whose grandfathers made up his world. This is not simply a literary loss; it is a break — a very recent and disastrous one — in the continuity of a group history. Jews who get a certain spiritual tonic from the reflection that they are somehow related to the creators of the Bible and of its ethical values forget that the relationship was passed on to them by the men who begot their fathers. Who were these men? Under what circumstances did they nurture the relationship for transmission? What tone and colour had their lives? What purpose did they conceive themselves to be serving in their obstinate fidelity to the relationship? What hopes had they for themselves — and for their grandchildren?

Are these questions irrelevant, or perhaps even improper, in a world which is in the throes of a tremendous transformation and must keep its eyes on the future? Not if they are put in the right spirit — one of human curiosity, of affection, and, if you like, of decency. We might even add, of modesty. It is not a wholesome thing to believe that we and our posterity will find all the answers; for some of them were discovered in the very imperfect past. The study of history will never become obsolete, and a knowledge of one's grandfathers is an excellent introduction to history. Especially these grandfathers; they were a remarkable lot.

CHAPTER II

Man in a Forest

❈

A CLUMSY wagon drawn by a dispirited nag crawls along the narrow path which leads through the forest from the city of Boiberik to the village of Anatevka. The man on the driver's seat, a little, bearded Jew in a ragged capote, keeps his eyes half closed, for he has no inclination to look on the beauties of nature. His stomach is empty, his heart is in his tattered boots. All day long, from summer dawn to summer dusk, he has been loading and unloading logs of wood, carting them from the edge of the forest to the railroad station of Boiberik. He started out without breakfast, did without lunch, and has yet to have his supper. It will not be much of a supper. The rouble a day he earns — when he earns it — will not buy a day's food for ten stomachs, one of them a horse's, even though nothing is deducted to clothe nine bodies — his own, his wife's, and those of his seven daughters. Seven of them, and not a single son; seven hungry daughters and a hungry wife, waiting for him and his rouble at the other end of the path. Little wonder if, for all his hunger, he shows no haste as he sits up there driving homeward.

Driving? That is hardly the word. He has not the

strength to drive, and it is all the horse can do to keep the ramshackle wagon crawling along, while the shadows of the trees grow longer and longer until they seem to become, as the man mutters to himself, " as long as the Jewish exile."

The forest is silent; no leaf rustles, no bird sings. Nothing is heard except the creaking of the cart, the dull klop-klop of the horse's hoofs and, occasionally, the mutter of the man's voice when his disconsolate meditations become audible. Now and again he does indeed make a driver's gestures; he lifts up the whip and brings it down again, but it is done listlessly and without conviction. What sense is there in lashing the animal? He expostulates with it instead, or, rather, explains the situation, for he is the kind of man who, however bitter his heart and however empty his stomach, does not lose sight of the larger aspect of things.

" Pull, miserable monster! " he mutters. " Drag, wretched beast in the likeness of a horse! You're no better than I am! If it's your destiny to be Tevyeh's horse, then suffer like Tevyeh, and learn like Tevyeh and his family to die of hunger seven times in the day and then go to bed supperless. Is it not written in the Holy Book that the same fate shall befall man and beast? "

Then the man Tevyeh bethinks himself and takes back his argument. " No! " he says. " It is not true. Here I am at least talking, while you are dumb and cannot ease your pain with words. My case is better than yours. For I am human, and a Jew, and I know what you do not know. I know that we have a great and good God in heaven, who governs the world in wisdom and mercy and loving-kindness, feeding the hungry and raising the fallen and showing grace to all living things. I can talk my heart out to Him, while your jaws are locked, poor thing. True, a wise word is no substitute for a piece of herring or a bag of oats; and if words could fill stomachs my old woman, God bless her, would be supporting all of us, and half the world besides. ' Children he wants me to bear,' she says, ' seven of them, no less. What shall I do with them? Throw them into the river? Breadwinner! Tevyeh of the golden hands! Answer me! ' She said it yesterday, and the day before, and the day before that, and she'll say it tonight. Sweet homecoming! What shall I answer? Nothing. For she is a woman, and the Holy Books are closed to her, the sayings of the sages are beyond her. Her wisdom, alas, is of another kind: an expert without equal at handing out a dinner of curses and a supper of slaps. What else should she have learned, being the wife of Tevyeh? "

The shadows of the trees are beginning to merge into one vast dimness. The sadness deepens in Tevyeh's heart, and all kinds of unbidden thoughts rise up in him — not the rational thoughts of a thinking man, but primitive ideas and imaginings. He sees the faces of friends and relatives long dead peering out at him from the rising wall of darkness. He remembers doleful stories of untimely deaths, of murder and robbery, of demons which haunt the forest in unimaginable likenesses, dragons, serpents with tongues a mile long, many-headed monsters.

" As the Holy Book says," he mutters, " man is dust, and his foundations are of the dust; which, rightly interpreted, means that man is as weak as a fly and stronger than steel. Thou hast made us a little lower than the angels. It depends what you call a little, doesn't it? Lord, what is life, and what are we, and to what may a man be

likened? A man may be likened unto a carpenter; for a
carpenter lives, and lives, and lives, and finally dies. And
so does a man."

So, against the rising tide of despair, Tevyeh tries to
spin the thread of rational discourse. But he feels the waters engulfing him, and he knows it will not do. Despair
is a sin and a blasphemy, despair is unbecoming to a man
and a Jew. He will not give way. He will address himself
to the Throne of Grace, he will have it out with the Almighty, with the One who lives for ever. And suddenly
Tevyeh realizes that the hour for *Minchah* — afternoon
prayer — is almost gone. Ah, that explains it! He pulls
up, steps down from the cart, and, holding the reins, begins to pray. And he prays in a manner all his own. He
repeats by heart the prescribed prayers, word for word,
from beginning to end, exactly as they are set down in
the book; but while his tongue follows the ritual, his
mind accompanies it with interpolations and interpretations and commentaries which have never been heard
before.

" Blessed are they that dwell in Thy house (Right! I
take it, O Lord, that Thy house is somewhat more spa-
cious than my hovel!) . . . . I will extol Thee, my God,
O King (what good would it do me if I didn't?) . . . .
Every day I will bless Thee (on an empty stomach, too) .
. . . The Lord is good to all (and suppose He forgets
somebody now and again, good Lord, hasn't He enough
on His mind?) . . . . The Lord upholdeth all that fall,
and raiseth up all that are bowed down (Father in
heaven, loving Father, surely it's my turn now, I can't
fall any lower) . . . . Thou openest Thy hand and sat-
isfiest every living thing (so You do, Father in heaven,
You give with an open hand; one gets a box on the ear,

and another a roast chicken, and neither my wife nor I
nor my daughters have even smelt a roast chicken since
the days of creation). . . . He will fulfil the desire of
them that fear Him; He will also hear their cry and will
save them."

Having thus reached the end of the *Ashre,* the first
part of the afternoon prayer, Tevyeh turns his face away
from the setting sun and looks eastward into the darkness, in the direction of the Holy Land, taking up his
station for the Prayer of the Eighteen Benedictions,
which must be repeated in complete immobility. But
scarcely has he begun with " God of Abraham, God of
Isaac, God of Jacob " when a demon takes hold of his
horse; for without warning, without visible or compre-
hensible cause, the exhausted creature breaks into a wild
and idiotic gallop, and Tevyeh, clinging to the reins,
pants after it, sobbing breathlessly:

" Thou feedest all things in mercy, and keepest faith
with the sleepers in the dust. (Stop! Indecent creature!
Let a Jew say his prayers, will you? If ever there was a
sleeper in the dust, O Father, it's me, Tevyeh, the father
of seven. Did I say dust? In the mud, O Lord, in the filth
of life! A thousand million curses in your bones,
wretched animal! Couldn't you find a more fitting moment for displaying your talents? Lord of the world!
Those others, the rich Jews of Boiberik, who do not
have to lug wood to the railroad station for a rouble a
day, but live on the fat of the land in their country cottages, *they* know Your grace and kindness. Father in
heaven, why not I? Am I not a Jew, too? Where is justice,
I ask, where is fairness?) . . . Look Thou upon our poverty (no one else cares to look upon it — stop!) . . . .
Send us a healing, O Lord, for our sickness (we managed

12

to get the sickness without Your help, thank You) . . . .
Have mercy upon us and be compassionate unto us (that
means me and my wife and my hungry children — and
may this horse be carried off by a black year!) . . . . And
may it be Thy will that we be restored (yes, that we, all
Thy children, the children of Israel, return once more
to the Holy Land, and rebuild Thy temple, and offer
Thee sacrifice, to the singing of the priests and the Levites as in the days of yore) . . . ."

At this point, as suddenly and as imbecilically as it had
set off on its wild gallop, the horse comes to a dead stop,
and Tevyeh finishes his prayer standing still and facing
east, the sweat pouring down his face and beard.

CHAPTER III

Tevyeh the Dairyman

❀

THIS is Tevyeh the dairyman you have just met —
and why dairyman you shall learn in the sequel — Tevyeh, the best-known and best-loved figure in the world
of Sholom Aleichem. A little Jew wandering in a big,
dark forest, symbol of a little people wandering in the
big, dark jungle of history. For the moment he is only
Tevyeh the drayman, the wage-slave; the God in whom
he believes with all his heart, whom he loves and prays
to at least three times daily, whom he addresses intimately with affection, irony, sympathy, reverence, impudence, and indestructible hope, the Omnipotent One
who sits on high while we grovel here below, has not yet
wrought with his child Tevyeh the great miracle concerning which you shall learn in the proper place. We
meet Tevyeh for the first time while he is still the Jewish
Man with the Hoe, bowed (who deeper?) with the
weight of centuries; the burden of the world is on his
back, but — here is the supreme difference — the emptiness of ages is not in his face.

It must be repeated, because it is the key to our understanding of Tevyeh: the emptiness of ages is not in his
face. We must approach him with caution, curiosity, and

liking, but not with the impulse to classify. He is not to be disposed of so simply. If he were just Markham's brother to the ox, you could write heroically about him and make him the springboard for a grand, revolutionary utterance. But Tevyeh will not let you strike an attitude in his behalf; he is not docile material for your fits of cosmic righteousness. Should you begin to orate at him he will listen, despite an empty stomach, with the closest attention, and just when you think you are at your irresistible best he will interrupt you with a disastrous misquotation from the Holy Books; he will disconcert you with the suggestion that he cannot be patronized on that high level. You want to remake the world? By all means! Let's sit down and talk it over. You would remove oppression, injustice, want, and persecution from among mankind? The idea is not at all bad. But first of all I should like to know who you are, and I should also like you to know who I am.

In short, Tevyeh is the indestructible individualist, and this is not to be misinterpreted as anarchist. He is, in a baffling way, a blend of individualist and traditionalist. Yet he is also something of the revolutionist; and, indeed, it is more revolutionary to believe in God and take Him to task sensibly than not to believe in Him and denounce Him in unmeasured language. Here too, however, Tevyeh is in the tradition. The orthodox Jewry of which he is a part is not unacquainted with protests directed at the Lord of the Universe for His mismanagement of human affairs. There was, for instance, the Saint of Shpolle, "the grandfather," who once summoned God to a regular trial. Yes, he of Shpolle appointed nine other judges and, himself acting as the tenth, cited the Eternal to appear before them. Or, rather, since God is everywhere, the judges simply entered into session and took the presence of the Defendant for granted. Three days, behind closed doors, the Court of Ten prayed and fasted and consulted the records, the Torah, the Books of the Sages, and the Responses. And then, not hastily, not in the heat of argument, they issued their verdict, which was against the Defendant. They pronounced Him guilty on two counts: first, that He had created the spirit of evil and had let it loose among the Jews; second, that He had failed in His manifest duty to provide adequate sustenance for Jewish women and children.

Not that it seems to have done much good, Tevyeh is ready to admit. Still, you can't dismiss it as a trifle. Such great and learned rabbis cannot have been wasting their time. And, in any case, you simply cannot leave God out of the reckoning. You cannot ignore His Torah and the long line of the generations which have died to keep it alive. So, whatever you propose to do for Tevyeh and the world, kindly remember that he is an orthodox Jew, and no rearrangement of the universe is acceptable or even thinkable which will not leave room for his religious practices.

For instance every morning, at sunrise or shortly before, Tevyeh has to say his long morning prayers, the *Shachris,* and he has to say them, on week-days, with the prayer-shawl over his head, and the phylacteries on brow and arm. It's no good arguing with Tevyeh on this point. It is worse than useless to talk to him of superstition, mummery, and the opiate of the masses. He will have only one answer, delivered in a Talmudic singsong: " If all the persecutions of the ages, and all the bitternesses of exploitation, could not prevent me from repeating the prayers of my fathers, shall I be made to fall away from

16

them in a world of freedom? " But the *Shachris* is only a beginning. During the day Tevyeh must take time out — and he does it, as we have seen, under the most discouraging circumstances — for certain other prayers. Do what you like with Tevyeh, chain him to a galley, yoke him to a chariot, starve him, break him, he is going to say his three prayers daily. And when the Sabbath comes, he will not work. You must make up your mind that Tevyeh the coolie, or Tevyeh the dairyman, simply will not work on the Sabbath, from sundown on Friday to sundown on Saturday. No labour-leader in the world has ever been so insistent on the forty-eight- or forty-hour week as Tevyeh on his six-day week. The Sabbath is the Lord's day; that is, it is Tevyeh's day for rest in the Lord. He will not work on that day, he will not carry money about, he will not touch fire or tear paper or do anything that savours of the slavery of the body. He will not work, either, on the two days of the New Year, or on the Day of Atonement, or any other of the festivals. You will neither bribe, bully, nor persuade him into such transgression. For the Sabbath and the festivals are all that are left to him; they are the last citadel of his freedom. On those days he will pray, meditate, and refresh his spirit with a little learning. He may be hungry; he will contrive to rise above it. He may not know where the next day's food will come from, either; he will contrive to forget that, too.

There never was such obstinacy! It must not be thought, either, that Tevyeh, crushed under the double burden of the Jewish exile and the worker's slavery, clings to these practices merely as a grim protest. Not by any means. He enjoys them, thoroughly. He loves the Sabbath and the festivals. He loves prayer. And when

17

the Passover comes around, he rejoices in the liberation from Egypt exactly as if he himself had just marched out of bondage. On Purim he is gleeful over the downfall of Haman, and on the Day of the Rejoicing of the Law he is ecstatic over the gift from Sinai.

Where does Tevyeh belong, and why is he so beloved of the Jewish masses — that is, of the Yiddish-speaking proletariat? We shall perhaps find the answer later on, when we encounter him again. At this point we can say that Tevyeh was not proletariate, not even in the days when he sweated hungrily from morning till night lugging the felled tree-trunks from the forest to the railroad station. Nor was he middle-class, not even after the miracle, when God had raised him from the dunghill and transformed him into Tevyeh the dairyman. He is always just a Jew making a living, and he is proletarian in the sense that he believes in only one way of making a living — namely, by the labour of one's hands. As Tevyeh the dairyman he worked, and the family worked with him. Wife and daughters milked the cows and goats, churned the butter and pressed the cheese; Tevyeh was the deliveryman, travelling back and forth through the forest between his cottage near Anatevka and the rich summer homes of Boiberik.

Just the same, Tevyeh is something of a businessman too; and at once we must set against this the fact that the ways of the business world are not in him. The idea of making money by the handling of money, or by the mere manipulation of words and documents, is alien to him. In this he is at the opposite extreme from his distant relative Menachem Mendel, who is perhaps the second most famous figure in Sholom Aleichem's world. Menachem Mendel is the *Luftmensch*, the manipulator, the *schlimihl* of the exchange, the wild man from whose dreams of sudden riches and pyramided finances God guard all of us. And to clear Tevyeh completely, we must add at once that Menachem Mendel is not even his relative. He is related to Goldie, Tevyeh's wife, being a second or third cousin three or four times removed.

Only once did Tevyeh let himself be tempted into Menachem Mendel's insane world, when he took out all his savings, every bit of one hundred roubles, and gave them to Menachem Mendel to turn into a fortune. He lost them, of course, for Menachem Mendels do not make money, either for themselves or for others. " Serves me right! " was what Tevyeh said, and spat out three times. " Is it money you want, Tevyeh? Then sweat for it, break your back, tear your guts out, plough the sands with your nose — but don't expect anything for nothing."

In talking of Tevyeh we must avoid at all cost the highfalutin; still it must be said that he represents, fundamentally, the inextinguishable spirit in man. Created for laughter by the greatest of Jewish humorists, he turns out to be, on more careful scrutiny, a type of aristocrat. He is a descendant of martyrs and scholars; and whatever happens to him, the marks of his lineage are ineradicable. He cannot abide ignorance and grossness in human beings. He will not even admit that poverty and oppression are adequate excuses for utter want of spiritual interest; and certainly he will not accept the blanket exoneration: " What can you expect of a man under such a system? " System or no system, a human being must retain some residue of uncorrupted spirit, or forfeit Tevyeh's respect.

This much is implied for Tevyeh in being a Jew, for he thinks of himself as an ordinary, everyday Jew. He

would laugh heartily if someone called him an intellectual or a scholar. He cannot interpret the intricacies of
the Talmud or the mysticisms of the Kabbalah. But he
is at home in the Bible, and in Rashi's great commentary
on it. On Friday evenings and Saturday afternoons he
will not fail to read through the week's portion of the
Pentateuch, translating it into the vernacular. In leisure
moments he will dip into the Mishnah, or into the Ethics of the Fathers, where it is written: " Say not: ' I will
study when I have the time,' for then you will never have
the time." Such things Tevyeh considers the minimum
requirements of the simple Jew; these, and decency, and
faith in God, and a drop of brandy on occasion.

We shall see that the chronicle of Tevyeh's life is, except for the miracle near the beginning, one of uniform
calamity. Yet it is read for laughter by tender-hearted
people. Not what happens to Tevyeh is funny, but how
he takes it. We might call him Tevyeh the unextinguish-
able. We might add, rather helplessly, that sometimes he
puts us in mind of a Job with a sense of humour and
without the happy ending, and sometimes of Charlie
Chaplin.

CHAPTER IV

The Townlet of the Tiny Folk

❀

I̲N one sense Tevyeh the dairyman stands at the centre
of Sholom Aleichem's world as its best-known and best-
loved inhabitant; in another sense he is a peripheral figure, not being a townsman, and belonging in time to a
transitional generation. For there are two ways of using
this phrase, " the world of Sholom Aleichem." We may
take it to mean the entirety of the record, the whole living and changing canvas in its passage through forty
years; or we may restrict it to that which is most typically
and intimately Sholom Aleichem.

If we choose to blend both meanings, we must think of
Sholom Aleichem's world as a series of irregular concen-
tric circles. The inmost circle consists of that part of Russian Jewry — more specifically White Russian Jewry —
which had retained most consistently the ancient ways
and forms of life. The language of this inmost circle was
Yiddish, which is often, and quite misleadingly, described as an offshoot of Middle High German with an
admixture of Hebrew and Slavic. Etymologically nine
tenths of the words commonly used in Yiddish are in
fact of German origin, but the tone and spirit of the language are as remote from German as the poetry of Burns

is from the prose of Milton. The Jews of Kasrielevky and Kozodoievka and Teplitz and Mazeppavka, in Sholom Aleichem's typical time-period — seventy or eighty years ago — also had a smattering of Russian — enough, that is, to do business with the peasants. Anyone among them with a sound reading and writing knowledge of Russian was a suspicious character; he was on the road to assimilation, to shortening of the beard and gaberdine, removal of the earlocks, consumption of forbidden meats, and the final horror of apostasy.

In the next ring there is a certain degree of modernization and Russification. It lies under the sign of the Haskalah, the Jewish Renaissance of the nineteenth century, which operated in Hebrew, but revived this ancient language for secular purposes repugnant to the denizens of the inmost circle. The study of Hebrew in any but a religious connection was therefore of a piece with the shortening of the gaberdine. Actually the first protagonists of the Haskalah were intensely Jewish; many of them were even completely orthodox; they said their prayers, donned the prayer-shawl and phylacteries, fasted on the Day of Atonement and the Ninth of Ab, blessed the new moon, and even emptied their pockets once a year into flowing waters as a sign that they were emptying themselves of their sins. As to those festivals which had a nationalist tinge, like the Passover, or Channukah, they created a new enthusiasm of observance rooted in their hope of a new era for Jewry. But the Haskalah did lead to secular knowledge, Russian high schools and universities, political movements, and other shifts of interest and emphasis.

The outer fringe of the Haskalah therefore merged with the third ring, which Jews often reached direct,

without the intervention of modernized Hebrew. There you might hear the words " superstition," " mouldy old ways," " greasy pietism," applied to the sanctities of the inmost circle. The denizens of the third, and fourth, and fifth rings — the divisions may be multiplied indefinitely — clipped their beards or even shaved them off, discarded even the abbreviated gaberdine for the short coat of the gentile, did not bless the Creator of the universe every time they drank a glass of water or answered the call of nature, and, passing through these stages to forgetfulness of the Day of Atonement, finally passed out of Jewish life altogether either by way of baptism or the revolutionary movement. There were still others, of course, who were not so purposive and who merely became fed up with being Jewish, a condition which the Jews of the inmost circle regarded as a kind of pathological sinfulness, as if a man were to say that he was fed up with breathing.

These irregular circles were in flux, too. We must not think of Jews passing systematically through successive peripheries, generation by generation. At the close of the nineteenth century the son of a Jew in the dwindling inmost circle — which still, however, occupied a larger area than any of the rings — would reach the outermost limits at a single bound. Nor must we think of the process of dissolution in ideological terms only. The world, the flesh, and the devil crept toward the citadel: card-playing, stock-exchange gambling, State lotteries, the fever of careerism, the lure of the big cities — of all these Sholom Aleichem takes account, and he has much to tell us about Odessa and Kiev, and of the queer Jewish types, or rather types of Jews, which appeared in them. But it is in the little places, the Jewish townlets and villages which were the strongholds of the old Jewish ways, the isolated, mediæval, Yiddish-speaking communities, that his heart remains; this is, in the restricted sense, Sholom Aleichem's world.

Kasrielevky, " the townlet of the tiny folk," is the core of that world: Kasrielevky, the place of his childhood, which appears in the geography books as Voronov, in deepest Poltava. He had a special reason for renaming Voronov Kasrielevky, though he does not tell us why he calls Kiev Yehupetz. Kasrielevky comes from the word *Kasriel* — and before we translate *Kasriel* into English, something must be said about Sholom Aleichem and poverty.

It would not be wrong to add to Sholom Aleichem's other titles that of the troubadour of the poor. He had an extraordinary love of poor people, and thought them the most marvellous of human beings. Poverty was not in his eyes — as it was not in the eyes of his " poor " — just the miserable absence of possession. It was that too, of course; but it was primarily a great calling, an art and a career. It had an extraordinary range of nuances — a pauper, a beggarly pauper, a pauper on seven levels, a church-mouse — beg pardon, synagogue-mouse — of a pauper, a crawling pauper, a howling pauper, a whale of a pauper, a cosmic pauper. These are not literal translations of Sholom Aleichem's classifications of pauperdom; they are merely intended to convey the exuberant lyricism to which the subject moved him. There is something impish in his love of the poor, something defiant, too; it was as if he were telling the rich: " You think the world is yours because you have the money. *I'll* show what we can do with poverty."

A special type of pauper, set apart but occurring on

every level, is the Kasriel, the jolly pauper. We might be tempted to call him the Jewish " Paddy-without-a-shirt," were it not that in many respects the Kasriel is very different indeed from the Gaelic sleeper under the hedges. To begin with, the Kasriel is anything but a *cheminot* or a bohemian, and he does not even pretend to despise riches. Second, his gaiety is not instinctive, but reflective, and has more than a touch of the sardonic. " God hates a poor man," says Sholom Aleichem. " The proof is that if He didn't, He wouldn't make him poor." Third, what makes poverty an art, a calling, and a career is the refusal to be thrust out of the world. Paddy-without-a-shirt cannot really be called poor, any more than the birds can be called poor. But the Kasriel, the true Kasriel of Kasrielevky, meets his poverty like a man and a hero. In his religious code, the Kasriel is a martinet; the rich man will not outdo him in piety. The Kasriel is a home body, deeply attached to his faithful and fecund wife. He is concerned with the education of his sons and the marrying off of his daughters. He obeys scrupulously all the six hundred and thirteen regulations of the Jewish code, carries the ritual fringes next to his body, kisses the *mezuzzah* on the lintel every time he leaves or enters the house, chants a loud Amen in the synagogue from his standing-place near the door, and defies the rich man to have a larger portion in God. To do all these things on any of the levels of pauperdom above classified, and to remain uncrushed and unabashed, calls for spirit, ingenuity, and a special sense of humour; the Kasriel has them.

Kasrielevky, then, is the town of the Kasriels. To be sure, it does not belong to them, but they make it what it is, and in that all-important sense it is theirs. Kasrielevky is also Kozodoievka and Bohopolie and Bohslav and any one of a hundred Jewish or half-Jewish centres in old White Russia. The town itself is a jumble of wooden houses clustering higgledy-piggledy about a market-place at the foot of a hill. All around is the spaciousness of mighty Russia, but Kasrielevky is as crowded as a slum, is in fact a slum. The congestion is not produced by external pressure alone; there is internal shrinkage, too. What are they shrinking from? Perhaps the loneliness and formlessness of space, perhaps the world of the uncircumcised, perhaps the brutalizing influence of untamed nature. They fear the bucolic. They fear, instinctively, to become the Man with the Hoe, not because they live any better than he, but because his jaw hangs down. *Their* jaws are in perpetual motion, though seldom for purposes of mastication. They are the greatest talkers in the world; and for a neat epigram, an apt Biblical quotation, an ingenious piece of commentary, a caustic phrase, or a good story they are ready to pawn their ragged capotes.

The streets of Kasrielevky — let us be courteous and call them that — are as tortuous as a Talmudic argument. They are bent into question marks and folded into parentheses. They turn back upon themselves absentmindedly, they interrupt themselves as if to admit an anecdote. They run into culs-de-sac like a theory arrested by a fact; they ooze off into lanes, alleys, back yards, like a thesis dribbling into an anticlimax. Sewerage and paving are as unknown in Kasrielevky as the steam train. Of course the Kasrielevkites — and not all of them are Kasriels — have heard of sewerage and paving and trains and are in part disposed to believe in their existence while remaining sceptical as to their value. One must say in part, because they cannot deny that in Yehupetz there are houses and streets of stone; the business of the train, however, is another matter. A Kasrielevkite merchant — obviously not a Kasriel — once had occasion to visit Moscow. Returning, he reported that he had ridden in a train for three quarters of an hour. Asked to explain the contraption, he sat down with pencil and paper and produced a diagram. There was the wagon in front snorting fire and smoke; there were the wagons behind, obediently following it on the rails. No sign of a horse, inside or outside. He swore by all that is sacred to a Jew that there was nothing more to it. What was one to make of that? On the one hand, why should a respectable householder and merchant imperil his immortal soul with uncalled-for oaths about non-existent things? On the other hand, were the Kasrielevkites ignorant peasants, to be taken in by a traveller's fables? There was only one sensible way out of the impasse. The Kasrielevkites believed every word the traveller uttered, but still refused to believe in trains.

At the heart of the dense labyrinth of Kasrielevky is the market-place, with its shops, booths, tables, stands, butchers' blocks. Hither come daily, except during the winter, the peasants and peasant women from many miles around, bringing their live-stock and vegetables, their fish and hides, their wagonloads of grain, melons, parsley, radishes, and garlic. They buy, in exchange, the city produce which the Jews import, dry goods, hats, shoes, boots, lamps, oil, spades, mattocks, and shirts. The tumult of the market-place of Kasrielevky is one of the wonders of the world. Paris, say the Kasrielevkites, is a dog by comparison. For besides the lusty haggling in Russian-Yiddish and Yiddish-Russian, there is the bleating of goats, the braying of donkeys, the neighing of horses, the clucking of hens, and on top of it all, persistent and piercing, the chorus of children's voices from the *cheders,* the one-room Hebrew schools, which are gathered about the market-place. Here, too, the Kasrielevkites have built their synagogues, prayer-houses, and Chassidic chapels, where services are not decorous and subdued, as among Christians, or among modernized Jews, who are afraid of God (there is a difference between fearing God and being afraid of Him), but noisy, hearty, enthusiastic, and even slightly riotous.

In the far-off days of Sholom Aleichem's childhood, before the assassination of Alexander II and the May Laws that followed, the relations between the Jews of Kasrielevky and their peasant neighbours were by no means unfriendly. However, they could not be called intimate, or affectionate, except in isolated instances. One got along, God be thanked. But nowhere in the world do peasants trust merchants, whether of the same race or not. And it was not on racial grounds, either, that many of the peasants had to be watched. They had covetous eyes and quick fingers. Little Sholom Aleichem himself used to be set by his mother, on busy market days, to keep a sharp eye on the buyers, especially the women with the roomy bosoms and voluminous shawls. They had a way of taking things to their bosoms, deftly and casually — a shoe, a hat, or even a candle. When you caught one in the act you merely retrieved the article, and business went on. No harm done, nothing to make a fuss about. But the watchword was " Two-ten! " — two eyes versus ten fingers.

The merchants of Kasrielevky, properly so called, could be counted on the fingers and toes of a normal man. Most of the market-place was occupied by pedlars, hangers-on, parodies of commission men, women with a basket of eggs or a bundle of old clothes. And the richest Jew in Kasrielevky could be bought out on the lower margin of four figures. Rich or poor, pedlars or artisans, their livelihood was drawn from the market-place, and from the semi-annual fairs. It depends, naturally, on what you call a living. A genuine Kasriel was content to say: " Well, it's better than nothing." Yerechmiel Moses, the Hebrew teacher, blind in one eye and short-sighted in the other, used to wear spectacles without lenses. Asked why, he would answer triumphantly: " Well, it's better than nothing, isn't it? "

CHAPTER V

The Eternal House

❀

THE glory of Kasrielevky, its peculiar treasure and heritage, was the old cemetery, at the opposite end of the townlet from the new cemetery. The new cemetery, too, was not particularly new; its graves were beginning to crowd the wooden fence, and toward the end of Sholom Aleichem's cycle the Kasrielevkites were greatly exercised over what they would do in case of a pogrom, for the new persecution increased the number of burials and at the same time imposed restrictions on the purchase of land.

The exact age of the old cemetery — the Jews call a cemetery " the eternal house " — no one knew. There were tumbled and worn tombstones, and fragments of tombstones, which might date back to the days of the Crusades, those mediæval Christ-enthusiasms which drove the Jews west to east, as the nineteenth-century nationalist enthusiasms were about to drive them east to west. And it is not impossible that hereabouts, and perhaps on this spot, Jews had lived and died and been buried when Yehupetz-Kiev was still waiting for the sons of Rurik and baptism into Christianity. But many of the names that could still be deciphered were those of famous rabbis, scholars, saints, and martyrs. Every century had yielded its quota of martyrs, but the richest harvest had been garnered by the old cemetery of Kasrielevky in the days of the Haidamaks, the peasant-rebels of the time of Bogdan Chmelnitzky, a more savage Petlura of the 1600's. Chmelnitzky will be remembered, or at least mentioned, as long as Yiddish is spoken, for he has passed into a folk saying: " Since the days of Chmelnitzky." But, most curiously, the phrase is devoid of horror or resentment, and is generally used as a marker to denote antiquity. The emotion associated with the name has long ago evaporated. The Kasrielevkites, like nearly all Jews, felt more strongly about Haman and Pharaoh and Hadrian (may their bones be broken!) than about Chmelnitzky. After all, a people with such a long record simply cannot bother to hate every one of its persecutors.

It was with other preoccupations that the Kasrielevkites would visit the old cemetery. This was the one piece of earth which they regarded as their own, for it was drenched with tradition. Here, under the roots of the trees, were assembled God knew how many generations which had lived and died in the faith, and sometimes for it. The Kasrielevkites were intensely conscious of their forefathers not simply as their progenitors in the flesh, but as successive guardians and transmitters of the only way of life which they considered possible, the men and women who had run without faltering in the relay race toward the Messiah. A visit to the old cemetery of Kasrielevky was partly a pleasure-jaunt, partly a pilgrimage; for, apart from everything else, this was the one clear space of green grass and flowers and shadowing trees where Jews felt at home.

With the high motive of spiritual awe was mingled one

of self-interest. The illustrious dead were also friends at court; they were close to the Throne of Grace, intimates, buddies one might say, of the Ancient of Days. What was more natural than that their offspring should implore their intercession? But for this purpose the " new " cemetery was used more than the old by the Kasrielevkites. A Jew — more frequently a Jewess — in the last extremity of poverty or sickness, would go or send someone to the grave of his parents with a message to be delivered direct to the Almighty. Sholom Aleichem, returning after many years to old Kasrielevky, which was by then new or near-new Kasrielevky, went to the cemetery as an act of piety. He was simply paying his respects, one might say. But even in those advanced days — at the beginning of the twentieth century — the cemetery was still the last resort of the defeated. He saw suppliants lying on the graves, women mostly, and heard their frantic appeals.

" Mother, darling Mother," wailed one woman, lying flat on the ground, " if you could only rise and see what has happened to your daughter, the apple of your eye, your tender little Sarah Pearl! If you would only know how I and my little ones are abandoned and forlorn, since that Israel of mine, that husband whom you made me marry, fell sick, coming home from the fair, and took to his bed! Mother, good sweet Mother, what am I to do now? Who's going to pay for Hershel's next term? Who's going to pay Henzil the tailor? Do you hear me, Mother? "

He heard another who came not to beg, but to render a report to her dead husband and to offer him her congratulations. " *Mazel tov*, my husband in the true world, congratulations and good luck! I'm marrying off our oldest daughter, our first one, but I haven't a rouble for her trousseau, and not the first kopeck for the first installment on the dowry. Where am I to get it, my husband? Where? Answer me! Shirts, dresses, shoes, underwear — and then the wedding itself, food, musicians, waiters — where am I to get it all? I'm going off my head with worry, lest the match should come to nothing. Husband, answer me! What shall I do? To whom shall I turn? "

In regard to such personal and intimate difficulties one turned to one's closest dead relatives. They might not have the standing, in the upper world, of the mighty scholars and martyrs of old time; but they could make up for it in persistence and importunity. After all, you may be better off enlisting the frantic sympathy of a true friend of no importance than the stately benevolence of one of the great who has never known you personally. But whomever you invoked, the calm and lordly dead of the centuries, or the excitable intimates of a year ago still warm with worry, you were following an accepted custom when you came to " measure the graves."

Both cemeteries, the old and the new, were always fullest with suppliants during the " ten penitential days " — the dread interval between the New Year and the Day of Atonement. It is then that the accounts are drawn up in heaven, and the fate of every man and woman settled for the next twelvemonth: who shall be raised up and who cast down, who shall live and who shall die, and what the manner of his death shall be — by pestilence, by asphyxiation, by disease, by hanging, or by drowning. During that interval of heart-searching, confession, and supplication, ending irrevocably with the blast of the shofar on the night of Yom Kippur (for the books are opened on the New Year, closed and sealed on the night of Yom Kippur), the old and new cemeteries of Kasrielevky were throbbing centres of life. Then even the Kasriel forgot his gaiety, for he was concerned now not with his status in this foolish world, but with the realities of eternity.

Among all peoples the repositories of the dead are sacred places, and honourable burial a sacred right; everywhere a decent exit from life, whatever the accepted form, is regarded as equal in importance with life itself, if not more so. But among the Jews of Sholom Aleichem's world the cemetery, the eternal home, was the object of a special and indescribable passion, and the dread of being interred among *goyim*, gentiles, heathen, in " alien " soil, an abiding obsession. " Do what Thou wilt with me, O God, only let me lie at last in Jewish earth! " Was this attachment to its graves the protest of a landless and wandering people, demanding at least in death the permanence of tenure which was denied it in life? Was it the tacit hope: " At least in death I shall be left in peace "?

For to the natural piety which normal people feel with regard to cemeteries, the Jews added the peculiar complexes of their position and experience. They projected their insecurity in a gentile world beyond death, and death was a little less chilly in crowded and consecrated ground. Besides, as in life they had felt that only their fellow Jews could understand their troubles, so in death they wanted to have the sympathetic company of their own. We must not wonder that when the fear of pogroms swept over Kasrielevky, the Kasrielevkites found time to worry about the inadequacy of the cemetery.

There is a traditional and typical piece of Jewish humour which incorporates this national fixation. A young

Jew about to be conscripted into the army is addressed by a friend with the following exhortation to cheerfulness: " There's really nothing to be depressed about, if you consider the chances sensibly. You're being taken into the army! Well, one of two things will happen: either there's a war or there isn't. If there isn't, what have you to worry about? But even suppose there's a war, one of two things will happen: either you'll be sent to the front or you won't. If you're not, what is there to worry about? But even suppose you're sent to the front, one of two things will happen: either you'll be wounded or you won't. If you're not, what is there to worry about? But even suppose you're wounded, one of two things will happen: either you'll recover or you won't. If you recover, what is there to worry about? But even suppose you don't recover, one of two things will happen: either you'll be buried in Jewish earth or you won't. If you're buried in Jewish earth, what is there to worry about? But even suppose you're not buried in Jewish earth? Well then, well then " — here the speaker pauses, perplexed — " well then, brother, you're certainly in one hell of a fix."

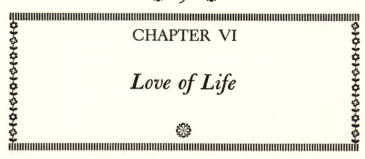

CHAPTER VI

Love of Life

ET's drop these dismal subjects and talk of cheerful things," Sholom Aleichem was wont to exclaim impatiently. " Tell me, what's the latest about the cholera in Odessa? " Let us leave the cemeteries of Kasrielevky and talk of cheerful things — of poverty, disease, and suffering and the indestructible cheerfulness of the Kasrielevkites.

What was it that made them predominantly cheerful in the midst of such discouragements as no other people has ever faced for half so long a period of time? Chiefly it was their boundless love of life.

But we must understand this phrase in their sense. " Love of life " is for most of us a cant phrase with which we glorify self-love. He is a lover of life who is avid of experience, who derives unusual and continuous satisfaction from living; for him the world is a vast smörgåsbord table, and he passes nothing up as long as his stomach works. He loves life for his sake, not for its sake. The Kasrielevkites loved life in a much more literal and direct sense. They so loved it that there could never be enough of it around them. The multiplication of life was a commandment and a joy. They would have liked to crowd out the universe of dead matter, transforming it into innumerable Jews (Kasrielevkites, of course) testifying to God and the Torah.

There was also the matter of the *Kaddish,* the Sanctification, or mourning prayer. It was a dreadful thing for a Jew to die without leaving behind at least one son to say the *Kaddish* for him at the appointed times. Jewish scholars will assure you that the *Kaddish* differs entirely from Masses, in that it is merely a prayer of glorification, uttered at set times, such as anniversaries, in connection with the memory of a dead parent, but having no purgatorial value. And in fact the text of the *Kaddish* contains not a single reference to the dead and is devoted entirely to praise of God. Which is only an illustration of what is wrong with scholars; for whatever the original intent of the *Kaddish,* however lofty its original purpose, it is accepted universally as a potent intercessory ritual. Poor Tevyeh the dairyman, having seven daughters and not a single son, tells us that after Goldie's death he, leaving the village, hired a *Kaddish* for her memory. Sholom Aleichem himself recalls how he and five brothers stood up to say the *Kaddish* in the first week of mourning for their mother.

" There were six of us, one already married and a little householder. You should have heard us deliver that *Kaddish!* It was a pleasure! Our relatives beamed with pride, and strangers envied us. One of our relatives, Blume, exclaimed: ' When a woman has six sons like that to say *Kaddish* after her, how shouldn't she go straight to paradise? Either that or else the world's coming to an end.' "

In this fifth decade of the twentieth century a million grandsons and great-grandsons of the Kasrielevkites, in

New York, Boston, Chicago, San Francisco, hold on to the *Kaddish* as the last vestige of their Judaism. They learn about it — some of them — only when they bring their dead to the cemetery. They learn to repeat it from little specially printed cards, on which the Aramaic words appear in Latin letters. In the busy sections of the great cities there are occasional synagogues into which come darting American businessmen, taxi-drivers, waiters, salesmen, looking for the man who will explain to them where and how they can say their *Kaddish*. Whether these moderns place a purgatorial value on the prayer, or whether they revert to it for lack of some other gesture of respect and memory, no one knows. But it is all that remains in them of Kasrielevky — that, and perhaps the Day of Atonement, and a funny Yiddish word or two, and, when it has not been changed, a name that keeps them out of certain jobs and country clubs.

We might debate endlessly whether the *Kaddish* was only a rationalization of the desire to have children, or whether it was actually an effective propaganda for larger families, such as modern statesmen are unable to duplicate. But vast families were the norm. There was nothing extraordinary about Tevyeh's seven daughters beyond their obstinate unanimity of sex. Sholom Aleichem himself was one of a dozen brothers and sisters, more or less. He does not seem to recall, he certainly does not bother to record, the exact number. The Kasrielevkites were incurably reckless about the having of children. " Let there be life " was the tacit motto.

Out of this addiction to the raw material of humanity sprang the peculiar position and role of the *shadchan*, the marriage broker, whose degenerate descendants have brought the ancient profession into disrepute. I will **not** assert that the old-time *shadchan* was an idealist *pur sang*, and that the modern marriage broker is a mercenary trader in sacred values; or even that the average of successful *partis* was higher among Kasrielevky's *shadchonim* than among our modern matrimonial bureaus. The point is that the *shadchan* looked upon himself as a divine instrument, and upon his calling as part of the divine order. God Himself was a supreme Matchmaker, and few of His activities were so exacting. It is solemnly affirmed by the sages of blessed memory that God puts as much effort into the pairing of each couple as He did into the dividing of the waters of the Red Sea. Every decent Jew was at heart a *shadchan;* and the two professions on which every failure could fall back were those of the *shadchan* and the Hebrew teacher for children.

This does not imply contempt either for the teaching of children or for the marrying off of Jew and Jewess. On the contrary, to teach children their letters, and bring man and woman together in holy wedlock, was everyone's imprescriptible right. Do we hold the vote in contempt because it is withheld only from technical lunatics and small-time criminals?

Childlessness was the great frustration. The difference between our outlook on children and that of the Kasrielevkites is mirrored in the difference between their outlook on the unmarried of both sexes and ours. For us the old maid is a comical figure, and she occupies a considerable place in our vocabulary of humour. In Kasrielevky an old maid was a specifically tragic figure; you no more joked about her than about cancer. On the other hand the " old bachelor," who has at worst a neutral status in our modern world, was definitely ridiculous in the eyes of Kasrielevkites. A woman did not re-

main unmarried by choice; a man did. Therefore he was
a spiritless poltroon, or a selfish oaf, or a twisted creature; and since impotence could not be assumed, for the
man had never tried, he was a wilful sinner on top of
everything else. He took life and did not replace it; he
made no attempt to provide himself with a *Kaddish;*
and he was indifferent to the perpetuation of Judaism
and the multiplication of its protagonists. Let no such
man be trusted.

In short, to be unmarried was sinful, improper, unnatural, and unreasonable. Poverty was no excuse. As
long as a man could beget and a woman bear, the unmarried state was to be condemned. Widows and widow-
ers were not exempt from the obligation. The dearest
and most beloved husband or wife had, in this respect,
no claim beyond the grave. It was taken for granted that
when the earth had lain a year on the departed one, the
survivor would remarry; and it was not in bad taste for
a *shadchan* or a relative to suggest a match to the widow
or widower a few weeks after the funeral. Sholom Aleichem remembers how, on the last day of the official week
of mourning, his father sat weeping for his dead wife,
wringing his hands, and crying: " God, God, what shall
I do, what shall I do now? " and how the widower's
brother, himself choking with tears, answered him
abruptly: " What shall you do? That which all Jews do.
You shall, with God's help, marry."

Does this sound heartless? Let it be said at once that
love between husband and wife was as strong in Kasrielevky as anywhere else in the world. Not heartlessness,
but a fierce attachment to life spoke in the Kasrielevkites. We respect grief, but we do not think well of a
man or woman whom a bereavement incapacitates for

further living; for that is emotional self-indulgence. And among the Kasrielevkites living was meaningless without the creation of more life.

To bring about a marriage was as meritorious an act as a Jew could perform. It became a public festival when the beneficiaries were two poor people who could not pay for the wedding and were treated to it by their neighbours; and if the bride and bridegroom contrived to be orphans as well as poor, the community stock took an upward leap in heaven. Indeed, the marrying off of orphans was both the highest form of charity and an act of community atonement for sin at large — hence, also, a specific against pestilence.

One of the grandest weddings which Kasrielevky ever beheld was that which Sholom Aleichem's own father arranged between Feigele, nicknamed the Ashmedai, or demon, and Moses Hirsch, a poor tailor. Feigele was a servant girl in the house of a certain Lifschitz, a distant relative of Sholom Aleichem's family, who lived in the tiny village of Hlubke and was the only Jew for miles around. Feigele, a hot-blooded young creature, was running wild for lack of a husband. It had gone so far that she had taken up secretly with Chvedor, the son of the village clerk, and for him she was robbing the household in the nights. She seems to have been a girl with some imagination. To cover up her thefts she managed to make it appear that the house was haunted by a poltergeist, who not only abstracted articles of value, but tore the pages from the sacred books, turned tables and chairs upside down, spilled out the milk, and carried on generally with the pointless malice of his species. Reb Lifschitz, a great simpleton of a Jew, came with the horrifying story of the poltergeist to Nochum Vevik Rabinovitch, Sholom Aleichem's father, who, for all his rigid piety and orthodoxy, was anything but superstitious. To make a short story shorter, Nochum Vevik and his younger brother Nissel came out to Hlubke to lay hands on the demon in the night; and laid hands instead, of course, on Feigele the Ashmedai and Chvedor.

Chvedor was carried off to the local prefect and threat-ened with prison if he did not return the stolen goods. Feigele was carried off to Kasrielevky and, before you could say " social adjustment," married to Moses Hirsch, a sturdy lad with a powerful fist. The Rabinovitches themselves gave away the orphan bride. All Kasrielevky came to the wedding, not excluding gentile officialdom. A finer wedding could not have been expected by the most respectable or richest girl in town. The dinner was cooked by the matrons of Kasrielevky; beer and wine flowed like water; the fiddlers fiddled into the white hours, and Nissim Rabinovitch danced a *kasatzky* with the prefect himself, to the glory of human brotherhood and the stupefaction of the beholders.

Need it be said that the prescription worked? The true story of the poltergeist remained a secret between the Rabinovitches and the Lifschitzes. Feigele the Ash-medai became a pious and prolific matron in Israel, a model of good works; Kasrielevky was enriched by a new generation of Kasriels, life was added to life, and a vast sum was chalked up to the credit of the Kasrielevkites in the heavenly registers.

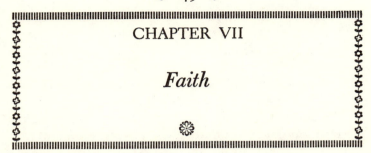

CHAPTER VII

Faith

✿

"Dᴇ *l'audace*," said the Frenchman, "*toujours de l'audace, encore de l'audace!* " The Kasrielevkite, without the French dramatic flair, placed the emphasis on faith, on *bitochon*. " A Jew must have *bitochon*. If he hasn't got it, he's not a Jew, but an unbelieving atheist."

Literally, the Hebrew word *bitochon* means certainty, assurance, trust, or security. In the mouth of a Kasrielevkite it expressed the ultimate principle of life. " Never say die," " down but never out," " *nil desperandum*," " *élan vital*": put all these expressions into a retort and distil the mixture, add a dash of derision and a consciousness of forty centuries of history; the result is a mere suggestion of *bitochon*. " As long as your teeth are chattering, you know you're still all right."

There is presumably a measure of instinctive faith in every form of life, part of the equipment of survival; there is also, presumably, a limit to what human beings are prepared to endure before they throw up the sponge. Of such measures and limitations the Jews knew nothing. Possibly this bland ignorance of theirs has been a continuous irritant in history. Some Jewish thinkers, at least, have thought so. For by every standard of reason, and even of propriety, the Jewish people should long ago have disappeared from the stage of history. It has refused to do so. Whatever rationale we construct for this exasperating inability of the Jewish people to play the game and acquire the habit of death, we must recognize the presence of the Kasrielevkite's *bitochon*.

The motif of the last-minute rescue from impending destruction stands out in the early Jewish records. When Laban was about to fall on Jacob, God warned the attacker in a dream; when Joseph lay abandoned in the pit, the Midianite merchants came along; when the children of Israel were at their last gasp in Egypt, Moses appeared; when they stood at the Red Sea, death by steel on one side, death by drowning on the other, the waters were divided; when the remnant in Babylon seemed ready to follow the ten tribes into oblivion, Ezra arose; when Antiochus Epiphanes had all but extinguished the national existence, Judas Maccabæus was sent to them; when Rome was closing in on Jerusalem, Jochanan ben Zakkai wheedled out of the conqueror the harmless concession of the academy which was to nullify the defeat. This sort of thing had been going on for so long that the Kasrielevkite, to whom the Bible was a daily newspaper and Haman a contemporary, did not know the meaning of surrender or despair.

"When need is highest, God is nighest." It is altogether proper that Tevyeh the dairyman should stand on the threshold of Sholom Aleichem's world, and that the miracle of his redemption should be the first story in the twenty-eight volumes which make up the collected works of Sholom Aleichem. We left Tevyeh, it will be remembered, in the midst of his prayers, the sweat of his pursuit and the tears of his supplications running down

his beard, in the darkening forest outside Boiberik.
What lay before him? Immediately, the disconsolate
journey home, to a wife and seven daughters as hungry
as he; permanently, a life of brute labour, nakedness,
and ignominy. And suddenly, out of nowhere, without
rhyme or reason — or rather, let us say like a true Kasrielevkite, out of the divine grace, with every rhyme and
reason — came the great reversal, and darkness was transformed into light, gloom into gaiety, lamentation into
rejoicing. The Red Sea was divided, the hosts of Sen-
nacherib were slaughtered, Antiochus was routed, and
Haman was hanged on a gallows fifty cubits high. Before
that evening was over, Tevyeh the coolie had been lifted
out of the abyss of want and worry, and set upon the
mountain top of affluence. His horn was exalted, his cup
filled to overflowing, and a table prepared for him in the
presence of his enemies.

" Get to the point," I hear someone say, and I should
like to do it, but it is not easy, for we are moving in a world
of talkers in which the preamble was usually the point;
and it takes a little time to build up a decent anticlimax.
For what is expected of Tevyeh by now? That he stumble
on a buried treasure of fabulous magnitude? That Elijah
the Prophet, patron of the poor, appear to him with the
Kabbalistic secret of the philosopher's stone? But we are
not dealing in fairy tales. The world of Sholom Aleichem
is a world of everyday people and reasonable incidents.
In such a world it is enough that Tevyeh should come
into unexpected possession of thirty-seven roubles and a
milch cow.

And as to whether this is really an anticlimax, let us
hear Tevyeh's own exordium to the exciting story, as he
himself gave it to the transcriber:

45

" I tell you, Mr. Sholom Aleichem, if a man is destined to win the great lottery of life, he needn't lift a finger in his own behalf. He just sits and waits, and it comes on its own four legs right into his house. It doesn't call for an ounce of brains. And if it's the other way round, if a man is destined to live out his life on Pharaoh's plagues, he can plead and argue till he's blue in the face; it won't do him a bit of good. This I know from personal experience, and from the miracle of my own life."

And then Tevyeh goes on to the great events of that evening, relating them in his own peculiar way, which we will by no means let him do here: how, when he had ended his prayers, he perceived approaching him two mysterious figures in the likeness of female women; how his first thought was: " Demons! " and his second: " Robbers! "; how the mysterious figures turned out to be two elderly Jewesses who had lost their way in the forest and had been wandering about since early that morning; how they implored Tevyeh to take them back to Boiberik, where their families were no doubt searching for them frantically; how Tevyeh — with his own family waiting for him frantically at home — hesitated and almost gave the miracle the slip: dark forest, lost females, knight-errantry were not in Tevyeh's line, either; how he took the women back to Boiberik, cursing himself all the way for not having put a good stiff price on his services in advance; how, when he drove up to the great summer cottage — it belonged to a famous millionaire who was positively known to be worth at least a hundred thousand roubles — where the women lived, there was loud rejoicing and thanksgiving; how, when he was asked how much he expected to be paid, Tevyeh fell into a sweat, thinking: " Father in heaven, what shall I do?

46

I'm afraid to ask for one rouble, they may be prepared to pay two; I'm afraid to ask for two roubles, they may think I'm crazy! "; how, before he knew it, he had burst out with " Three roubles! " and, when the shout of laughter had subsided, apologized, saying: " If a horse with four legs can sometimes stumble, how much more a man with only one tongue? "; how the millionaire who was positively known to be worth at least a hundred thousand roubles drew out a monstrous wallet and put down, before Tevyeh — you'll never guess it! — a ten-rouble note, crimson as a peony; and how the others at the open-air table added their contributions, fives and threes and twos, while Tevyeh stood there, his knees trembling so that he almost fell in a faint; how, as her own special gift to her rescuer, the older of the two women told him to come the next day and she would let him lead home a milch cow whose dugs had been dried by an evil eye ("Don't you worry," said Tevyeh, fervently, " the cow isn't born yet that my old woman can't get milk from ") ; and how, on top of it all, they loaded his cart with good things, fresh yellow loaves, roast quarters of chicken, parcels of boiled fish, and jars of chicken fat and preserves.

All this Tevyeh tells, circumstantially, in detail, with many quotations and misquotations from Sacred Writ, with many philosophical reflections and historical parallels, and if at first you were disappointed by the modesty of the miracle, being no Kasrielevkite, the telling of it reminds you that there are miracles and miracles, and you realize that this one was not among the least. And if the miracle is not enough, think of Tevyeh's home-coming that night: how he burst in on his wife with a riotous " Good evening, my Goldie, good evening, my

47

spouse! *Mazel tov,* congratulations, and joy to the hour! "; and how foolish Goldie, smelling liquor on his breath (they had not let him depart without a drink), began to rail: " A black and blistering *mazel tov* to *you*, my Tevyeh, my spouse, my breadwinner! What holiday is this? What wedding have we, what circumcision feast, for *mazel tovs?* "; to which Tevyeh, bringing in the good things, replied: " It is a holiday, and a wedding, and a circumcision feast rolled into one! Wake up the children, wife, light the samovar, let there be eating and drinking! What! Do we live more than once? "; how, when the amazed and sated children had gone to sleep again, Tevyeh showed her the pile of money, which they counted over — twice times eighteen roubles and one extra — and he assured her that he had come by it honestly, by his own courage, ingenuity, foresight, and labour (forgetting for the moment that if a man is destined to win the great lottery of life he need not have an ounce of brains); and how they sat up half the night debating what was to be done with so vast a capital, and quarrelled six times and made up six times, and finally decided that besides the milch cow which Tevyeh was to bring home the next day they would purchase another and set up in the dairy business; which they did, in order that the words of the Psalmist might be fulfilled: " He lifteth up the poor man from the dunghill," and that Tevyeh the dairyman might be given to the world.

This was the first and last of God's beneficences to Tevyeh, who thereafter has nothing to relate save disaster following on disaster, as we shall see; and if the substance of the beneficence was a little less than massive, that of his disasters is guaranteed to give full satisfaction, so that at least we cannot complain of the average. Were it permitted to scrutinize the purposes of the Almighty, we might even ask whether Tevyeh was not lifted up in order that he might the more resoundingly be brought down, and whether God had not merely decided that a man so beset with sordid cares was unfit for the higher suffering in store for him.

CHAPTER VIII

One Man to be Envied

❀

Now, since life, as Sholom Aleichem assures us, is a blister on top of a tumour, and a boil on top of that, is any man to be envied? Yes, one such man there was, and he not an emperor on his throne, and not even a Rothschild in his counting-house, but a certain Kasrielevkite, Reb Melech, the cantor in the old synagogue.

Of Reb Melech the cantor we know almost nothing except the manner of his death and the magnificence of his funeral. But he was a cantor and therefore poor; a Kasrielevkite and therefore blessed with many children. We are told further that in his prime his voice was a thing of wonder, and when he opened up on a psalm or blessing, it was with the roar of a lion, so that the four walls of the ancient synagogue trembled and the windows rang. In his old age he was still a mighty man of prayer, but thunder had given way to lamentation. He was a great weeper, and an infectious one; and when he interpolated a heart-broken " Oh, Father, Father in heaven," the whole congregation wept with him, and you could almost hear the rustle and splash of tears, especially in the women's gallery.

Was it for this gift that Reb Melech was to be envied?

By no means. Held in esteem, yes, but not envied. Reb Melech was, after all, only a prayer-leader, the messenger of the community to the Throne of Grace; undoubtedly a good messenger, one that would not easily be turned back, but pushed his way past doors and intermediaries and let his voice be heard by the Master Himself; still, only a messenger, with nothing more to say than was entrusted to him. What Reb Melech did by way of duty for fifty years was commendable, but not enviable; if he became a legend and a byword in Kasrielevky, it was for the manner of his death.

For Reb Melech the cantor died in harness; or, if that expression is a trifle indecorous in connection with Reb Melech and his calling, let us say that he died like a hero on the field of battle. Though that expression, too, is not altogether felicitous, smacking more of the Homeric than the Hebraic. Reb Melech died in the midst of prayer, while he stood before the congregation weeping, as only he could, for its welfare. But this was not on a week-day, and not on the Sabbath, and not on a festival like Pentecost or Booths, but on the dread Day of Atonement itself; and not at the beginning or in the middle of the services, his task undone, but at the very end of the Day of Atonement, when the fasting Jews of Kasrielevky, exhausted with confession and repentance, were awaiting the last call of the ram's horn. It was as if, just before the gates of heaven closed on the sealed orders for the coming year, Reb Melech resolved to make his last intervention in person and, abandoning his spent and useless body before the Ark of the Covenant in the synagogue of Kasrielevky, swung upward through the seven heavens to the Throne itself.

Who knows for what unrevealed merits Reb Melech

had been chosen for such a glorious end? They must have been uncommon even among the elect, for no one in Kasrielevky had heard tell of so perfect a close to a human life. Was it possible that Reb Melech was one of the Perpetual Thirty-six, the unacknowledged saints in whose merit the world is sustained from generation to generation, and who are renewed like an Academy of Immortals? They carried the frail body of Reb Melech out of the synagogue and returned for the *Neilah*, the final words. The next day Reb Yozifel the Rabbi delivered the funeral oration, and proved by many ingenious texts that Reb Melech had proceeded immediately to the portals of paradise, which were flung wide open for him as for a distinguished guest. And quite forgetting that he was speaking to a dead man, Reb Yozifel closed the oration with these words: " Go in peace, Reb Melech! Go in good health! Happy be thy journey and successful thy mission! "

The town was empty that day save of those who could not walk and had no one to carry them to the cemetery. The market-place was abandoned, the Hebrew schools were emptied, the streets silent. For ever after, when the name of Reb Melech was mentioned, it was with a sigh, and a wistful smile, and the words: " Ah, there was a man to be envied! "

CHAPTER IX

Sabbaths and Festivals

❈

HE THEORY which assigns to the Jews a major role
in the creation of European capitalism leaves unex-
plained one very odd circumstance. The words which
have to do with banking and finance are largely of Italian origin: " account " and " discount " from *conto* and
disconto; " bankrupt " from *banca rotta,* the broken
bench of the merchant expelled from the *borsa,* and
" bank " from *banco;* while in many European countries
the pawnshop is called the *Lombard,* and its coat of arms
consists, not of a Jewish candelabrum or Shield of David,
but of three balls, the *palle* of the Florentine Medici. On
the other hand, the words which the Jews have made in-
ternationally familiar have nothing to do with business.
" Halleluyah," " Amen," " cherubim," " Gehenna," and
" Eden " seldom appear in histories of economics or the
reports of commercial attachés.

These words come, of course, from the Bible, to which
the affirmative interest of the world in the Jews is confined. What the world does not know is that the same religious intensity continued to exist in the Jewish people
until very recent times. Life and religion were indivisi-
ble for the Kasrielevkites; they did not think of religion

as of something tagged on to life, something separate, de-
tachable, and optional. Their grandchildren and great-
grandchildren in the American cities have rabbis, synagogues, temples, Sunday schools, or even Yeshivas; they
have activities, holy days, and high holy days; they have
organizations and *landsmanschaften,* Zionist societies,
B'nai B'riths, anti-defamation leagues, lodges, unions,
cultural groups, men's clubs; and all of these things, including even the rabbis and synagogues, are additions
and increments, in no way reproducing the folk whole-
ness of the Jewish life of Kasrielevky.

What did a Kasrielevkite work for all week? To reach
the Sabbath and celebrate it. What did learning consist
in? The Bible, the Talmud, the sacred books generally,
the literature of the sages. What was music? The ornament of prayer. The cobbler at his bench, the tailor
squatting on his table, hummed a liturgical melody.
Where did the Kasrielevkite find art? In the carvings of
lions on top of the Ark of the Scrolls, in the embroidery
of the curtains, in the crowns on top of the Scroll-holders,
in the incense boxes and beakers for the ceremony of the
Departure of the Sabbath, in the illustrations of the Hag-
gadah, the Passover prayer-book.

That which we call religion, and for which the Kasrielevkites had no name, because for them it was simply
equated with being human, distinguishes the world of
Sholom Aleichem from every other world that has ever
been reproduced by a regionalist writer. For nowhere
else is it natural for a simple, unlettered man of the people to speak as does, for instance, a certain drayman,
whose name we do not know, but who has his say on
the beauty of the Sabbath:

" A man wouldn't know what to do, I tell you, if God

54

hadn't given us the Sabbath, a gift, a real gift, out of His grace. When the Sabbath comes I'm a different man, do you hear? I get home betimes on Friday afternoon, and the first thing of course is the baths, if you know what I mean. There I sit on the top row of the steam room and get myself scalded from head to foot. That puts a new skin on me. Fresh as a new-born babe I dance home, and there on the table are the two old brass candlesticks, shining like stars, if you know what I mean, and the two big Sabbath loaves; and there, right beside them, are the winking Sabbath fish, sending out a smell that takes you by the throat. And the house is warm and bright and fresh and clean in every corner. So I sit down like a king, and open the Good Book, and go twice over the week's portion. Then I close the Book, and it's off to the synagogue. What a homecoming after that! When I open the door and sing out: ' Good Sabbath ' you can hear me at the other end of town. Then comes the benediction by candlelight, and the drop of good old whisky, that sings right through me, if you know what I mean, and then the Sabbath supper — the shining fish, and the golden soup, and the good old yellow carrots in honey. That night I sleep like a lord, if you know what I mean. And where am I going in the morning? Why, to the synagogue, of course, as I'm a man and a Jew. And back from the synagogue it's the real Sabbath meal again, the grand old chopped radish, and the good old onion, and the jellied calf's foot, if you know what I mean, with a proper smack of garlic. And when you wake up after your Sabbath afternoon nap, and your mouth's dry, and there's a sourness in your belly, if you know what I mean, what's better, I ask you, than a quart or two of cider? Then, when you're good and ready, and fresh and strong, you sit down to the Good Book again, like a giant, and off you go! Chapter after chapter, eh? Psalm after psalm, at the gallop, like the mileposts on the road, if you know what I mean. . . ."

So speaks a man of the people. We do not know who he is. He appears and vanishes. We only hear the deep voice, we see the broad, round smiling face, the massive build. What, indeed, would he do, without the Sabbath and the festivals? You cannot content *him* with a ritual detached from the texture of his life, with something called " religion " on which he pays a respectful call every now and again, hat in hand.

This was Jewishness at its earthiest, of course, worth remembering because our attention is generally directed to the Jewishness of the more learned. Each in its own way the various levels of the Kasrielevkites were interpenetrated with this omnipresence of their folk religion, asserting itself tacitly in their daily lives, and emerging into more explicit expression on the festivals.

Of all festivals the Sabbath was the mightiest, and the obligation to be happy on the Sabbath took precedence over every earthly consideration. If the fast of the Ninth of Ab, for the destruction of the Temple, fell on a Sabbath, it was deferred to the next day; so was the fast of the Seventeenth of Tammuz, for the breach in the walls of Jerusalem; and the fast of Gedaliah, for the assassination of the last Governor of Jerusalem. Only the fast of the Day of Atonement could not be displaced by the Sabbath. No personal sorrow could interfere with the recurrence of this weekly ascension into heavenly bliss.

But did the Kasrielevkites, by and large, observe the Sabbath in this spirit? They did. There was something miraculous in the regularity of the weekly cycle; for how can men summon up, at a given signal, and at fixed intervals, an inspiration of the heart? There were of course certain exercises prescribed in the orthodox ritual. The eve of the Sabbath was sacred to love in all its senses, and the night sacred in particular to the love of husband and wife. Every Friday, between afternoon and evening prayers, the more pious Jews — they were the majority — would chant from beginning to end the Song of Songs, which is the love-song of King Solomon. Nothing could have been further from their minds than the aphrodisiac effect of that Oriental duet; if they thought at all of the meaning of such phrases as " Thy breasts are like roes which feed among the lilies," it was as rabbinical exegesis. The breasts of the dusky Shulamite represented Moses and Aaron, the co-founders of the people of the law. Verse by verse they would transpose the piercing sweetness of erotic strophe and antistrophe into a subtle allegory of the eternal, passionate bond between God and Israel. But it is probable that this very sublimation only served to concentrate the veiled impulse of the flesh. And no doubt the wine of the Friday evening played its part, as did the cleansing of the house, the richer meal, the lights, the singing, and the leisure.

But all this ingenious ritual of morale would have remained bare and unfruitful mechanics without the inward predisposition of the people. It would have degenerated — and of course it sometimes did — into bleak pietism. But while old Kasrielevky was old Kasrielevky the Sabbath did not fail.

The commandments and prohibitions of the Sabbath, which to the grandsons and great-grandsons of the Kasrielevkites are at best only the vestiges of an interesting folklore, and at worst an irksome and witless regimenta-

57

tion, were for their forbears the very opposite of burdens
and privations. They were the appropriate ornaments of
a day which had nothing in common with other days.
Time and consciousness had a special colouring for the
twenty-four hours of the Sabbath, and a savour created
for the occasion in remotest times; yes, according to the
tradition, God created the Sabbath before He created
the world, and perhaps created the world for the sake of
the Sabbath — as a great poet suddenly thinks of an immortal phrase and has to write a poem in which to in-
corporate it. That one did not ride on the Sabbath (a
pious Kasrielevkite would not have said that one *could*
not, or *dared* not, as if confronted with a mere prohibi-
tion) , that one did not touch or kindle fire, or handle a
writing implement, or do any manner of work even if it
were pleasurable, was for the Kasrielevkite gravely and
exquisitely proper. No, these were not prohibitions at
all; they were melodic utterances of the spirit of the
Queen Sabbath, and a transgression wounded them as a
false note in the playing of a piece of music wounds the
ear of a musician. We are told that Rabbi Nachman of
Bratzlav once received an important telegram on the
Sabbath. He could have circumvented the spirit of the
law which forbids the tearing of paper on the Sabbath,
and observed its letter, by sponging the flap until the
envelope came loose. So a bleak pietist would have done,
as certain bleak pietists today use a depilatory instead of
a razor to get rid of their beards, the razor (of old the
only known remover of beards) being forbidden. Not so
Reb Nachman of Bratzlav. He kept the closed telegram
before him all that Sabbath day, observing with delight
how unimportant its contents had become by comparison with the bliss of the Sabbath.

58

A true Kasrielevkite would have regretted the loss of any one of the injunctions which reflected the gracious division of the week into the sacred and secular. The dearness of the Sabbath was a faint foretaste of the sweetness of paradise; the ordered procession of its laws a hint of the perfectibility of human behaviour, and of the time when men would perform lovingly the duties to which they now yielded rebelliously, if at all.

On a Sabbath afternoon in the summer a townlet like old Kasrielevky belongs to a dream world. The Sabbath siesta is a traditional if not a formal obligation. The children are quiet; Father is sleeping the sacred sleep of the Sabbath afternoon. The market-place is deserted: no peasants, no traders, no horses, no goats, no bleating, no braying, no dealing, no chaffering. It is forbidden to carry money with one on the Sabbath — what could you use it for if business has come to an end? It is even forbidden to think of money and business on the Sabbath. You must be at peace, you must have Sabbath within you, body and spirit must know the tranquillity and beatitude of the day ordained at Sinai.

The Sabbath siesta is not a long affair. Who wants to sleep away the loveliest of days? Half an hour passes, an hour at most. Then you hear, issuing from the delapidated houses, and hanging over the crooked alleys, sweet, haunting melodies in a minor key; not formal songs, but vague chants, carrying not formal phrases, but half phrases, words and half words, repeated over and over again. Melancholy but not depressed, suppliant but not importunate, the voices linger over the townlet with the tenderness of bells. " Ah, Father—Father—bim —bom—Father in heaven—ai—ai—look upon us— bim—bom—Thy people—Father—ai—ai—King—"

59

The words and half words, the melodies, the grace-notes, say nothing and say everything. They are mnemonics, mysterious and meaningless to the outsider, intimate, lucid, and vivid to the insider, evoking dimly a long history of homelessness, of faithfulness and hope. As the sadness of great stretches of space informs the songs of the Russian peasant, so the sadness of great stretches of time haunts the truncated words, the elisions and repetitions of these minor Jewish chants. " Life is hard, God is good, a time will come, bim-bom, remember Thy people, hard, good, people, Father — ai, Father, little Father — " And meanwhile the Sabbath is slipping away, the Queen is preparing her departure, the harsh world, the daily struggle, the bitterness of life, stand at the gates of the evening. Get everything you can out of this heavenly interlude, an hour or two of prayer, an hour or two of study, in the synagogue or at home. Till the moment of the Separation comes, and with incense box uplifted, his family gathered about him, the Kasrielevkite takes regretful leave of the Sabbath, and his wife sings, in homely Yiddish, the valedictory of Reb Isaac of Berditchev, Reb Levi Isaac the Compassionate.

Where are the Sabbaths and festivals of old Kasrielevky today? They will not be found in Kasrielevky, or Kozodoievka, or Bohopolie, or Teplitz, or Boiberik, for those townlets of Sholom Aleichem's world have been utterly transformed, and the good has vanished with the bad. In transatlantic cities there are aging men and women who knew Sholom Aleichem's world at first hand, and some among them have deliberately cut loose from orthodoxy, while others have drifted with the tide into the new forms of life. But even those who have tried their hardest to conserve the old forms know that " it is not as it used to be," for whatever their own practices and inclinations, the ancient setting no longer exists. What kind of Sabbath is it, I ask you, which leaves the world around you utterly unchanged from the week-days? The shops are open, the market-place is filled, the horses neigh, buyers and sellers chaffer, the El or the surface car thunders past the synagogue, and the Sabbath siesta is a day-mare in a din of blaring radios and yelling children playing baseball in the street. And all the surviving Kasrielevkites, the traditionalists and modernists alike, remember now and again with a nostalgic pang the far-off magic of those sacred hours, those transfigured interludes of the Sabbaths and festivals for which even progress and freedom have found no substitute.

CHAPTER X

From Passover to Passover

❀

Oₙ the Sabbaths and festivals the Kasrielevkites
simply went off into another world — a feat of self-trans-
lation so remarkable that to the outside observer it suggests a split personality. So it was, to some extent; but
the inside observer, or participant, knew that the division was deliberate; it was nurtured by an ingenious technique; and its discontinuities were mitigated by preparation on the one side, recollection on the other. There
was fusion rather than confusion. Heaven, the Holy
Land, and daily life, a world of symbols and ideas and a
world of very ordinary substance, coexisted in the individual Kasrielevkite. Yet somehow the Kasrielevkite,
when you knew him, did not impress you as a neurotic
or a freak. On the contrary, he was refreshingly whole
and harmonious, if distinctly not commonplace.

No doubt it calls for an effort to understand how a
wretched little householder — a Jew, a pauper, an exile,
an object of persecution — could sit down to the Passover ceremonies at home and feel that he was a king, his
wife a queen, and his children princes and princesses,
yet come out of the Passover cheerfully free from delusions of grandeur. (Delusions of persecution, it may be

noted, the Jew has never had: he has not needed them.)
The difficulty is increased by the fact that this same
householder might be celebrating the festival of the liberation on the *matzos* and potatoes of charity. No matter; when the table was set and the family ranged about
it, the spirit descended on the assembly. Itzik Meyer of
Kasrielevky was told to feel that he himself, with wife
and children, had marched out of Egypt, and he did as
he was told. He felt that he himself had witnessed the
infliction of the ten plagues on the Egyptians, he himself
had stood on the farther shore of the Red Sea and seen
the walls of water collapse on the pursuers, drowning
them all to the last man — with the exception of Pharaoh, who was preserved as an eternal witness for the
benefit of the Torquemadas and Romanovs. Itzik Meyer
rejoiced, genuinely and heartily, and his wife and children rejoiced with him.

No Jew in old Kasrielevky ever lacked the means for
the observance of the Passover. Sholom Aleichem assures
us that a Kasrielevkite had never died of hunger during
this festival; or if he had, it was because of the hunger
which he had endured on the other three hundred and
fifty-seven days of the year. For it was a principle in Kasrielevky that for the Passover you either gave or accepted
charity. There were no neutrals; and for eight whole days
no Jew was in want — which is perhaps more than can
be said of any other community in the world.

The Passover celebrated the Exodus, the defeat of tyranny, the birth of a nation; but it also celebrated, if less
consciously, spring and renewal. What a happy rumpus
in the homes of the Kasrielevkites in preparation for
the Passover! What a cleansing and scouring and hunting out of traces of leaven! And what a time for the chil-

dren, who are the special objects of the pedagogic symbolism of the Passover! Before the Passover begins, Father
must go through the house with a lighted taper in
his hand to make sure that no leaven has been left in
the corners — although everyone knows that he is doing
this for fun, and not in distrust of Mother's thorough-
ness. At the table of the *seder* — the evening ceremonial
and grand dinner of the Passover — Father sits leaning
on a cushion, to show off his royalty. On the table are
the covered *matzos,* and the platter with multiple food
symbols — the shank-bone in memory of the Temple,
the bitter herbs in memory of the bitterness of life under Pharaoh, the *charosoth* in memory of the mortar between the stones of the buildings which the Jewish slaves
erected in Pithom and Rameses. There is a wine-cup for
every celebrant, even for the youngest, which must be
drained — theoretically at least — four times in the
course of the ceremony. There is also a special wine-cup
for Elijah the Prophet, who will enter at a given signal
and drain that one, too — also theoretically at least.
There is also one *matzoh* which will be broken into two
parts, one of which will be wrapped up and hidden
away, to be divided and eaten at the close of the meal.
And if a child should manage to steal the hidden half of
the *matzoh,* called the *afikomon,* he — or she — can de-
mand a ransom for it, and this time not theoretically, either. Nor does anyone expect Father to be particularly
vigilant about the *afikomon* — that would bespeak an
inattention to the service less excusable in him than in
the youthful *matzoh*-snatcher. So the ceremony begins,
with the youngest child asking the classical four questions, and everyone joining in the reply: " Slaves we
were to Pharaoh in Egypt. . . ."

64

" Slaves we were! " And what are they now? It is not easy to answer. For on the one hand they have stated explicitly, at the outset of the service: " Now we are slaves, next year we will be free, now we are here, next year we will be in the land of Israel "; and on the other hand they are living through liberation, they sit at the table clothed, ready to rise and depart, waiting for the call. They are slaves and freemen simultaneously; they are servants and kings. But, above all, they are happy.

This is what we must remember, that the festivals were made for happiness, and the Kasrielevkites would not let themselves be done out of their last privilege. Possibly they had no right to be happy; possibly the outsider will exclaim, irritably: " I don't believe they were really happy." If they were not, they were giving a remarkably good imitation.

To be sure, we shall have to use the word " happiness " in various senses; for every festival had its shading of mood, from the solemn exaltation of the Day of Atonement to the gaiety of Simchas Torah — the Rejoicing in the Law — which marked the end and beginning of the yearly cycle of Sabbath readings from the Pentateuch, and the hilarity and downright buffoonery of Purim, which commemorated the discomfiture of Haman. But Passover and Pentecost and Booths (which together with the New Year and the Day of Atonement made up the five major festivals) were times of radiance.

On Pentecost the Kasrielevkites rejoiced for the giving of the Ten Commandments at Sinai, which may seem a little perverse since it was there that the troubles of the Jews began, and for the wheat harvest of Palestine, which was more reasonable, since they had reaped it once and expected to reap it again — some day. Pious Kasrielevkites sat up all night for the Pentecost, studying the Bible and the Talmud; and the pious and the less pious alike (there were no impious Kasrielevkites to speak of) accounted it meritorious in some obscure way to eat dairy dishes on Pentecost, with plenty of milk and cream and cheese.

The festival of Booths or Tabernacles comes next to the Passover in the richness of its symbolism and the completeness of its hypnotic translation; for during that week the Kasrielevkites dwelt in booths, like their forefathers in the wilderness. Not literally, of course. Every Kasrielevkite built himself a charming, ramshackle imitation of a cabin next to his own house; the roof was of branches and leaves; the walls were hung with fruits and vegetables; and all of it suggested much more the autumn harvest huts of Palestine than the aridity of the wilderness. In this booth the Kasrielevkite took his meals with his family during the festival, wind and weather permitting. Into this booth came an odorous reminder of the Orient, a palm branch and a citron — the *lulav* and the *esrog* — imported from Palestine or Korfu, for the special prayer of the festival. And here Kasrielevky dreamed itself back into the Holy Land, or, if you like, merely assumed its other personality.

Of course not one Kasrielevkite in twenty could afford to own for himself the exotic appurtenances of the festival, the *lulav* and the *esrog* imported from Mediterranean shores. So a Jew who owned one would make the rounds of his neighbours' booths. Or else the beadle of the synagogue would perform this duty with the communal palm branch and citron. On the festival of Booths you would see, hastening through the morning streets of Kasrielevky, bearded Jews in black capotes with a yellow citron in one hand and a cluster of palm branch in the other — fantastic apparitions to all but the Jews themselves. A Jew with a citron of his own was widely envied. Moishe Yenkel, who lived in a townlet near Kasrielevky, waited ten years before he could buy one for himself; and a terrible tragedy happened. Leibel, his little son, was so fascinated by the precious and sacred fruit that he crept down from his bed in the night, took the *esrog* in his hand, and, seized by a frightful and blasphemous curiosity, bit off the head, thereby rendering the *esrog* unfit for ritual use. Sholom Aleichem thinks the incident worth recording, and I certainly think it worth mentioning.

Echoes of the old jollity of Palestinian harvests sounded in the booths of the Kasrielevkites, and prayers of a rustic people were rehearsed with great earnestness by a nation of workers and merchants. On the last days of Booths, Leib the tinsmith and Yossie the haberdasher and Simon Ellie the tailor and Reb Melech the cantor, and Reb Yozifel the Rabbi — the rich and the poor, the prominent and the obscure — assembled in the synagogue, took up clusters of willow, sang Hosannas, and prayed fervently for rain; not because they had a personal interest in the rainfall, but because Palestine might need it; that is to say, not the actual Palestine which lay a thousand miles or more to the southeast, and with which they had no practical connections to speak of, but the Palestine which Kasrielevky carried around in its heart, the Palestine that once had been and was to be again. And all this elaborate make-believe, this retention of an agricultural form of self-expression by thoroughly urbanized communities, was anything but a petrified ritual. It was taken in passionate earnest and had a fan-

tastic purposiveness. The Kasrielevkites were determined to retain, intact and ready for immediate applica-
tion, the psychological modes of a life on Palestinian soil
in case the Messiah should suddenly appear and lead
them back to the Holy Land. Out of this retention
sprang, in fact, the folk motivation of the Zionist movement. The grandsons of the Kasrielevkites are mostly in
America, where they are relinquishing, among other
things, the cultural paraphernalia of " the return "; but
a considerable number of them are actually in Palestine,
and their transition from a Russian urban life to a sub-
tropical agricultural life was tremendously facilitated by
the rituals of their grandfathers! What a curious vindication of a two-thousand-year plan!

Now, if the Kasrielevkites could put so much emotion
into remote memories and expectations and give them
such burning immediacy, how much more were they
stirred by the festivals of the New Year and the Day of
Atonement, which touched their quickest interests! For
the period of nearly two weeks enclosing these festivals
was the period of heavenly decision on all human desti-
nies. " The Days of Awe " were filled with repentance,
mutual forgiveness, and supplication. The grandeur of
the New Year and Yom Kippur services owed nothing to
external circumstance, everything to the imagination.
How much the Kasrielevkites did, with how little! Their
place of worship was a tumbledown wooden chapel
which could not hold more than three or four hundred
persons; but no Notre-Dame of Paris or St. Peter's of
Rome, with vast spaces, forests of pillars, great coloured
windows, and thunderous organs, was ever filled with a
more impressive inner magnificence than a Kasrielevky
synagogue on the Day of Atonement. Consider, for in-

stance, the shofar, or ram's horn, which is sounded in the synagogue in the Days of Awe, when the heavens are open. The shofar is, as a musical instrument, an unfortunate invention. It has less volume than a saxophone and less dignity than a trombone. The original users of the shofar on the hills of ancient Judea may have imparted to it a certain primitive ferocity; but when the *baal tekiah* of Kasrielevky blew into it, the shofar yielded, at best, a tremulous staccato fading into a bronchitic wheeze. And yet in the ears of the Kasrielevkites it was the trumpet of doom pealing from end to end of the universe, and their hearts contracted with fear. A modern Jew acquainted with nothing more than the respectabilities of Western synagogues has not the remotest notion of the glory and terror which filled the little tabernacles of Sholom Aleichem's world on Yom Kippur.

The famous *Kol Nidre* prayer, which opens the Yom Kippur services, is another instance of this transformation by the power of suggestion. In substance *Kol Nidre* is a legalistic formula intended to discourage the taking of vows, which are understood to be religious vows, as between man and God and not (as has been falsely represented) bargains between persons. It has no special beauty of diction; in the significance of its content it is inferior to a score of prayers occurring in the Yom Kippur service. But it opens the service, and it has been set to moving music. And so *Kol Nidre* became for the Jews an unanalysable symbol of the most solemn moment of the year. No one thinks of the meaning of the words; the association has transcended and obliterated the original purpose. *Kol Nidre* has become an eternal sanctity.

Israel Zangwill somewhere makes sarcastic comment on the custom of Western Jews who send one another greeting cards for the high holy days, on which the words appear: " Wishing you a happy New Year *and well over the fast.*" Kasrielevkites certainly wished themselves and one another a happy New Year, but the twenty-four-hour fast was nothing to make a fuss about. They did make a genuine fuss, however, about repentance and mutual forgiveness.

Noah Wolf, the butcher, for instance: a hard, rough man, who from one year's end to the other is the terror of his customers. A woman comes in and says, quite innocently: " Reb Noah Wolf, have you any fresh meat this morning? " And Reb Noah answers: " Fresh meat? Certainly not. Rotten meat, stinking meat, crawling meat is all I deal in." " Reb Noah Wolf, give me a good portion." " I'll give you exactly the portion you've earned." Why does Noah Wolf talk like that? He does not know. It simply comes out of him. But in the days of repentance Reb Noah Wolf is as meek as one of his own slaughtered lambs; and on the day before Yom Kippur Noah Wolf, burly, clumsy, heavy of speech, makes the rounds of his neighbours and customers, saying to each one: " If I've offended you with a harsh word, forgive me, and may you have a happy year." To which they answer: " You too, Reb Noah Wolf. May God forgive." And they offer him cake.

Or Ezriel the fisherman, whose tongue is as sharp as Noah Wolf's, and who adds to this virtue a universal suspiciousness that every customer is trying to steal something. And if you should happen to poke a finger into one of his fish, just to try it out, he's liable to pick up the fish and slap you across the face with it. And nothing to be done either; Ezriel is the only fish-dealer in town; you must buy from him or do without fish for the Sabbath.

The day before Yom Kippur he makes the rounds, and however hard he finds it, he says: "If I've offended you with a harsh word, forgive me, and may you have a happy New Year." To which they answer: "You too, Reb Ezriel. May God forgive." And they offer him cake.

And so with Gonte the Hebrew-teacher, and Moses Velvel the drayman, and Sanne the water-carrier, and Getzi the beadle, and all the others. "If I've offended you with a harsh word, forgive me." "You too, you too. May God forgive."

Noah Wolf and Ezriel and Gonte and Moses Velvel and Sanne and Getzi remained what they were, of course. What, then, was the good of Yom Kippur, if it did not make them better? Well, perhaps it prevented them from becoming worse.

CHAPTER XI

Kasrielevky on a Binge

❀

TWICE a year it is meritorious to get drunk in Kasrielevky, on the day of the Rejoicing for the Law, called Simchas Torah, and on Purim, the half-festival which commemorates the immeasurable devotion of Esther, the subtle wisdom of Mordecai, and the foiled villainy of Haman.

A Kasrielevkite talking of drink puts you in mind of vikings draining gigantic flagons to the bottom. He talks big. A Kasrielevkite actually drinking is much less formidable. The first thimbleful brings a joyous light into his eyes, the second thimbleful sets him dancing, the third extinguishes him. Three healthy peasants could have downed at one sitting all the brandy consumed in Kasrielevky on Simchas Torah and Purim and walked home erect. Hence the contemptuous Yiddish phrase: " A Jewish drunkard! " It is of a piece with the other folk phrase " A Jewish robber! " to which is attached the story of a Jewish highwayman who held up a merchant and demanded his life, or a pinch of snuff.

A highly suggestible people, as we have seen, they get drunk mostly on the idea of getting drunk, and become riotous with the mere thought of licence. On Simchas

Torah the town is in an uproar. The lads, the boyos, the buckaroos of Kasrielevky, a round dozen of them, dance in parade through the streets and force a way into the houses of the rich, where the householder must stand treat, serve them with cake and wine, or cake and brandy, or cake and beer — or else. Or else they will take it from the sideboard without his permission; and perhaps even insult him to boot. You never know what a Kasrielev-kite will do on the grand and glorious day of Simchas Torah, between his first and his third thimbleful.

The gay blades of Kasrielevky are strictly Simchas Torah blades. One neither sees them nor hears a chirrup from them the rest of the year. Just as certain American descendants of Kasrielevky are once-a-year Jews, on Yom Kippur, so the " *huliakes*," the roisterers, of Kasrielevky are once a year roisterers, on Simchas Torah. There are other " *huliakes* " who choose Purim for their binge. It appears that there are no Kasrielevkites capable of maf-ficking twice a year. Nor do the " lads " forgather even for milder jollifications at any other time. It is a strictly annual reunion.

Elik " the mechanic " is one of the Simchas Torah hooligans. Why he is called " the mechanic " is not re-corded. He is a tailor by trade, and by habit a teetotaller. He might perhaps incline toward the fiery drop on other days than Simchas Torah, but he has a wife and many children to support with his needle and shears, and noth-ing is left for self-indulgence. Kopel " the brain-man " is the second of the hooligans. He comes by his nickname honestly, for he has a tremendous forehead (" the fore-head of a prime minister," they say in Kasrielevky, where prime ministers are still respected) and is a thoughtful, even a gloomy man. Kopel is a shoemaker by trade and

spends the days of his years in a cellar dwelling, hammer-
ing tiny wooden pegs — iron nails are not often used in
Kasrielevky — into soles. His wife is a shrew, homicidally
garrulous. Mendel " the tinman " or tinsmith is the third
apache. His trade has eaten into his bones and skin and
nerves. His face is pallid, like unpolished tin, his beard
has a tinny look, and his voice is metallic. He mends
samovars and stoves, and earns about enough to buy water for gruel. You must buy your water in Kasrielevky,
from the water-carrier. The grits his wife has to buy;
she is a midwife, and earns very little, so that Mendel's
task of providing the water for the gruel is not a difficult
one. Moses Yenkel " the heretic " is the fourth in the
company; an elderly man, a watchmaker by trade. You
must not let yourself be frightened by his nickname. His
heresies are — at least in the eyes of moderns — exceed-
ingly mild. He does not believe in the evil eye, is not
afraid to cross a priest's path, does not regard an empty
pail as a bad omen, and makes fun (this is more serious) of the extravagant worship of Chassidim for their
rabbis. How did Moses Yenkel get that way? Kasrielevkites say that he has been affected by his occupation; the
mechanics of watches has given a mechanistic twist to
Moses Yenkel's thinking. The Kasrielevkites have not
heard of Paley, who found in a watch the confirmation
of his faith.

Such are the four leaders of the company, and not very
different is the spirit of the others. A quiet lot three hundred and sixty-four days in the year, but positive demons
on Simchas Torah. It must be remembered, however,
that all Kasrielevky rejoices on Simchas Torah, if not
with the alarming abandon of the " huliakes," at least
sufficiently to give warrant to their excesses. The high

point of the celebrations is reached in the synagogue, where on the eve and morning of Simchas Torah, the Scrolls are taken out of the Ark and carried in procession, by rounds, called *hakofos.* Everyone has his chance to join in a procession, and the bystanders press forward and kiss the sacred objects. To give you some idea of the pandemonium of Simchas Torah, it need only be said that on the occasion of the *hakofos* the girls are permitted to break into the men's section of the synagogue, and to join, not in the processions, of course, but in the kissing of the Scrolls. And if one girl here and there, bending down, kisses, instead of the velvet, gold-embroidered covering of the Scroll, the hand of the boy who carries it, who's to know? Such are the carryings on in Kasrielevky on Simchas Torah.

Purim is, if anything, madder and merrier than Simchas Torah. It is more secular in spirit, too; that is, to the extent that any festival in Kasrielevky can be called secular. There is the same wild drinking and dancing, the same rejoicing in the streets, the same high climax in the synagogue. Instead of the reading of the Torah, however, it is the reading of the Book of Esther that is the focal point of the celebration. It is read from beginning to end, with special cantillation, and amidst indescribable jubilation. The children in the synagogue — and, if you want to know, many of the adults, too — are provided with a special kind of rattle, called a *gragger;* and whenever the name of Haman (may his memory be blotted out for ever!) is mentioned in the reading, there is a tremendous rattling of rattles, stamping of feet, and general manifestation of high glee.

There are many, many jolly customs associated with Purim. There is the *hamantasch,* the Haman's pocket or

Haman's hat, a special cake, triangular in shape, with a sweet hard crust and stuffing of poppyseed and ground nuts and honey, which everyone must eat. Purim without *hamantasches* is *Hamlet* without the Prince. There is the sending of *shalachmonus*, platters of sweetmeats, to friends and relatives and acquaintances. There is the Purim play.

A certain family of Kasrielevky, that of Naphthali "with the legs," is famous for the unique role which it plays in the Purim celebrations of Kasrielevky, and envied for the enormous rewards which it gathers therefor. They call it, indeed, "the golden-handed family." We shall learn a great deal about Purim, and Kasrielevky, and Naphthali's family if we spend a few minutes on the reasons for the nickname.

To begin with, then, there are the long legs of Naphthali himself. He is the fastest walker in Kasrielevky, and if the Kasrielevkites were given, like other people, to such absurdities as athletic competitions, let us say walking matches, it would be Naphthali first, the rest nowhere. An obvious connection between Naphthali's long legs and the gainful exploitation of Purim at once suggests itself: Naphthali must make a mint of money on Purim delivering *shalachmonus*. No; *shalachmonus* is delivered by children and servant girls. It is Naphthali's uncountable children who bring home pocketfuls of tips on Purim. There is another and loftier connection between Naphthali's long legs and the festival of the triumph of Esther.

Naphthali is the producer of the one dramatic spectacle which is offered every year to the Kasrielevkites: the Purim play. He is producer, backer, designer, stage manager, coach, ticket-seller and playwright. In none of these functions are long legs an advantage. But Naphthali also plays the role of Memuchan, the chamberlain of King Ahasuerus, and Pooh-Bah of the Persian court. Who is it that carries the command of Ahasuerus, the foolish, tipsy, and uxorious King, to Vashti, his Queen, to display her naked beauty before the assembled guests? Yes, her naked beauty. The Bible text does not say " naked " outright, but how else are we to understand Vashti's refusal? Also, how else are we to interpret the verse: " To bring Vashti the Queen before the King with the royal crown, to show the people and the princes her beauty "? Why is only " the royal crown " mentioned? What was the matter with the royal robes? Obviously the Queen was commanded to show herself to the assembly in her nakedness; and even if the verse itself did not practically state this, we know that nothing better could be expected from a half-witted show-off like Ahasuerus. But to return to Naphthali. Who carries the message to the Queen? Memuchan. Who brings back the stupefying answer? Memuchan. With whom does Ahasuerus take counsel? Memuchan. Who is the ambassador to Mordecai? Memuchan. It's Memuchan here, Memuchan there, Memuchan everywhere. A Memuchan with short legs is a calamity in a Purim play. A Purim play simply cannot be written for a Memuchan with short legs.

Compared with this gift of Naphthali's, his other qualifications as playwright, stage manager, and so on, are of secondary importance. Not that they are by any means contemptible. For who in Kasrielevky besides Naphthali of the long legs can produce the ringing Yiddish verses of the Purim drama? Such, for instance, as the monologue of Memuchan in transit between Ahasuerus and Queen Vashti:

77

Behold me, everybody, Memuchan is my name,
And I am King Ahasuerus's chamberlain.
I must tell Queen Vashti to do the King honour
By coming before his guests without a single thing on her.
And if she proves to be a rebel and a backslider,
And disobeys Ahasuerus, then woe betide her.

Or the defiant answer of Queen Vashti, delivered in a singsong by Nosy Berel (the Purim play, like the Shakespearean drama, had no women) :

Come hither, all you women of Persia and Media,
And a most terrible story everyone shall hear.
Not only is my husband a disgraceful boozer,
But having a noble wife, he doesn't know how to use her.
He commands me to do a thing which, to my sorrow,
Is altogether against the laws of the Torah.

And so on, scene after scene, on the same inspired level, through the dethronement of Vashti, the election of Esther, the refusal of Mordecai to humble himself before Haman, the resolve of Haman to avenge himself by the liquidation of the entire Jewish people, the providential sleeplessness of the King, the banquets of Esther, and the downfall of Haman. It is no small task for Naphthali of the long legs to coach ten boys in their parts, design their costumes, paint the scenery, sell the tickets, and collect the money. But when Purim is over, Naphthali is reputed to have made a fortune.

That is not all. Naphthali's wife, Rivelle " the sweet," is an artist in her own right; not as producer and playwright, but as a baker of Purim sweetmeats, in which there is not a housewife in Kasrielevky who can hold a candle to her. Mysterious are the ways of Providence,

Why should Rivelle's genius be so curiously circum-
scribed? Why should she not be equally gifted in the pro-
duction of Sabbath bread, sponge cake or *knishes*? For
the obvious reason, of course, that then she would not
be " Rivelle the sweet," but " Rivelle the baker," which
would only raise the question: " Why should she be
' Rivelle the baker ' rather than ' Rivelle the sweet '? "
Some people are never satisfied. Better leave this question alone, then, and accept the simple fact that she is
" Rivelle the sweet," from whom half Kasrielevky must
buy its Purim sweetmeats.

Add that to Naphthali's income as playwright, producer, and so forth, and proceed to the item of Naphthali's children, carriers of *shalachmonus* on Purim. How
many children has Naphthali " with the legs "? Sholom
Aleichem does not tell us, just as he does not tell us how
many children there were in his own family. He contents
himself with the word " multitude." This is not careless-
ness but good manners. After all, what business is it of
ours exactly how many children Naphthali, or anyone
else, brought into the world? Do we have to support
them? Are they in our way? A well-bred Jew, compelled
to count the members of his or someone else's family, always says: " Well, Isaac is not one, Jakie is not two, Abie
is not three, Dovidl is not four, Beckie is not five, Hymie
is not six, Sarah is not seven, Joey is not eight, Leibel is
not nine, Aaron is not ten, and then there is little Rosie,
which makes a total of not eleven, may they live one hundred and twenty years." Very well, then, whatever the
number of children Naphthali does not have, every one
of them is old enough to serve as messenger and carrier
on Purim.

And still we have not exhausted the sources of Napth-

thali's income on Purim. Noah, the oldest son, was born
with a talent for woodcarving. Like every other artist, he
has had to fight his way through. Until he was eleven or
twelve years old he whittled or carved in secret, as far as
he could. When he was caught at it he was beaten black
and blue. Noah the idiot, they called him, Noah with the
penknife, Noah the wastrel, Noah the wood-fiend, Noah
the this, Noah the that. Until Noah, one Purim, was inspired to carve a rattle, for which an amazed neighbour
paid him two kopecks; after which it was, respectfully,
enviously, Noah the rattle-maker, Noah the genius.

Thus it was that Naphthali " of the legs" made
enough on Purim to see him and his family through the
Passover, with new clothes, new shoes, *matzos,* wine,
eggs, potatoes, and all the other necessaries of the festival. Whence it was a proverb in Kasrielevky that God
brought about the Purim for three reasons: that the Jews
of Esther's generation might be saved from destruction,
that the Jews of all other generations might rejoice, and
that Naphthali " with the legs " might make enough to
see him through the Passover.

We are now at the end of this incomplete account of
the festivals of the Kasrielevkites. A footnote remains to
be added, an additional attempt to answer the unanswer-
able question: What was there behind the fundamental
contentment of the Kasrielevkites, behind the frivolity
of Purim, the gaiety of Simchas Torah, the joy of Passover and Pentecost and Booths? I have spoken of the love
of life, as Kasrielevkites understood it, of *bitochon,* of
faith, of pride in the one true religion. To these mysteries let another be added: the overwhelming and tacit
belief in the Messianic outcome of history.

Sholom Aleichem remembers how his grandfather,

Moishe Yossie of Bohslav, used to talk about the coming
of the Messiah. Moishe Yossie was an old, old man, who
lived like an ascetic, brooding day and night over prayers and sacred books. He mortified his body, and never
ate meat except on Sabbaths and festivals, when mortifi-
cation of the flesh is forbidden. He was a mystic by constitution, a pawnbroker by profession; a sad, but not
gloomy old man, contemptuous of this world of ours, the
sole merit of which is that it enables you to practise the
virtue of charity. Only at rare intervals would old Moishe
Yossie discard the mantle of mournfulness, and that was
when — as on Simchas Torah — he was visited by ecstatic visions of the Messiah. It was true that centuries
might pass before God would release the Messiah for the
work of salvation; but it was also true that the Messiah
might already be on the way, preceded by Elijah the
Prophet. Old Moishe Yossie was a wanderer in the labyrinths of eschatology, for ever deducing from sacred texts
the duration of the exile.

Once little Sholom came into his grandfather's room
and beheld a marvellous sight. On the wrinkled, bearded
face of old Moishe Yossie rested a divine light, and the
words he murmured to himself were full of sweetness and
ecstasy:

" It is close at hand! The kingdom of Edom is drawing to a close. Come here, little one, and we will talk of
the end of days, and of the things that will be when the
Messiah comes."

Awed and fascinated, little nine-year-old Sholom listened to the revelation which had just been vouchsafed
old Moishe Yossie. Bliss, eternal bliss, for Israel the faithful one! The saints of all the ages were gathered, together
with the seraphim and the cherubim in their hierarchies,

81

about the throne of glory, and in the midst was the Ancient of Days, the King of Kings, the Holy One, blessed be He. Moishe Yossie had smelt the odour of roast Leviathan and of the Mighty Ox — and it was delicious. Moishe Yossie, the ascetic of this world, dreamed of mighty feasting in the world to come. For then it would be different — permissible, nay, meritorious, to eat of Leviathan and *Shor ha-Bor,* and to wash down the morsels with draughts of the Guarded Wine, which had been bottled and stored away in the celestial cellars from before the evening of the world's first Sabbath. Besides, this indulgence of the flesh — not the gross and ordinary flesh, but an exalted and transfigured flesh — would be accompanied by eternal study. The Hidden Light, which had reigned during the process of creation, would rest on the changeless scene, and the Almighty Himself, in His own dignity and glory, would serve the saints. Then, at a given signal, a temple, a thousand times more dazzling than that which Solomon built, would be lowered, all assembled and perfect, from the divine courts, to rest exactly on the spot where Solomon's Temple had stood, on the Hill of Moriah, where Abraham had made ready to sacrifice to God the son of his old age, Isaac. Diamonds and precious stones would flash on every side, and priests and Levites would sing on the stairs. . . . And here Grandfather Moishe Yossie can speak no more. His head is thrown back, his eyes are closed, his lips parted. A Chassidic melody issues from him, he snaps his fingers to the rhythm, and he sings: " Bim-bom, oh, Father, bimbom." And what would the supreme bliss consist in? Study, eternal study, the eternal session of the Academy on high, with God as the teacher, uncovering the secrets contained in every curl of every letter of the Torah.

In old Moishe Yossie the belief in the Messiah and in
the glorious redemption was more explicit than in most
Jews; but it was not deeper. We are speaking, naturally,
of the Jews of the inner circle, of Kasrielevky, of Sholom
Aleichem's world. Rabbi and drayman, carpenter and
ritual slaughterer, householder, pedlar, tailor, beggar —
the word Messiah was always on their lips. The ultimate
blasphemy was " to speak against God and His Messiah."
With such certainty of final triumph in their hearts, were
not Moishe Yossie and all the other Jews of Kasrielevky
and Kozodoievka and Mazeppavka and Bohslav and Bohopolie justified in celebrating their Jewishness? What
if — awful thought! — the Torah had been entrusted
to another people! Not that the nations had not had
their chance. The tradition tells that God offered the
Torah to nation after nation, only to have its onerous
terms rejected by all of them; until He came to the Jews,
who accepted: under duress, it is true — but why did He
not apply the same duress to the others? Perhaps because
He did not believe that they would endure the long test.
Four thousand years, most of them years of exile, the
Jews had endured, from Ur of the Chaldees to Kasrielevky. Look at it any way you like, you could not say that
it was meaningless and without purpose.

CHAPTER XII

A Tale of Two Cities

❀

It is a pity that we cannot continue for the remainder of this book in the same strain, all quaintness and mysticism, courage, gaiety, and piety, and charming, elfin little people. The microcosmos of Sholom Aleichem is a true replica of the world. He was not a modern novelist with a special line; he did not set out to be refreshingly idyllic or sternly realistic. He did not even set out to be a Yiddish writer. In a letter which he wrote toward the end of his life to an old friend he tells how, late one night, kept awake by business worries, he sat down at his desk and sought distraction by putting down on paper, in Yiddish, a fantasy of his own childhood. He did not invent; he merely recalled. He sent off the manuscript to a Yiddish periodical, and was dumbfounded to receive, together with the acceptance, an urgent request for more. Doubtless if it had not happened thus, it would have happened some other way, for he was destined to be the voice of Russian Jewry, and destiny always gets us — that's the business of destiny — but always by accident, as we think. From that time on he wrote, inexhaustibly. And still he was not what we call a writer. He was a speaker. He chatted about his world. Or put it this way: he let his world flow through him, as through a funnel. He uses ordinary language; his stories, people, and townlets have the quality of anonymity; they are not thought up; they happen to be there, and Sholom Aleichem calls our attention to them, casually. It is all one long monologue, the recital of a pilgrimage. Certainly it is all transfigured by the passage through his mind, but it is not distorted. The bad is there with the good, the hateful with the heartening; and so, as we retrace the path of his pilgrimage, we should be false to him, and to life, and to ourselves, if we omitted a single unpleasant picture or mood.

The bad in Sholom Aleichem's world, as in every other real world, is not independent of the good, but organically linked with it. Let us take the matter of prayer among the Kasrielevkites. A pietist cannot but be edified by the seriousness with which they took it. A Kasrielevkite, being usually a Chassid, regarded prayer as an act of intimate communion between himself and the Almighty. He knew that it was an affront to the Glory to utter prayer without complete absorption in the meaning of the words. The sages of blessed memory have stated explicitly that one reason for the destruction of Jerusalem had been the perfunctory and therefore empty devotions of the Jews in the latter days of the Second Temple. A true Jew gives himself utterly and without reservation to the contemplation of the Presence when he addresses it in praise or supplication. Reb Pinchas of Koritz, a great Chassidic Rabbi (his merit be our shield) said that God and prayer were one. It is written of Rabbi Akiba of old that in the ecstasy of his devotions he would leap from corner to corner of the room. And the Saint of Shpolle (it was he, we remember, who put God Almighty on trial) danced after prayer, so that the hearts of beholders melted; while of him of Berditchev, Reb Levi Isaac, also known as " the Compassionate," it was told that those who saw him at his devotions were cast into a spell by his visible unification with the invisible Presence.

It is disturbing to record that with this lofty Kasrielevkite concept of prayer went a rigid pedantry with regard to certain forms.

In the morning, for instance. You came into the synagogue for *Shachris;* you put on your prayer-shawl and phylacteries, with the appropriate benedictions, and you led off with the prayer beginning: " Give thanks unto the Lord and call upon His name." Then you followed up with the prayer beginning: " Blessed be He who spoke and the world was in being."

That was the accepted and the natural order. But wait. It was the accepted and natural order if you were a Kasrielevkite. Very different was the accepted and natural order if you were a Jew of Kozodoievka. There too you arrived early in the morning for the *Shachris.* There too you put on prayer-shawl and phylacteries with the appropriate benedictions. But instead of leading off with " Give thanks unto the Lord, call upon His name," following it up with " Blessed be He who spoke and the world was in being," you reversed the order. *First* " Blessed be He who spoke and the world was in being," and *then* " Give thanks unto the Lord, call upon His name." The rest of the service was the same in Kozodoievka as in Kasrielevky.

But what on earth is the difference? Don't ask me and don't ask Sholom Aleichem; and if you value your peace of mind, don't ask the Kasrielevkites or Kozodoievkites, either. Was there perhaps some profound difference between the structures of the two towns? There was not. Kozodoievka and Kasrielevky were as like as two peas: the same Jews, the same paupers, the same merchants and pedlars, the same ritual baths, synagogues, market-places, and cemeteries. The only outward difference had to do with goats. Those of Kozodoievka were distinguished in the matter of their horns, which they did not have. If this had any connection with the quarrel over the order of the prayers, a subtler analyst than Sholom Aleichem will have to detect it.

Now, it would happen that a Kozodoievka Jew would pass the night in near-by Kasrielevky and in the morning would, of course, go to the synagogue. He would put on phylacteries and prayer-shawl, and repeat the benediction like anyone else. But no sooner had the cantor and congregation started in chorus on " Give thanks unto the Lord " than the lone, protesting voice of the Kozodoiev-kite would be heard intoning: " Blessed be He." And when the Kasrielevkites had finished the first prayer, with the Kozodoievkite battling against the stream, *they* would start on " Blessed be He," and *he*, as obstinately as before, would work on " Give thanks unto the Lord."

Contrariwise, a Kasrielevkite visiting Kozodoievka, and attending morning prayers, would set the teeth of the congregation on edge by blessing Him when they were giving thanks, and giving thanks when they were blessing Him.

It is probable that visiting Kasrielevkites in Kozodoi-evka were more provocative than visiting Kozodoiev-kites in Kasrielevky, for the order of the prayers indi-cates that the Kasrielevkites were Chassidim, who prayed with great gusto, while the Kozodoievkites were non-Chassidim, and therefore less boisterous. At any rate, the strain between the two communities reached the breaking-point on one occasion, when a visiting Kasrielevkite was praying in the Kozodoievka synagogue. Not content with asserting his own order, and chanting: " Call upon His name " when all the others were chorusing: " Blessed be He who spoke," he made a point of it, by lingering loudly on the word " name." The Kozodoievkites might have let the Kasrielevkite ritual pass, as they had often done before. But that word " name," which the Kasrielevkite drew out at the top of his voice, with passionate roulades and trills and grace-notes and appoggiaturas and all manner of musical devices, not just " name," but " nay-yay-aya-nayay-ayay-yayayayame," was not to be borne. And what, I ask, did he want to do it for? Had anyone tried to stop him from exercising his rights and saying: " Give thanks unto the Lord, call upon His name," in a quiet, orderly fashion? Under what necessity was he to lift up his voice above all the others, and to draw out the word " name " with operatic repetitiousness a mile and a half? This was nothing but provocation, and as provocation it called for a retort; which the Kasrielevkite got from an enraged Kozodoievkite in the form of a resounding slap in the face, followed by another, and a third and a fourth, from other Kozodoievkites. In short, they fell upon the impudent Kasrielevkite and beat him within an inch of his life before they threw him out of the synagogue.

Thus began the great feud between Kasrielevky and Kozodoievka; and you must not imagine, either, that it was a comical, good-natured little feud, a kind of game, like that which the children play with wooden swords and paper helmets on the thirty-third day of the Omer. No, it was Rome and Veii, Athens and Megara, Florence and Pisa. On the other hand, we must not carry it too far. Actual bloodshed there was none. It was not in a Kasrielevkite or a Kozodoievkite to stick a knife into a human being, Jew or non-Jew, or to send an arrow into him from ambush. But the wars of the Chassidim and Misnagdim, whether of Kasrielevky and Kozodoievka or of two other neighbouring Jewish townlets divided in the faith, were not at all funny. Anger, hatred, envy, came into play. There were thrashings and mutual excommunications. Marriages between children of the hostile communities were as unthinkable as between the children of Montagues and Capulets. There were appeals to the governmental authorities, who were baffled by the origins of the quarrels, being unable to imagine that Jews too were addicted to the imbecilities of *homoousion* and *homoiousion*. There were Kasrielevkites and Kozodoievkites who became informers to the police: such and such a one was peddling socks without a licence, so and so was fermenting wine illegally.

A very unedifying business: two adjacent Jewish communities filled with spite and rancour against each other, all in the name of the common Father of Jew and gentile. The vendetta between Kasrielevky and Kozodoievka lasted for many years, perhaps for a generation, perhaps longer. It did not end until old Kasrielevky became new Kasrielevky — that is, until the twentieth century dawned on Russia, bringing with it enlightenment, modernity, and pogroms. Further on in this pilgrimage we shall see in what manner the two communities became reconciled.

CHAPTER XIII

The Judgments of Reb Yozifel

❀

Lilies that fester smell far worse than weeds," sang a poet unknown to old Kasrielevky — a poet old Kasrielevky might have loved because as many commentaries have been written on him as on the Talmud, and as many interpretations grown up round his text as round that of the Torah. The Kasrielevkites were so organically interpenetrated with religion that they had nothing to be good with except religion, and nothing to be bad with except religion. (Somewhere among the old prayers there is one which runs approximately thus: " O Lord, let me worship Thee not only with my good inclination, but also with my evil inclination.")

Shalachmonus, the sending round of sweetmeats on the festival of Purim, was not a religious rite, properly speaking. But it had a semi-religious character, and in any case it was a charming tradition; certainly it added, or was supposed to add, to the jollity of the celebration and the sweetness of life.

The Kasrielevkites sent one another plates of *hamantasch,* a delicacy already described, of *teiglach,* tiny squares of dough boiled in honey, chopped nuts and spices, of cakes, tarts, biscuits, cookies, scones with rai-

sins and scones with currants; they sent one another everything that the ingenuity of the housewife could de-
vise with flour, eggs, milk, sugar, fruits, and an oven. All
day long, as we have seen, boys and girls, messengers and
maidservants, scurried through the streets of Kasrielevky,
carrying gift and return gift from neighbour to neighbour, acquaintance to acquaintance, relative to relative,
and receiving a little cash reward — Purim money. A
lovely and gracious tradition it was, which gave a special tone and colour to Purim, the most secular of the
festivals.

Lovely and gracious, that is to say, in the spirit, and
for that matter in the execution too, most of the time.
But how can one ensure a lovely and gracious tradition
against petrifaction into the formal and snobbish? How
can we prevent the gifts of Father's Day and Mother's
Day and Wedding Day and Birthday and Christmas
from degenerating into — well, into missiles instead of
missives? Consider a housewife of Kasrielevky, with her
Purim list of relatives, in-laws, friends and acquaintances,
each one of whom had to be considered individually.
There were gradations and standards and precedents,
featherweight distinctions in the sending and return of
shalachmonus; particularly in the return, if you happened to be the first recipient. For instance, two *hamantasches,* five cookies, a currant scone, and a slice of honey
cake called exactly for one *hamantasch,* two tarts, eight
biscuits, and a raisin scone, or its equivalent, three slices
of honey cake, a slab of *teiglach,* two currant scones, and
three cookies. Of course the size of the slices and the
density of the baking also entered into the reckoning.

You had to know your way about these usages; it was
a question of feeling rather than of weights and meas-

ures. You had to be the possessor of a massive memory, as well as of a delicate sense of social values. For a disparity in gifts was permissible, or, rather, expected, as between the poor and the well-to-do; the former were not abashed to receive a plateful of good things out of all proportion to their own sending; the latter did not expect in return more than a token greeting. But God help you if you sent more than you received to one whose inferior status was not established and acknowledged; or less than you received if your own inferiority was not similarly established and acknowledged. The *nogid,* or rich man, ranked everybody except the other *negidim;* the trustees of the synagogue were in the upper brackets; the Rabbi, the cantor, and the ritual slaughterer were in the middle class for substance, but high up for honours. There were class and personal distinctions, individual and group subtleties — all in all an etiquette as complicated as the hierarchies of the Byzantine court and the rigid ceremonial compulsions of the hidalgos. And people knew their rights and stood on them.

A particular sense of delicacy was needed by the first sender of *shalachmonus,* especially as the gifts might be crossing and still had to correspond to the weights and measures of the code. Here was where memory came in, the *shalachmonuses* of previous years, the relative standing of the parties, and the interpretation thereof in *shalachmonus* rating.

How deep the code went, and what calamities might follow from the contravention of it, we learn from the incident of the two Nechamahs, or rather of their employers. Nechamah the black and Nechamah the red were two servant girls. Nechamah the black worked for Zlota, the wife of Reb Isaac the storekeeper, and her pay was four and a half roubles the season — six months — with clothes and shoes. Nechamah the red worked for Zelda, the wife of Reb Yossie the storekeeper, and her pay was six roubles the season, no clothes and shoes. On a certain muddy Purim — that is to say, on a certain Purim, for the festival occurs in the early spring, when the unpaved streets and alleys of Kasrielevky were covered by six inches of ooze — Nechamah the red and Nechamah the black came face to face as they were carrying their covered trays of *shalachmonus*, Nechamah the red on her way to the employer of Nechamah the black, and vice versa. A happy meeting! The girls were tired with delivering gifts in all quarters of the town. So they sat down on a doorstep to swap experiences, compare tips, and revile their employers.

Thence they proceeded to show each other the contents of their respective trays. Nechamah the black was the bearer of an appetizing square of strudel, two big honey cakes, a fish-shaped cake stuffed with ground nuts and sugar, and a slab of poppyseed cake rich with honey. Nechamah the red carried a fat *hamantasch*, black with poppyseed, two " cushion cakes," so called from their shape and softness, a golden cookie starred with black raisins, a slab of tart, and two cherub cakes. As any Kasrielevkite expert could have told you, the gifts were balanced to a nicety, both in respect of each other and of the relative social status of the senders.

Who would have thought that from this casual encounter of two servant girls would ensue a *cause célèbre* never to be forgotten in the annals of Kasrielevky? And who but a Kasrielevkite could understand, and even sympathize with, the circumstances? Beginning with loose, idle talk, the two Nechamahs, tired and hungry, as

93

well as rebellious and envious, passed from the scrutiny
of each other's trays to the consideration of conspiracy.
What would be the harm, they asked, if an equal quan-
tity of sweetmeats were removed from each tray, leaving
the balance where it had been? Thus, if the strudel disappeared from the tray of Nechamah the black, and the
golden cookie from the tray of Nechamah the red, the
gifts of Zlota the wife of Reb Isaac and of Zelda the wife
of Reb Yossie would still be perfectly matched. One
could go further: if a honey cake faded from the tray of
Nechamah the black, accompanied by a cushion cake
from the tray of Nechamah the red, the equilibrium
would still remain undisturbed. And was it not more fitting that the said strudel and honey cake and cookie and
cushion cake should go to the feeding of the stomachs of
the Nechamahs rather than the vanity of their employers?

Said and done; which showed they were only two foolish servant girls; for they left two fatal considerations
out of the count. Zelda the wife of Reb Yossie and Zlota
the wife of Reb Isaac would remember what they had
sent, but see only what they received. There was, moreover, the unalterable status established and maintained
throughout the years.

Thus it was: Nechamah the black brought her de-
pleted shipment to Zelda, the wife of Reb Yossie, who
uncovered the tray, took one glance, and uttered a shriek
which woke from his afternoon nap her husband Yossie,
Yossie the Washrag as the Kasrielevkites had named him
because he was the most henpecked husband in Kasrielevky.

" Tell your mistress," hissed Zelda to Nechamah the
black, " that I hope she lives till next Purim and doesn't
get a nicer *shalachmonus* than this from anyone in town."

94

Nechamah the red brought her diminished offering to Zlota, the wife of Reb Isaac, who uncovered the tray and almost fainted. She could not call to her husband, Reb Isaac, because he was not at home. One-a-year Isaac was *his* nickname, because every year, without fail, his wife brought forth a baby. That was the way of the Kasrielev-kites; they gave a man a nickname and it stuck. Reb Isaac might live to the age of ninety, and cease to procreate at the age of seventy, but it would be One-a-year Isaac till the day of his death.

" Look at this *shalachmonus,*" gasped Zlota. " May all the nightmares of my life, and the nightmares of the lives of all my ancestors, be visited upon the heads of my enemies! Is this a *shalachmonus* or a joke? Take this back to your miserable mistress, do you hear? " Wherewith the wife of One-a-year Isaac thrust out of doors Nechamah the red and sent her back to Zelda, the wife of Yossie the Washrag.

It would have been bad enough if One-a-year Isaac and Yossie the Washrag had been mere acquaintances. They were friends, which was odd enough since their two dry-goods stores stood side by side on the market-place and they were for ever snatching away each other's customers. But friends they were. They lent each other a couple of roubles now and again, they came to each other's homes on Friday evenings for the Sabbath bene-diction, and in the winter they went into each other's stores to warm up at the stove or play a game of checkers. Their wives, too, were on friendly terms, exchanging pots and scandal, pouring out their hearts to each other, and taking counsel on their domestic problems. Friends have, of course, larger foundations on which to erect a quarrel than have mere acquaintances. On the morning following this Purim, Reb Yossie the Washrag and One-a-year Isaac, well primed by their respective wives, opened their adjacent stores as usual and stationed themselves at their respective doors, each one waiting for the other to say " Good morning " in order that he might not answer. Customers being scarce that raw spring day, Reb Yossie and Reb Isaac stood there grimly, hour after hour, till their wives arrived.

" Isaac," said Zlota, acidulously, " why don't you thank your friend for the wonderful *shalachmonus* he sent us yesterday? "

" Yossie," said Zelda, poisonously, " have you returned adequate thanks for the noble present you received? "

" I don't speak to a Washrag," announced Reb Isaac loudly.

" I wouldn't answer a One-a-year," responded Reb Yossie.

There you had it! The battle was joined. In less time than it takes to put on a prayer-shawl, the husbands were in each other's beards, the wives in each other's hair. The market-place came to life; half the town assembled to separate the combatants or to join in the mêlée. The air was filled with questions and answers: " *Shalachmonus*," " insult," " *Shalachmonus*," " fit for a beggar," " *Shalachmonus*," " *Shalachmonus*," " *Shalachmonus*." Before the day was over, One-a-year Isaac and Yossie the Washrag invaded the office of the prefect, Pan Milinievsky, to lodge charges of libel, assault and battery, and malicious slander. With them came their wives, relatives, acquaintances, and enemies.

It is as shocking to report as it would be dishonest to deny that recourse to Pan Milinievsky the gentile on matters connected exclusively with internal Jewish differences was only too frequent. Particularly was this true in the autumn, round the time of the festival of Booths and Simchas Torah, the Rejoicing for the Law. But no season of the year was exempt from such scandals. There could always be an explosion over precedence in the synagogue, over privileges denied or honours misplaced. Feivel, the son of Chantze Mirke, got the most coveted section of the Torah to read out on a Sabbath morning when obviously it should have gone to Chaim, the son of Leah Dvosse; Kiveh One-eye was called twice in one month to roll up the sacred Scroll, and Deaf Itzig not even once in two months. Pan Milinievsky, a Russian with a high forehead and a vast beard, had been prefect of Kasrielevky so long that he spoke Yiddish like a native and even understood something about the delicate problems of precedence and social status in the synagogue. A decent enough man, considering that he was a gentile and an official; reasonable enough in the taking of bribes and, though an anti-Semite, devoid of viciousness. A trifle impatient, though, as he showed again on this occasion. For having tried for over an hour to get a word in edgewise between the accusations and counter-accusations of Zlota, Zelda, Isaac, Yossie, and their partisans, he rose to his feet and roared: " Get out! Get out! The whole kit and kaboodle! Go to your Rabbi! "

So the litigants and their partisans streamed toward the house of Reb Yozifel, the old and honoured Rabbi.

Patient, wise, long-suffering Reb Yozifel! He cannot be introduced casually. I must digress and present Reb Yozifel according to his merit. He was an old man even in old Kasrielevky, and he lived on into the wonders and terrors of new Kasrielevky. The word " rabbi " has been denuded, among us moderns, of the connotations which

clung to the word *" Rav."* Reb Yozifel, the *Rav* of Kasrielevky, has not his like among us. To say that he was a
scholar and saint is to give him his formal due. He was
the conscience of Kasrielevky, its purer self and its suffering heart. Himself without sin (you would not have
dared to suggest this in his presence), he did not believe
in the sinfulness of others. He saw only childishness and
error. No man, in his view, was wicked by choice. It was
all misunderstanding. If you only listened to the " sinner," if you gave him a chance to talk himself out, you
would discover nothing but good intention gone astray.

Now, just as an instance of Reb Yozifel's way with
" sinners " (let Zelda and Zlota and Isaac and Yossie and
the rest of them wait awhile), there was the matter of
the Old People's Home which Reb Yozifel set his heart
on, and of the rich Jew — not a Kasrielevkite — who do-
nated the money for it. This was in later years, in the period of new Kasrielevky, when they were building the
station for the railroad which the Kasrielevkites did not
believe in. The rich Jew in question was a contractor; a
St. Petersburgher; a modernized man; one of the Poliakovs, whose name was mentioned in an awed murmur,
like that of the Brodskys and Rothschilds; and he came
to Kasrielevky on business.

When a Jew comes to Kasrielevky on business the
town organizes itself round him. His room is beleaguered
by merchants, messengers, brokers, pedlars and commission men. Within an hour of his arrival Kasrielevky
must know his name, his occupation, the nature of his
mission, the size of his income, and the probable length
of his stay. Privacy? Reticence? Kasrielevky knows not
these things. All Jews are brothers; all Jews have a share
in the world to come and in each other's present business.

But this man Poliakov — of *the* Poliakovs or not — was an unnatural phenomenon. First, he took two whole rooms for himself at the Kasrielevky inn; second, he shut himself up and refused to receive anybody; third, he stationed a man at his door (did you ever hear the like?), and if you wanted to see him, you had to be announced.

Reb Yozifel and two of the leading householders of Kasrielevky, the *crème de la crème* of its respectability, called on the said Poliakov, and for some reason or other the guardian at the door had left his post. So they entered unannounced, whereupon the fantastic St. Petersburgher, coming out from the inner room, fell upon them in a rage and ordered them out as if they were, God forbid, robbers, or beggars.

The two householders fled, but Reb Yozifel, frail, tottering old Reb Yozifel, stood his ground, and began to explain, in his quavering voice, that this was a holy matter, an Old People's Home for which he was collecting funds, and that he was offering the stranger a share in paradise in exchange for a donation. The man Poliakov, beside himself at the impudence of the funny old Jew in the mediæval gaberdine, lost himself completely, and before he knew what he was doing, he had slapped old Reb Yozifel in the face, so that Reb Yozifel's skullcap fell to the floor, and he stood there bareheaded for several seconds, perhaps for the only time in his life.

Slowly and thoughtfully Reb Yozifel bent down and picked up his skullcap; slowly and thoughtfully he faced the stranger.

" That," said Reb Yozifel, " was for me. Now what will you give for the Old People's Home? "

When Reb Yozifel came out and rejoined the terrified committee, his face was flushed — one cheek being un-

99

accountably redder than the other. But he had the promise of the man Poliakov of St. Petersburg that an Old
People's Home would be built in Kasrielevky.

That, as I said, was years later. At the moment Reb
Yozifel's home has been invaded by the tumultuous
crowd turned away so unceremoniously by Pan Milinievsky. And here the scene was repeated, with this difference, that Reb Yozifel made no attempt to wedge in a
word. He let the hours pass while the room resounded
with the clamour of accusation and counter-accusation:
" *Hamantasch,*" " *Shalachmonus,*" " insult," " beggarly,"
" Washrag," " One-a-year."

They quieted down at last and demanded judgment,
which Reb Yozifel, as *Rav,* was bound to render. Never
had he been known to fail in this duty, no matter how
complicated or embittered the dispute. Indeed, Reb
Yozifel was famous for his judgments — you shall hear
shortly of his subtle solution of an insoluble problem in
the case of the Mayers and the Schnayers — not less than
for his sanctity.

But before judgment came the summation of the case,
which Reb Yozifel began with a heart-broken sigh.

" We stand," he said, " on the threshold of the Passover, the great, the holy festival — the festival, it may
be said, without an equal. Thousands and thousands of
years ago our ancestors went forth from Egypt in freedom, and traversed the Red Sea dryshod. What a festival! What a sea! What a miracle! Forty years they wandered thereafter in the wilderness, having received the
Torah at the foot of Sinai, that marvellous Torah in
which it is written *ve-ohavto,* and thou shalt love, *re-echo,*
thy neighbour, *komocho,* as thyself. Ah, what a Torah
God gave us! And how shall we honour it? With quar-

rels, with foolish disputes, with vanities? Is it not a desecration to prepare thus for the Passover? Come, children,
we have serious business before us. We must begin to
consider what shall be done in this town of ours for the
poor, who must celebrate the Passover like all the others. Have we yet made a list of what they need, in the
way of eggs and potatoes and chicken-fat — not to mention *matzos,* of course? But stay! There is a quarrel to be
composed, a judgment rendered. Let us begin the summation once more. The Passover is approaching! The
Passover! What a festival! Our forefathers went out of
Egypt in freedom, and traversed the Red Sea dryshod.
And after that they wandered forty years in the wilderness, having received the Torah at the foot of Sinai!
What a Torah! A Torah without an equal! Do you know
what that means? . . ."

And so Reb Yozifel went on with his summation, in his
weak, sad voice, and one by one the partisans began to
sneak from the room; one by one they withdrew, and
after them the litigants, each one going thoughtfully and
shamefacedly home, to wonder what the excitement had
been about, and to prepare for the great and holy festival of the Passover.

Could King Solomon have done better?

CHAPTER XIV

A Seat by the Eastern Wall

✿

EVEN more famous than the judgment he rendered in the *shalachmonus* dispute was Reb Yozifel's solution of the seemingly unmanageable case of the Mayers and the Shnayers.

The Mayers and the Shnayers were not two groups of people; they were two brothers, twins. They were referred to in the plural because though by convention one was known as Mayer and the other as Shnayer, it could not be said with certainty which was which; therefore each one of them was potentially both a Mayer and a Shnayer, and taken together they were the Mayers and the Shnayers.

In babyhood and boyhood they had been indistinguishable. The one who had issued first into the light of day had been given the name of Mayer; the one who had followed thirty minutes later, that of Shnayer. But who could guarantee that very early, when they had been bathed together, dried together, and put to sleep together, Mayer had not become Shnayer and Shnayer Mayer? Not that it really mattered at first, or that they themselves cared. They accepted the advantages and disadvantages of occasional confusions in the true spirit of brotherhood. If Mayer (or Shnayer) was sometimes praised in place of Shnayer (or Mayer), why, Shnayer (or Mayer) sometimes escaped punishment which fell by error on Mayer (or Shnayer). They did not even demur when the exasperated Hebrew-teacher, remembering at the end of the day that one of them had earned a thrashing, but unable to tell one from the other, thrashed them both, to make sure, and added: " What's the difference? It'll stay in the family."

It did not matter and they did not care, for there was a great bond of affection between them, which continued even after they had become grown men, easily distinguished from each other by the black beard belonging to Mayer (or Shnayer) and the red beard belonging to Shnayer (or Mayer). By convention blackbeard was Mayer, the elder; redbeard Shnayer, the younger. But no one, least of all the Mayers and the Shnayers, thought of going behind the convention to the original fact. And thus it might have been until the end of their days if there had not arisen a question of inheritance when their father died.

Reb Samson was the father of the Mayers and the Shnayers; a Jew held in high esteem for his character, his honourable antecedents, and his beard. Reb Samson Beard, they called him; a poor man, but a scholar and a saint. The inheritance which he left his older son consisted neither of fields nor houses nor merchandise, and certainly not of gold and silver. It consisted — and let no man smile at this — of a seat by the eastern wall of the old, old synagogue of Kasrielevky, a seat next to that of Reb Yozifel himself, and therefore all but next to the holy Ark itself; a seat which had descended from father to oldest son in a line reaching back into the unremem-

bered past, beyond the days of Mazeppa and Chmelnitzky the butchers.

When the seven days of special mourning and
the thirty days of milder mourning had passed after the
death of Reb Samson Beard (peace be upon him!), the
quarrel began. Said blackbeard, whom convention called
Mayer the older: " The seat by the eastern wall is mine,
for I am the older." Said redbeard, whom convention
called Shnayer the younger: " No! On two counts. First,
no one knows who is the real Mayer the older, and the
real Shnayer the younger. Second, you, who are called by
mere convention, but without reason, Mayer the older,
have a rich father-in-law to whom God has given only
daughters, and he has his seat by the eastern wall. At the
proper time, one hundred and twenty years hence, you
will inherit his seat for yourself; whereas I, who am
called by convention, but without reason, Shnayer the
younger, have a father-in-law as poor as myself, without
a seat by the eastern wall."

An impasse, a Gordian knot. The Mayers and the
Shnayers repeated their arguments and would not cede
so much as an inch. On successive Sabbath mornings,
when the seat had to be occupied officially, blackbeard
and redbeard, Mayer-Shnayer and Shnayer-Mayer, came
earlier and earlier to the synagogue, to anticipate each
other. When a month or so had passed they arrived on a
Sabbath morning simultaneously, and before the beadle
had had time to open the door. Then ensued, in the holy
place, and on the holy day, a scandalous scene: Shnayer-
Mayer and Mayer-Shnayer rolling on the floor of the
still empty synagogue and tearing at each other's Sabbath gaberdines, to keep each other from occupying the

seat. Such a desecration had not been witnessed before by the oldest Kasrielevkite.

There was nothing left for it but to submit the claim to the judgment of Reb Yozifel. That same evening, after the ceremony of the Leavetaking from the Sabbath, the Mayers and the Shnayers appeared at the home of Reb Yozifel, and with them — how could it be otherwise? — the hosts of their partisans. And as always Reb Yozifel listened, with a sweet, patient smile, to argument and rebuttal as put forward by the Shnayers and the Mayers, their wives, hangers-on, friends, and acquaintances — not to mention the innumerable " neutrals," " lovers of justice," " friends of peace," " guardians of the good name of Kasrielevky," and the like. Hour after hour Reb Yozifel listened, letting the torrent flow over him like a patient rock in a turbulent river. When the spate was exhausted and every insider and outsider had had his say, Reb Yozifel lifted up his mournful, quavering voice and addressed himself thus to the Mayers and the Shnayers:

" Gentlemen, hear me. I have listened to your claims and arguments, and to the arguments of your good friends, and I have reached a conclusion which I know will please both of you. Not only will it please both of you, but it is wholly in accordance with the principles of truth and justice. My conclusion is — mark it well — that both of you are right. For it is true that you are the sons of one father, a fine father, God rest his soul, a finer father no Jew ever had; and it is equally true that each of you may consider himself the heir of your father. The pity of it is that he left you as your inheritance only one seat by the eastern wall. Not much of an inheritance, some would say, but they err. A seat by the eastern wall

of the old, old synagogue of Kasrielevky. It is surely dear
to you, and properly so, and all honour to you that you
feel thus. Here, however, lies the point: as it is unnatural that one man should occupy two seats simultaneously, either by the eastern wall of the old, old synagogue
of Kasrielevky or anywhere else, so it is unnatural, even
impossible, that two men should occupy the same seat
simultaneously. For instance, I put my hand thus on the
open page of this sacred book " — and Reb Yozifel put
his trembling, transparent hand on the page of the Talmud, in the reading of which he had been interrupted
— " and it is this hand, not the other, which is in contact
with the sacred words. How can my other hand be in
contact simultaneously with the same sacred words? It
cannot. And why? Because God has so created the world,
and the understanding of man cannot penetrate the mystery. And so, gentlemen, we are back at the original
question. What *are* we to do with the two brothers, each
one of whom may be the older, and to whom their father — God rest his soul, a finer father no Jew ever had
— left as an inheritance a single seat by the eastern wall
of the old, old synagogue of Kasrielevky? Are we to divide the seat, split it in two? Alas, gentlemen, a seat by
the eastern wall of the old, old synagogue of Kasrielevky
cannot be split in two, as we split, let us say, an apple:
' Here, you eat one half, you the other.' Is there, then, no
answer? Yes, gentlemen, there is an answer to this, as to
all other problems, for those who will follow the spirit
of the sacred books. And what is the answer? Hear me
carefully."

Here sly old Reb Yozifel paused and let his listeners
rack their brains for several moments.

" The answer is," he continued, " that you shall both

sit by the eastern wall, side by side in peace and honour. How? Simply enough, gentlemen. There is, next to your father's seat — God rest his soul! — another, namely, mine. Two seats by the eastern wall. One of you shall sit in one seat, the other in the other. And if you raise the question where shall I be sitting, I will answer with still another question. Where, in what chapter and verse, is it written that I, Reb Yozifel, must occupy a seat by the eastern wall of the old, old synagogue of Kasrielevky? For let us consider the matter closely. What is a synagogue? It is a holy place. Why do we go to the synagogue? To utter prayer. To whom? To the Supreme Judge. Where is the Supreme Judge? The earth is filled with His glory. And if the earth is filled with His glory, what matters east or west, north or south in the synagogue? What matters the eastern wall or the standing-place by the door? To what shall this situation be likened? It shall be likened to two servants of a King, who approached their master for a favour, and in the midst of their petition, ay, in the very presence of the King, flew at each other like wild animals. What think you the King did? He had them removed, with all courtesy, outside the palace, saying: ' If it's a fight you want, must I be the spectator? Get you gone outside, and fight to your hearts' content, but my palace is not an arena.' "

And here Reb Yozifel paused again, most cunningly, as if he had lost the thread of his argument. Then he continued: " Yes, where were we? I have rendered judgment, that both of you shall sit by the eastern wall. Now go home, gentlemen, in peace, as becomes two brothers, and let your father, who is in paradise, speak up before the Throne of Grace for you and for us and for all good people."

When the next Sabbath came around, the Jews assembled in the old, old synagogue of Kasrielevky beheld a strange spectacle. The Mayers and the Shnayers were stationed at the door, among the poor and humble. Neither Reb Yozifel nor the beadle could persuade either of them to come forward and occupy one of the adjacent seats; seeing which Reb Yozifel resumed his place by the Ark, and the Mayers and the Shnayers stood on their feet till the services were over. So it was the following Sabbath, and the Sabbath after that, and the Sabbath after that, as long as the Mayers and the Shnayers lived. And a seat remained for ever vacant by the eastern wall of the old, old synagogue of Kasrielevky. What a waste!

CHAPTER XV

Kasrielevky on Kasrielevky

❧

SUCH were the judgments of Reb Yozifel, and such
the quarrels and reconciliations of the Jews in old Kasrielevky. Such at least were some of them, for there were
others, and they shall appear in the record. But the time
has come to interrupt the narrative and to ask certain
questions. Where is the famous inner unity of the Jews,
where the unbroken conspiratorial front against the gentile world? What has become of the immemorial accusation that the Jews regard themselves, individually and
collectively, as the salt of the earth and the only recognizable handiwork of the Almighty?

If anti-Semites were genuinely interested in the sins
and shortcomings of the Jews, the chief of which, we are
told, is their immeasurable spiritual arrogance vis-à-vis
the rest of the world, they would look for their material
among the Jews themselves; that is, in what the Jews say
of themselves among themselves. But this suggestion has
two drawbacks. It presupposes " genuine interest," which
in turn implies an objective and human relationship;
and investigating the delinquencies of the Jews, the anti-
Semite would perforce stumble upon their virtues, which
is by no means to his purpose.

For really appalling remarks about Jews you must go to the Jews themselves. Now, I do not mean modern Jews in flight from anti-Semitism. They know nothing about themselves as Jews, and very often their attitude toward themselves and other Jews may be summed up in the inversion of a highly immoral advertising slogan: " Such unpopularity must be deserved." I am talking still of Sholom Aleichem's world, and of what Kasrielev-kites said about Kasrielevkites. Only it must be remembered that their biting comments, made intramurally, did not spring from hatred or terror; and they were not part of a sustained and programmatic anti-Jewish thesis. At bottom Kasrielevkites did not mind adverse comment on themselves. Nor, for that matter, do the less panicky among their descendants. What they object to, whether they quite know it or not, is the practice of linking such comment with an implied vindication or even explanation of anti-Semitism. They object as strenuously, and as justly, to the compromise view: that all the Jews are hated, by certain misguided people, because of the un-doubted faults of some Jews — from which it would ap-pear that if there were only nice Jews, there would be no anti-Semitism. Why, they ask, should not all humanity be hated because of the undoubted ugliness of some hu-man beings? But of course all humanity *is* hated by some people: to wit, the ugly ones themselves. Jews who have not been morally shattered by anti-Semitism feel instinc-tively that even the compromise " explanation " of anti-Semitism is itself poisoned with anti-Semitism; and they flare up when some " well-wisher " undertakes to dis-cuss their inadequacies *in connection with the problem of anti-Semitism*. For no such connection exists in reality.

The strictures that spring from love are always more

penetrating than those that are prompted by hatred. Who could accuse Tevyeh the dairyman of hatred of his own people? But he knew the faults of the Jews — none better. And Sholom Aleichem does not play the censor with his characters. When God had remembered Tevyeh and lifted up his head, transforming him from a starving slave into an independent producer and merchant, he was only too well aware of the envy and suspicion which he aroused in the hearts of fellow-Jews. " Will you ever hear a good word about yourself from your own kind? " he asks Sholom Aleichem. " Never. All they know is to poke their noses into your business and try to find out what's going on in your kitchen. They see Tevyeh the pauper suddenly milking two cows of his own, and they can't be at peace. Where did he get them? Is Tevyeh dealing in contraband goods, counterfeit, moonshine, stolen merchandise? Ho-ho, says I to myself, break your heads, little brothers, you'll never find out. And for that matter, Mr. Sholom Aleichem, though I produce the finest butter and cheese in these regions, I've never received a word of praise from a single Jewish customer. Many's the time I've been asked by gentiles to serve them. ' Tevyeh,' they say, ' we've heard you're a very decent man, even though you are only a lousy Jew.' Do I ever get such a compliment from one of our own kind? Not on your life."

There is a whole folklore of Jewish self-criticism and self-deprecation, quite unconnected with any theories of anti-Semitism. There are indigenous anecdotes and phrases which have not their like among other peoples. " A small people," they say of themselves, " but a nasty one." And " We have a God in heaven, God help us so; but has He got a people on earth, God help him! " More elaborately a question is asked in the regular style of the Biblical commentators: " How comes it that in the Book of Esther the name of Haman the villain is mentioned before that of Mordecai the saint? " And the answer is: " Because no one in his right senses ever starts with a Jew."

The Jews of Kasrielevky knew themselves, then, to be full of sin. They described themselves as an envious lot, scurrilous, rancorous, touchy seekers of honour, oppressors of the poor. They said that a Kasrielevkite could not bear to see his neighbour making a living. They used to say: " If a Kasrielevkite were to cut off his nose some day and show himself in the market-place, be certain that the very next day at least one more Kasrielevkite would appear in the market-place sans nose. Why? Because at least one Kasrielevkite would have argued: ' If it pays him to cut off his nose, why shouldn't it pay me? ' "

The richest Jew of Kasrielevky — of old Kasrielevky, that is—was probably worth not more than a couple of thousand roubles. But every Jew who was suspected of "riches" lived too long in the eyes of the other Kasrielevkites; at least, so said the Kasrielevkites. And they backed it up with a story. A Kasrielevkite once conceived the idea of selling the secret of immortality to Rothschild. Having trudged across Europe on foot, he managed somehow to make his way into the presence of the fabulous multimillionaire and convince him of the genuineness of the offer. " How much? " asked Rothschild. " Three hundred roubles," said the Kasrielevkite, desperately. " Here is the money," answered the banker; " now for the formula." " It is as simple as simple can be," explained the Kasrielevkite. " Pack up and come to live in

Kasrielevky, because there a rich man has never been known to die."

Because he was the mirror of Kasrielevky, presenting the image of his own world to his own world, and to no one else, Sholom Aleichem had no thought of " making a good impression," of practising concealment or distortion. Besides, he was himself a Kasrielevkite, and could not be anything else. A long time ago, in the early days of the First World War, he sat with a group of us on the porch of a hotel on the New Jersey coast and told us something about the autobiography he was then writing. I, a youngster of twenty, sat and stared at him, who was already a living legend among his people. A slightly gnome-like elderly little man, with a clever, wrinkled face, kindly, satirical eyes, and a gentle voice, full of tenderness and slyness. Even in repose his face suggested irrepressible amusement, as though invisibly on the tip of his nose a joke were ever balanced neatly on its centre of levity. You would have taken him for a Hebrew-teacher, a small town Rabbi, perhaps even for a wise old shopkeeper given to books and close observation of his customers; certainly an attractive, even a fascinating personality, full of years and suffering and accumulated comment on life, but not, in heaven's name, a literary genius.

He told us of the name he had chosen for his autobiography, the first volume of which had not yet appeared in print. *Fun'm Yarid — Back from the Fair*. He said: " When a man starts out in life he's like a Jew setting out for the fair, to make his fortune. What impatience, what excitement and hope, what dreams and expectations! ' Don't stop me! I've no time for idle talk! ' The

113

world is waiting for him. He's liable to miss a great bargain, a fateful meeting with a rich merchant. Who knows
what's in store for him? But when the day is over, the
same Jew, returning home, is quite another man. He
walks slowly, thoughtfully. He's got all the time you
want. He knows everything now — nothing was waiting
for him, no fortunes, no rich merchants, no fateful en-
counters. He's ready to talk."

Then he added something so characteristically his own
and yet so characteristically Kasrielevkite that we could
not tell whether he himself had invented it or whether
he had picked it up and made it his own in the telling.

" When a man gives an account of what befell him at
the fair, he must always be considerate of the feelings
of his neighbours. He must be careful not to wound his
fellow Jews, but strive rather to be at one with them. For
it is written in the Ethics of the Fathers: ' Separate not
thyself from the community,' which means, among other
things, do not break in thoughtlessly and selfishly with
something that jars on your listeners. Unity in Israel!
Let us never forget that principle. So, for instance, if I
went out to the fair — in a manner of speaking, of
course, for I never attended fairs except as a child, with
my father — when I went out to the fair and did well,
sold everything at a good profit, and returned with pocketfuls of money, my heart bursting with joy, I never
failed to tell my neighbours that I had lost every kopeck
and was a ruined man. Thus I was happy, and my neighbours were happy. But if, on the contrary, I had really
been cleaned out at the fair, and brought home with me a
bitter heart and a bellyful of green gall, I made sure to
tell my neighbours that never since God made fairs had
there been a better one. You get my point? For thus I

was miserable and my neighbours were miserable with me."

This is Kasrielevky, and this is how Kasrielevkites talked about themselves. Is such self-denigration sickly? It only sounds so out of its context, which is the totality of a people's life, sustaining the people in its own culture and maintaining in proper balance all its moral and psychological elements. The Jews have probably been, since their beginnings, more self-critical than any other people. They have in fact produced a literature of self-criticism which incidentally constitutes the supreme moral utterance of mankind. From the worldly point of view it is not prudent to speak ill of yourself in the presence of others. They will take you at your word, and cap the list of your acknowledged weaknesses with the unacknowledged one of masochism. You have an inferiority complex, which is only the reverse side of a superiority complex.

But if they felt thus about themselves, whence the conviction of the Kasrielevkites that they *were* God's chosen people after all, the protagonists of the only religion worth the name, and the earthly representatives of the Divinity? Strange as it may sound, this point of view was not only not incompatible with their consciousness of sin, but an organic part of it. It was because they had undertaken to be so much better that they felt themselves to be so much worse. An objective outsider would say that they exaggerated their shortcomings — that is, if he did not know how high a mark they had seriously set themselves. A modern Jew defends himself with this negative observation: " We're no worse than others." To which the Kasrielevkite would have retorted with the anecdote of the two quarrelling business partners, one of whom cried: " You rogue, you thief, you liar, you swindler, I'm just as honest as you."

We can now understand certain other reasons for Jewish sensitivity to criticism from the outside. That criticism is not aimed at the uncovering of the real defects of the Jews (which are the defects of all other peoples, or at least the defects which all other peoples would develop in similar circumstances) and their correction. Such a program would not mention the Jews, except along with everyone else. The critic may not be an anti-Semite, but he uses the language of one, and the anti-Semite is not at all concerned with improving the moral condition of the Jews. He has quite another purpose or set of purposes: the construction of a horrendous legend of world Jewry, the externalization of his own unconscious dreams of a world without conscience, the projection of a wild, ruthless, secretive, and systematic hatred of mankind. It is the creation of a Devil for the purpose of Devil-worship in the form of Devil-hatred.

When the " criticism " has a less portentous origin it still touches Jews on the raw, for apart from lacking relevance and constructive intention, it is catastrophically related, in the Jewish mind, with an ancient and implacable hostility which has pursued the Jews through the ages like a nightmare. This is also true of ordinary, vulgar abuse which people should be able to take in their stride. Call an Italian a " wop " and he responds normally with a twinge of irritation; call a Jew a " sheeny " and his mother's milk curdles in him as his flesh remembers the bestialities of Chmelnitzky and the insanities of Hitler.

Internally free of illusions as to their moral superiority in their daily behaviour, the Jews were nevertheless aware that world anti-Semitism was not based on Jewish iniquity, but on ideal Jewish values. What stuck in the crop of the anti-Semite was the whole system of moral categories which Jews and the Jewish people had evolved, to the discomfort of mankind — and their own. But it is not easy to understand why, feeling thus, the Jews, let us say the Kasrielevkites, did not get out from under while they still had the opportunity. Why did they not disassociate themselves from their forefathers, the creators of Judaism and Christianity? Why did they not flock to the baptismal font while the offer was still good, and thus acquire the privileges of the normal quota of human sinfulness, while repudiating any responsibility for the trick which the Jews of old had played by putting the Bible over on the Western world? Why, on the contrary, did they celebrate with glee the acceptance of the Torah at Sinai and the publication of the Biblical literature, announcing themselves the partners of the original miscreants?

Was it their belief in the Messiah, in the world to come, and in their own ultimate vindication? Was it their belief in the reward? Perhaps it was. And perhaps, behind these ostensible motives of prudence, there was a streak of obstinate honour which their descendants can no longer display because the choice has been withdrawn. In any case, the Kasrielevkites did not think highly of themselves, but they took it for granted that a Jew who refused to carry any longer the immemorial burden of his Jewishness had blotted out his own name from the book of life.

CHAPTER XVI

Old and New Kasrielevky

❀

How shall I begin to tell you of the cataclysmic changes which came over Kasrielevky in the course of some forty years and made a new Kasrielevky out of old Kasrielevky? I could — and, depend on it, I will — give you a detailed list of unheard-of innovations which the Kasrielevkites of Sholom Aleichem's childhood did not foresee in their maddest dreams. Most of them are easily described, being externalities; those that reached deepest, however, had to do with the spirit, which must be treated circumstantially; and perhaps the best lead will be the incident of new Kasrielevky's most famous " expropriation."

" Expropriation? " you ask. " You mean — ? " Yes, I mean the real thing: expropriation as a part of revolutionary technique, the most modern form of Robin Hoodism and (for local colour) Stenka Razinism. For new Kasrielevky stood in the midst of awakening Russia, the Russia of strikes, constitutions, Nihilism, Social Democracy, and talk of the bourgeoisie, exploitation and the toiling masses, of Karl Marx, Lasalle, Bebel, Kropotkin, Plekhanov, and Jaurès. Mediæval religious Russia had not been able to break into the stronghold of Jewish separatism; modern revolutionary Russia was more successful. Even Kasrielevky, which was not Odessa, or Kiev, or Warsaw, with their proletarian masses, began to move with the current.

The great expropriation of Kasrielevky was precipitated by the breakdown — the first in the town's history — of the Passover charity system. Since the days of Chmelnitzky and before, it had not happened that the poorest families of Kasrielevky should not be provided with supplies of *matzos,* potatoes, chicken-fat, and *matzoh* meal to see them through the eight-day festival of the Exodus. But on this particular Passover the incredible happened. It had been a bad winter; business had been scarce, unemployment plentiful. The committee discovered that there were twice as many " takers " as " givers " that year, and its resources were exhausted long before the crowd besieging the office had anywhere near been satisfied. Benjamin Lastetchky, a *nogid,* a rich man, chairman of the committee, sat perspiring behind the desk, and repeated: " There isn't any more! We've spent every kopeck! Don't be offended! "

" Thank you," said the paupers. " May you live till next year and apply to us for Passover food." And they went out with crimson faces, cursing the rich.

The last to apply were not so easily dismissed. They were certain young men, with Samuel Abba Fingerhood at their head; workers, without families to support, but hungry for all that. They, queerly enough, were more obstreperous than the family men, probably because Benjamin Lastetchky not only turned them away, but added the standard observation: " You're young and strong, you can work for your Passover supplies." It is amazing how a man with money or a job attributes his security solely to his superior ability, and at the same time looks upon the presumably inferior ability of the destitute as a deliberate misdemeanour.

It was with a clean conscience — had he not done his best? — that Benjamin Lastetchky went home, put on festive garb, and sat down with his family to the *seder* ceremony and dinner of the first eve of Passover. A rich table, a happy family, king and queen, princes and princesses, with newly bathed bodies and shining faces; and freedom in the air, for had they not all — in accordance with the tradition — just marched out of Egypt? The youngest boy sang out the traditional Four Questions, and everyone broke into the great chorus which is the reply, and which begins: " Slaves we were to Pharaoh in Egypt." At which moment there was a knock at the door.

A knock at the door in the midst of the *seder* ceremony! Impossible! No Jew of Kasrielevky is abroad at such an hour. And no gentile had business with Benjamin Lastetchky at such an hour. But the impossible was repeated, a second time, a third time, a fourth, and successively louder and more insistently. Zlota the servant girl was sent to open, and in marched the young men, with Samuel Abba Fingerhood at their head.

The family stared, open-mouthed. Benjamin Lastetchkys' heart took refuge in his festival shoes. " Happy Passover! " he quavered. " Welcome. What good news brings you here? "

Samuel Abba Fingerhood had no good news. He had a lecture, half in Yiddish, half in Russian. It was a lecture on the selfishness of the rich and the misery of the poor, and on the shocking contrast between the opulent table at which the Lastetchkys were celebrating the holy festival and the desolation and hunger of himself and his comrades. It ended with a command: " Get up from the table and we will sit down and celebrate in your place! And let no one go to the window or try to call the police if you want to see the light of day tomorrow. Comrade Moses, the bomb! "

Comrade Moses, a shoemaker, came forward and placed on the table a large, black, and most sinister-looking cylinder. The Lastetchkys, king and queen, princes and princesses, rose from the seats, ranged themselves about the walls, and stood there as motionless as Lot's wife after she had turned round to look at the burning cities of the plain. Thus they stood while the comrades celebrated the Passover and made havoc with the dinner. They left not a bite of food, not a drop of wine, and with every glass they toasted their reluctant hosts: " Happy festival! Good health, comrade bourgeois! God grant that a year from now you belong to the ranks of the proletariat! " And when they finally withdrew, sated with piety and Passover fare, nothing was left on the table but the prayer-books and the sinister cylinder.

Half the night went by before the terrified Lastetchkys dared to approach the table and put a finger on the instrument of death placed there by Comrade Moses the shoemaker. It turned out to be nothing more desperate than a large shoe-polish can filled to the brim with *matzoh* meal.

New Kasrielevky! How could old Kasrielevky have forevisioned something called " expropriation "? It could not even have dreamed of a day when poor Kasrielevky Jews would be left without the means to observe the

Passover; and no doubt there is a connection between the two impossibilities. How much had come to pass in those forty years! New Kasrielevky had paved streets and water-mains. No more mud, and no more water-carriers. New Kasrielevky had a tramway system. Horsecars, of course, and the lines double-tracked only part of the way, so that sometimes tram would encounter tram on the single track, and there would be a tremendous to-do about who was to back up — but a tramway system all the same. New Kasrielevky had Jewish children who could not speak Yiddish. Russian, yes; French, yes; German, yes. But not Yiddish. New Kasrielevky had no *shadchan*, or marriage broker; it had instead a " mediator," who did not " arrange marriages," but " negotiated alliances." Soloveitchik the mediator was the son of Sholom the *shadchan*, and you might have found it difficult to distinguish between the professions of father and son. But a " mediator " is not a " *shadchan* " — it is a question of the spirit.

What forty years can do! The old " *chevrahs*," or religious brotherhoods and associations, were nearly all gone: the " Mishnah " brotherhood, for the study of the sacred books; the " Clothers of the Naked," the " Visitors of the Sick," the " Supporters of the Fallen," for various charitable labours. New organizations had taken their place: Cultural Societies, Yiddishist Societies, Hebraist Societies, Dramatic Societies, Workers' Societies, and so on without end. Old Kasrielevky had known no other drama than the Purim play; new Kasrielevky had two theatres, both of them empty most of the time. Old Kasrielevky had known no other music than that of the synagogue; new Kasrielevky had two Choral Societies. Why *two* Dramatic Societies and *two* Choral Societies? The answer is that though everything else might have changed, the spirit of imitation, envy, and competition had not disappeared with old Kasrielevky.

Old Kasrielevky had been without a local publication; new Kasrielevky had two Yiddish dailies, the *Skullcap* for the orthodox, the *Bowler Hat* for the moderns. Not that the *Skullcap* and the *Bowler Hat* were not both modern in their methods. They lacked nothing which may be found — or might have been found forty years ago — in the newspapers of the great outside world. They had their news columns, their interviews, their feature articles, their thrilling novels in thirty or forty or four hundred instalments, their advertising departments, and of course their platforms. The *Skullcap* stood for tradition, orthodoxy, and Hebrew (though it was a Yiddish newspaper) ; the *Bowler Hat* stood for progress, modernity, and Yiddish. The rivalry between the *Skullcap* and the *Bowler Hat* was conducted with a ferocity which would have startled the gun-toting editors of the Far West in the early days of Mark Twain and Bret Harte.

The battle between Hebrew and Yiddish in Kasrielevky, and in European Jewry generally, was a highly confused one. The revival of Hebrew was an integral part of the Zionist movement, which aimed at the establishment of a Hebrew-speaking Jewish homeland in Palestine. The insistence on Yiddish was a feature of the (generally) anti-Zionist labour movement in Jewry, which equated Hebrew with superstition, reaction, and nationalism. And yet the spread of secular Hebrew was fought bitterly by the extreme orthodox, the more so as the Haskalah, the Jewish renaissance of the nineteenth century, with its cries of " Down with the ghetto walls! Down with our mediævalism and separatism and superstitions! " was conducted in Hebrew. The Haskalists as a group despised Yiddish, the language of the ignorant masses and of the courts of the Chassidic rabbis. They called it a jargon. They associated it with all the spiritual stigmata which the long exile had produced in the Jewish people. The Haskalists were therefore passionate modernizers in their own way. But so were the left-wingers among the Yiddishists, who fought the rise of Hebrew because it was, among other things, the barometer of the growing Zionist movement. To make confusion worse confounded, the Zionist movement had its own strong leftist wing, Hebraist and radical. The powerful labour movement of Jewish Palestine — the outstanding feature of the present-day homeland — stems largely from Kasrielevky; and in Palestine the struggle between Yiddish and Hebrew was to a large extent the struggle between secular Zionism and socialism on the one hand, and Messianic Zionism and reaction on the other. The complicated struggles of Kasrielevky were also transferred to America, where they meshed with new internal conflicts, social, cultural, and religious, so that it is quite impossible to guide an outsider through the labyrinths of Jewish life. All he needs to be told is that ot all modern myths that of " Jewish unity " is the most incomprehensible to Jews on the inside.

However, we are still in Kasrielevky, at the beginning of the twentieth century. It is not, in the sense I have mentioned, Sholom Aleichem's Kasrielevky any more. He has written a great deal about it, of course, but the world which is peculiarly his, the world which uttered itself through him, making him a folk figure rather than a writer, is gone for ever. In new Kasrielevky Sholom Aleichem is a visitor and observer; the humorist has been transformed into the satirist. We must be careful how we take him now; the record must be translated back, here and there, from the language of invention into the terms of the underlying reality. Not that he ever misrepresented; he merely intensified the effect. But this is something we do not feel about his utterances when he is in the midst of his own world.

He certainly did not misrepresent the divisions and hostilities of the new Kasrielevky. He did not misrepresent the social changes. We feel he is always telling the truth, but this time from a point of view. For Kasrielevky is no longer *sui generis;* it is part of the great world, and it therefore invites parallels. Indeed, we know Sholom Aleichem is telling the truth because what he says of Kasrielevky other satirists have said of other cities. What could be more universal, for instance, than his description of the provincial cultural life of new Kasrielevky? The literary evenings, the banquets to visiting celebrities, the rivalries of local poetasters, the irrepressibility of local orators, the interminableness of chairmen's introductions — are not these to be found everywhere, from Middletown to Stoke-on-Trent? All these things exist in new Kasrielevky. The snobberies of the middle class, the cultural fads in music, languages, and authors, the importation of women's modes from Paris (really from Yehupetz, but who's going to find out?) , the rise of summer resorts (old Kasrielevky would have stared incomprehendingly at you if you had talked of " vacations " and " resorts ": are not the Sabbaths and festivals enough? Or do you need your resorts because you do not rest on the Sabbaths and festivals which God gave us?) — these came in with Russia's first industrialization, child labour in factories — Kasrielevky had that too — and the general dissolution of the special character of old Kasrielevky. Kasrielevky was reading Artzibasheff and Tolstoy, dancing the two-step and the tango; Kasrielevky had movies and *cafés chantants,* and practised mixed bathing at the summer resorts. Mixed nudism would not have horrified old Kasrielevky more; for that matter, even mixed dancing was a pagan depravity in the eyes of old Kasrielevky. Dancing, like music and art, or even more than these, belonged to religion. Chassidim danced together to the glory of God, as David had danced before the Ark. And when the Rabbi himself joined in the dancing, or executed a *pas seul,* heaven opened and the angels looked down, gaping. But this business of young men and women wriggling in contiguity to the strains of an orchestra — it is good to think that Reb Yozifel never heard of it, much less saw it. Automobiles, telephones, electric lights he probably could not keep outside the range of his observation; but what should Reb Yozifel, the nonagenarian, be doing in a dance hall or at a modern wedding?

Sholom Aleichem, however, saw it all, and because his life was rooted in old Kasrielevky his emotions were at war with new Kasrielevky: his emotions much more than his mind. There is a strange streak in Sholom Aleichem, who belongs with his heart to old Kasrielevky, but with his intelligence to the revolutionary world. He reminds one of certain Jewish leftists — there are many such — who cannot help sneaking into a synagogue on the Day of Atonement, and do so with only one prayer on their lips: namely, that the other Jewish leftists there do not see them.

You would have expected Sholom Aleichem to take sides in the struggles of new Kasrielevky; his human im-

pulses were with the underdog; instinctively he disliked
the upper class into which he had been born. But except
in this general way, he does not take a stand. His satirical
report on new Kasrielevky is impartially negative; he
laughs as heartily at the *Skullcap* and its " platform " as
at the *Bowler Hat*. He is neither a Zionist nor an anti-
Zionist, neither a believer nor an unbeliever. His affections are instinctive.

He tells a story which typifies the ferocious struggle
between the two newspapers. One day the Hebraists of
new Kasrielevky (whose organ, we must remember, was
the *Skullcap*) invited to the city a famous Doctor of Philosophy, a resident of Yehupetz, to deliver a public lecture. The Doctor arrived, delivered his lecture, sustained
the question period, and departed in peace — exactly as
might have happened in any other city. But because he
had been invited by the Hebraists, the report in the
Skullcap was eulogistic to the point of delirium, while
the report in the *Bowler Hat* was derogatory to the point
of defamation. In particular he was vilified because he
had dared to cast aspersions on the Jewish youth of Kasrielevky, with its shocking addiction to the cinema, indiscriminate dancing, and other un-Jewish practices.
Thereupon the *Skullcap*, on the next day, loosed the
torrents of its fury on the *Bowler Hat,* and asked sar-
castically what those ignoramuses, heathen, bath-house
attendants, bargees, illiterates, apostates, and shoe-shine
boys knew about Judaism and Jewish tradition. To which
the *Bowler Hat,* returning to the charge, answered with
another question: How was it that the Hebraists, the
pietists, the representatives of tradition and respectability, had dared invite to Kasrielevky, and had eulogized
to the skies, one who moralized the public while he him·

self had two sisters, one of whom had been baptized while the other was a common thief?

The riposte of the *Bowler Hat* exploded like a bomb in the camp of the *Skullcapites*. For a day or two they went about with their noses in the dust. Then a meeting of the editorial staff of the *Skullcap* was held, at which the question was discussed whether a telegram ought not to be sent to the Doctor of Philosophy asking him to verify or deny the allegations of the *Bowler Hat*. The staff was unanimous on the advisability of the step; the difficulty lay in the wording of the telegram. After all, the man might indeed have two sisters, one of whom had been baptized and the other of whom was a common thief; one could not very well ask him flatly whether such was indeed the case. A member of the staff had an inspiration and proposed that the telegram be worded thus: " How are your sisters? " The telegram was despatched, and a day later came the reply: " Which sisters? " To this unexpected answer the same genius on the staff of the *Skullcap* responded with: " Both your sisters." The Doctor of Philosophy in Yehupetz was apparently a patient man, for he replied: " I have no sisters." But the genius on the staff of the *Skullcap* was equally patient. " Have your sisters died? " he inquired. The Doctor of Philosophy answered promptly: " What do you want of me? I never had any sisters. I am an only child."

What a relief for the Hebraists! Their first act was to reprint the scurrilous statement of the *Bowler Hat* side by side with the exchange of telegrams. Let Kasrielevky and the rest of the world know what sort of people these were. Their second step was to send a complete copy of the relevant material to the Doctor of Philosophy, who immediately sued the *Bowler Hat* for libel, slander, and defamation of character. And when, in the course of time, the matter came up for trial, the Doctor of Philosophy appeared, armed with all his family documents, which proved that not only had he never had a sister, but that even his father and mother had never had sisters. He therefore demanded both a retraction and damages from the publishers of the *Bowler Hat*. Unfortunately the court could not see eye to eye with the Doctor of Philosophy, and ruled that inasmuch as the Doctor of Philosophy had no sisters, any derogatory remarks regarding these non-existent persons were meaningless and therefore could not constitute an infringement of the law.

Is the story true? Yes and no. It is not as true as the stories of Tevyeh the dairyman and Reb Yozifel. It is true in another way: symbolically, that is, and in the spirit. It is to be accepted as a moral. And this is the difference between Sholom Aleichem the satirist of new Kasrielevky and Sholom Aleichem the singer of old Kasrielevky.

CHAPTER XVII

The Reconciliation

❀

BETWEEN old and new Kasrielevky — that is, between the 1870's and the eve of the First World War — lay the assassination of Alexander II by Russian revolutionaries, the savage reaction under Alexander III, the period of Pobiedonostsev (the Russian Torquemada), the anti-Semitic May Laws of the year 1881, the exclusion of the Jews from the countryside, the creation of the Pale of Settlement, the enactment of educational and professional restrictions against unbaptized Jews, and the emergence of the *Protocols of the Elders of Zion*. German total anti-Semitism was already in the making, and its influence was transmitted into Russia by the court. French anti-Semitism, crystallizing in the Dreyfus affair, also had its repercussions in Russia. In general this period saw the transformation of anti-Semitism from a tacit prejudice into an explicit movement, and its partial transference from the religious to the political field.

Great changes came about in the relationship between the Jews of Kasrielevky and the surrounding gentiles, between Jacob and Ivan. The liberal interlude between the death of Nicholas I and Alexander III ended abruptly, and Russian Jewry became an important instrument of the reaction. It was a preview, in as yet imperfect form, of the Hitlerian exploitation of anti-Semitism, an attempt to impregnate a country with the Jewish issue.

Yet even in the palmy days of Alexander II the Jews of old Kasrielevky had not felt themselves to be too safe in the great ocean of Russian and gentile life. Historically speaking, they knew themselves to be in exile; they were tolerated; they were sojourners. Still, by comparison with what came later, they had felt tolerably secure. " There has always been Jew-hatred," they said. " There always will be. Yet we've managed somehow, and we always will."

The Jews had come to terms with their status. At least the days of Chmelnitzky were no more. The time of the " child-snatchers " was gone, too — the time of Nicholas I, when press-gangs would descend in the dead of night on a Jewish family, carry off a boy, and send him to the other end of Russia to be brought up — after the fashion of Turkish Mamelukes — as a soldier. Twenty-five years was the term of service, after which the soldier was permitted to return to his family, or what was left of it. Old Kasrielevky had a number of " Nikolaievsky " soldiers, living memorials of the bad days; but the Jews of old Kasrielevky could sleep of nights. There were no more press-gangs. In outlying villages the relations between Jews and Russians were often cordial, even affectionate. Everybody knew that at bottom Ivan was not a bad fellow; stupid, perhaps, and earthy, given to drink and occasional wife-beating, but essentially good-natured. That is to say, as long as he was left alone, as long as someone did not put a flea in his ear, as long as the higher-ups did not begin to manipulate him.

One could take a single village, a single family history, and trace through them the process of deterioration which was set in motion and kept going by the rulers of the country and their hirelings. For instance Nachman Verebivker of Verebivky. " Our Lachman " (they transposed the N into an L) the peasants used to call him; a massive, broad-boned figure of a man, a Jew, the son of Feitel Verebivker, who was the son of Aryeh Verebivker, all of the village of Verebivky. Once upon a time the family had been wealthy. Aryeh Verebivker had owned the village store, the village inn, and the village mill. His grandson Nachman had nothing but his house and vegetable garden, on which he worked, together with wife and children. Still, " our Lachman " was a somebody in Verebivky. The peasants respected his intelligence; they sought his advice on the planting of crops; they liked to talk with him about the goings on in the great outside world. And closest of all was Kuretchka, Nachman's neighbour, who would come to him when he had a toothache because Nachman had a certain lotion which brought instant relief, and who would send for Nachman's wife whenever his own wife was about to bring forth a child. Nor was Kuretchka one of your ordinary illiterate peasants. Kuretchka could read; Kuretchka could assimilate ideas — and that perhaps was Kuretchka's trouble.

With the coming of the " new " regime, Kuretchka read the papers more assiduously than ever, and a change came over his attitude toward " our Lachman." Kuretchka did not become unfriendly; on the contrary, he was a more frequent visitor than before. But he never failed to bring one of the " gazettes " with him, and to read out of it to Nachman. Now it was about a new Governor, now about a new anti-Jewish law, now about a new circular from the Minister of the Interior. And Nachman listened with a smile, though his blood ran cold; he listened with a smile because he would rather have died than give Kuretchka the satisfaction of seeing a frightened Jew.

Far deeper than the friendship between Nachman Verebivker and Kuretchka was that between their youngest sons, Feitel and Fedka, a little black-haired Jewish boy and a little flaxen-haired peasant boy, whose souls had grown together. Spring and summer and autumn they were inseparable; only in the winter-time, when storms raged and the snow-covered roads were impassable, they stayed home near the stove and longed for each other. And when the first warm spring day broke over Verebivky the boys flew out to join each other, and to wander over the fields to the river, where the ice was breaking up.

Once, after a winter that had been unusually long and severe, lasting, in fact, down to the day before Passover, the youngsters came together, as they had always done, and went joyfully, hand in hand, out of the village. This time they were so laden with things to tell, such an accumulation of adventures and discoveries, that they forgot about passing hours. They talked and talked and talked, as only children can, and it was only when the light was beginning to dim, and Feitel suddenly remembered that it was the eve of Passover, and that Mother would be waiting for him, to wash his head before the *seder*, and put a new pair of pants on him, that they turned back. And this was the picture which confronted them when they reached Feitel's house:

A crowd of peasant men and peasant women, peasant

boys and peasant girls, was gathered before the door. Kuretchka was there, the village headman was there, the village policeman was there, everybody was there, and everybody was talking at once, shouting, gesticulating. In the midst stood Nachman, his wife, and the older children. They too were talking, and the sweat was running down their faces. Suddenly the picture changed. Someone pointed out the approaching youngsters, and all faces were turned to them. Kuretchka and the headman and the policeman and everyone else were frozen into silence. Nachman Verebivker straightened up and laughed out loud — but what a laugh! Feitel's mother clapped her hands together and burst into tears.

What was it all about? Feitel never found out. He did not know why his father gave him a thrashing — a mild one, it was true, but administered with a queer, disproportionate depth of feeling. He could not understand why his mother murmured, in the midst of her tears: " O God, let this Passover end in peace! Would that it had ended before it began! " Nor did little Fedka fare any better. He too received a thrashing, a hearty one, which he absorbed philosophically; but he could not understand what all the fuss was about. He heard one of the village women telling his mother of something that had happened in the city: how Jews had trapped a little boy the day before Passover, had kept him in a cellar for twenty-four hours, and then " had set to work on him." Fortunately passers-by had heard the screams, and the child was rescued, but not before it had been cut in four places, four light cuts in the form of a cross. Fedka listened, and felt that somehow this story had to do with the excitement about him and Feitel. But why? And in what way? That he never found out.

There the incident closes, with two children bewildered by the incomprehensible behaviour of grown-ups,
leaving us to ask where the peasant woman got that story.
Was it a sudden resurgence of a piece of folklore, for
which no one in particular was responsible? We know
better. The poison in Kuretchka and in the peasant
woman and in millions like them was a mixture; part of
it an internal secretion which had been growing weaker,
part of it injection, which brought it to life again. There
were men, skilful, vicious, diligent, whose business it was
to reawaken the dormant folklore of anti-Semitism and
turn it to political account. Their purpose was not to
spread a certain point of view with regard to the Jews;
they were much more ambitious. They sought to call up
in the Russian masses, through the dark rebirth of anti-
Semitism, a general darkness of the spirit.

Their success was only partial, and therefore temporary. Perhaps it was because they lacked the demonic
will-power of their successors in Germany; perhaps because they lacked the technical equipment; and perhaps
because the Russian masses were not so tractable. Certainly the Jews were right in repeating, in that particular
instance (they were wrong in the instance of Hitlerite
Germany) : " We've always managed somehow, and we
always will." Jew-hatred never became a mania with any
considerable number of Russians, not even among the
rulers. It was a policy rather than an obsession. There
were kindly priests and humane officials. Besides, just as
Austria was once described as " an autocracy mitigated
by inefficiency," so Russian anti-Semitism might be described as persecution mitigated by dishonesty. The vast
majority of Russian officials were " takers " — they could
be bribed. Some provincial officials, town clerks, police

captains, prefects, might actually have a sort of fondness for Jews. Even after the accession of Alexander III, when anti-Semitism was incorporating itself in a vast code of laws, and the Jews were being represented as Russia's number-one problem, it was not unusual for a Russian official to be a regular visitor in a Jewish home. But rarely was the relationship natural, wholesome, or pleasant.

Mordecai Nathan, one of the " rich " Jews of Kasrielevky-in-transition, was on very good terms with the new prefect. There existed between them an excellent understanding based on a mutually contemptuous friendliness, which on the prefect's side was tinged with condescension, on Mordecai's with abjectness. The prefect liked Jewish brandy and Jewish gefillte fish, and in the matter of gefillte fish Temeh Beileh, Mordecai Nathan's wife, was one of the experts of Kasrielevky. Every Friday evening the prefect was a guest at Mordecai Nathan's for the hors d'œuvre. What an honour for Mordecai Nathan! The prefect himself, *natchalstve*, officialdom, the government in person! And what compliments he paid the Jewish people! " There's nothing like a piece of Jewish fish anywhere else in the world," he declared, and Mordecai Nathan and his wife melted with rapture. When the brandy had been drunk and the fish eaten, the prefect wiped his whiskers and withdrew, followed by a murmured blessing from Temeh Beileh: " Break your legs before you get home."

Bribing an official, keeping on his good side, had always been a life and death necessity for Jews. But in the old days the relationship had been recognized for what it was. In transitional and new Kasrielevky, thrown off balance by the strange rise of conspiratorial anti-Semitism, certain ugly overtones appeared. Mordecai Nathan might justify himself as his fathers had done: "My life is in that man's hands." So it was, but that did not explain the wretched feeling of elation roused in him by the visit of the prefect. It was no longer cold policy; it was no longer an "honest" transaction between oppressed and oppressor. Transitional and new Kasrielevky were not so sure of themselves as old Kasrielevky had been, and the root of the spiritual disturbance lay in this odd fact: Kasrielevky was losing its inner self-certainty vis-à-vis the outside world just when the latter was becoming worse, not better!

Kasrielevky now had its professional, careerist anti-Semite, a young man named Makar Pavlovich, a clerk in the city hall. We must distinguish between the respective attitudes of the prefect of Kasrielevky and of Makar Pavlovich toward the Jews. The former no doubt looked down on Jews; he considered them a queer lot; they dressed outlandishly, talked a gibberish of a language — in which he, like his predecessor, was himself not inexpert — were always up to sly tricks, had to be watched, were difficult to manage, and showed an inexplicable obstinacy with regard to their religion. Still, they were human. Makar Pavlovich's attitude was grimmer. Jews were not queer to him; they were sinister. They were a danger to Russia. They were practitioners of dark and horrible rites. They could not be managed; they had to be suppressed. In the famous formula of the Russian anti-Semitic leadership: "One third of the Jews would be baptized, one third would migrate, one third would die out" — that was the solution.

How did Makar Pavlovich get that way? Sholom Aleichem attributes it to little Makar's fights with little Jewish boys. It is startling to encounter this theory in Sholom

Aleichem; it leads back to the conclusion that if Jews were perfect in their behaviour from the cradle to the grave, the ancient Western folklore of anti-Semitism would die of inanition, and Pobiedonostsevs and Hitlers would have nothing to work on and no underlings to work through; or that Hitlers and Pobiedonostsevs themselves would never think of the Jews in any particular way. Some of the inner uncertainty of new Kasrielevky had crept into the soul of Sholom Aleichem.

The differences in outlook on the Jews between the prefect and Makar Pavlovich added up to this: bribing the prefect and toadying to him had at least a purpose; on Makar Pavlovich it was wasted. There was no coming to terms with him. Not that Makar Pavlovich was above taking bribes; not that he did not once come crawling to Mordecai Nathan to get him out of trouble when, as the result of his relationship with a certain young woman, he was in danger of losing his job and perhaps being sent to Siberia. Mordecai Nathan foolishly and ignominiously gave Makar Pavlovich the help he pleaded for, in which he was to be more condemned than for his abjectness toward the prefect. Makar Pavlovich was ready to derive personal advantage from his anti-Semitism, even at the hands of Jews, but not to mitigate it; anti-Semitism was his only stock in trade.

This dark picture of the deterioration of the Jewish position must not, however, be permitted to stand as it is. The Kasrielevkites kept some of their " bitochon." When Russian anti-Semitism was at its worst, they still said: " It could be worse." How pitifully right they were they did not realize, for they did not live long enough to be confronted with Hitlerian anti-Semitism. In the midst of edicts, exclusions, and pogroms Kasrielevky found consolation in a remarkable incident caused directly by these very evils — the wiping out (who would have foreseen it?) of the ancient feud between Kasrielevky and Kozodoievka.

That feud, it will be remembered, had centred on the question of the priority of the two prayers: " Give thanks unto the Lord," and " Blessed be He who spoke," and had been precipitated by the thrashing administered in Kozodoievka on the person of a Kasrielevkite. It had been in the good old liberal period, before the coming of the Pobiedonostsevs, the Krushevans, and the Makar Pavloviches, when Jews had had nothing more to worry about than the prayer-book.

One day the lightning flickered over Kasrielevky. A certain ritual slaughterer received from his son-in-law, who lived in Kishinev, a Hebrew letter which read as follows: " To my beloved father-in-law, whose name has penetrated to the ends of the world, and to my dear and beloved mother-in-law, greeting and peace. With faltering hands and trembling knees I write these words to you. Know that the storm has passed this way and left destruction behind it. No pen can describe it all. But we of the family are, God be praised, well — my wife, my children, and I. We came through the tempest with nothing more than a fright. . . ."

No mention of a pogrom; no mention was necessary. Long before the Jewish newspaper was received by Zeidel — at that time Kasrielevky's only subscriber — all Kasrielevky knew. At first there was some attempt, in true Kasrielevky fashion, to laugh it all off as a wild exaggeration. But Kasrielevky's laughing days were over. Then the newspaper arrived, and the worst was confirmed.

" Thank God it didn't happen here," said the Kasrielevkites, and added, again in true Kasrielevky fashion: " It *can't* happen here." Those are the very words reported by Sholom Aleichem. " It can't happen here."

Why couldn't it happen there? Simply because it had not happened before; simply because the Kasrielevkites did not want it to happen. But somehow the old Kasrielevky scepticism did not have the old ring. " Are you sure it can't happen in Kasrielevky? Quite sure? Has not Kasrielevky got its Makar Pavlovich? Will the prefect of Kasrielevky risk his job by trying to prevent a pogrom? Is he so enamoured of Mordecai Nathan's brandy and Temeh Beileh's gefillte fish? For that matter, is he afraid that he won't get Jewish brandy and gefillte fish after a pogrom, just as he did before? "

Because they could think of nothing else, they kept on repeating, with diminishing conviction: " It can't happen here." Until — how it began, with whom, where, was never discovered — a rumour spread through Kasrielevky, grew into a report, became a certainty, that three villages were on the march, hundreds of peasants, arms in their hands, murder in their hearts. The Philistines are upon thee, O Kasrielevky!

Then panic, furious, unreasoning panic, descended on Kasrielevky. There was a feverish running to and fro, a wild packing of household goods, a loading of possessions on wagons. The majority of Kasrielevkites had no wagons and could not obtain them. They loaded what they could on their backs. Fathers, mothers, wailing children streamed out of Kasrielevky that morning, fleeing they knew not whither or from what.

The town was left empty except for three persons: old Reb Yozifel, and Adam and Eve, the keepers of the baths

by the river. Reb Yozifel was no longer the *Rav* of Kasrielevky. He had been retired; on a pension, of course,
for it was unthinkable that Kasrielevky would forget its
honoured spiritual leader in his latter days. Not that the
Kasrielevkites paid old Reb Yozifel a pension, either.
Where were they to get the money after paying the new
Rav his stipend? The famous visitor Poliakov had not
yet slapped Reb Yozifel in the face and expiated it by
building the Old People's Home. And even when the
Old People's Home was built it remained empty because
there was nothing to run it with. It had been arranged
that Reb Yozifel, who had neither wife nor child, should
go to live with Adam and Eve by the river. Adam was
what they called the keeper of the baths, partly because
that was his real name, and partly because most of the
time he was almost as naked as the father of mankind;
and Eve was the name given to his wife because nothing
else would have done. Good, simple, sturdy people, they
accounted it an honour above their merit to give shelter
to the aged saint, and to support him out of the " income
of the baths." With them Reb Yozifel lacked nothing, chiefly because he needed nothing. They loved
him as they would have loved a father, and he them
as he loved all human beings, as if they had been his
children.

Well, on that memorable day Kasrielevky was in flight,
but Reb Yozifel would not budge.

" Rabbi! Rabbi! " pleaded Adam and Eve. " Don't
you know what's happening? "

" What is happening, my children? "

They told him of the reports: three villages marching
on Kasrielevky, hundreds of peasants with arms in their
hands and murder in their hearts.

Reb Yozifel listened patiently, as was his wont, and then began:

" Hear me, children! All these things that you tell me are childish and meaningless. Know that the Guardian of Israel sleepeth not and slumbereth not. Therefore sit down, and I will tell you a parable of a certain king — "

" Rabbi, what are you talking about? " almost shouted Adam. " Who wants to listen to a parable of a king? " And immediately big, burly Adam of the baths cut himself short. He would have liked to bite his tongue out. Was this the way to talk to old Reb Yozifel, the glory of Kasrielevky, its chief ornament even though he was no longer *Rav*? But Reb Yozifel answered never a word. He put on his prayer-shawl and phylacteries, he opened a sacred book, he took his place at the head of the table. And there he sat, looking so regal, so secure, that Adam and Eve were struck dumb. They too sat down wordlessly, their eyes fixed on the majestic figure of Reb Yozifel.

These three alone remained in the forsaken town. All the others, rich and poor, young and old, were driving their wagons or marching on foot in the direction of the big city of Yehupetz, by the road which leads through Kozodoievka and Mazeppavka. Half-way between Kasrielevky and Kozodoievka the two marching communities came face to face, bag and baggage, horse and foot: two communities in flight, in opposite directions. The sight of Kasrielevky in panic brought the Kozodoievkites to an abrupt halt; and the sight of Kozodoievka in panic did the same for the Kasrielevkites. The refugees faced each other as in battle array, and the following colloquy took place:

Kazrielevkites: " Whither bound, fellow Jews? "

Kozodoievkites: " The very question on our lips. Whither bound, fellow Jews? "

Kasrielevkites: " A business mission."

Kozodoievkites: " What? An entire community on a business mission? "

Kasrielevkites: " And what about you? Aren't you an entire community? "

Kozodoievkites: " But who said we were on a business mission? "

Kasrielevkites: " If not on a business mission, then where are you going? "

Kozodoievkites: " We're not going. We're running."

Kasrielevkites: " Now you're talking. And who said *we* weren't running."

Kozodoievkites: " Now *you're* talking. Whither are you running? "

Kasrielevkites: " Whither are *you* running? "

Kozodoievkites: " In your direction. And you? "

Kasrielevkites: " In yours."

Kozodoievkites: " And what will you do in Kozodoievka? "

Kasrielevkites: " The same as you in Kasrielevky."

Kozodoievkites: " Then what's the sense of your running to Kozodoievka and our running to Kasrielevky? "

Kasrielevkites: " Obviously so that we can change places."

Kozodoievkites: " Joking aside, what *are* you running for? "

Kasrielevkites: " What are *you* running for? "

Thus, or approximately thus, the leaders of Kasrielevky and Kozodoievka fenced with each other on the open road, concealing the shame of their panic under a sour jesting. But the talk died down, and Kasrielevky

143

and Kozodoievka stood looking at each other helplessly. Ah, God, what they had come to! They remembered suddenly that they were not on jesting terms, not even on speaking terms. They remembered the follies of the past, the mutual excommunications, the thrashings, the appeals to the authorities, the lawsuits; and the tears began to steal down their cheeks. There and then the great reconciliation took place. Kasrielevky householders shook hands with Kozodoievka householders, champions of the priority of " Give thanks " with fanatics of the priority of " Blessed be." It was an unofficial and unexpected Day of Atonement, without the prayers and the ram's horns. The two communities parted from each other with kisses and heart-felt good wishes. Kasrielevky returned to Kasrielevky, and Kozodoievka to Kozodoievka. There was, as it happens, no pogrom in either community that year, but the ancient feud was buried for ever. If only the results of anti-Semitism had always been so salutary!

CHAPTER XVIII

A Special Kind of Anti-Semite

❀

HERE lived in ancient Palestine, some two thousand years ago, a Jew by the name of Nahum Gimzo, and this Jew had neither arms nor legs, besides which he was totally blind. It had not always been so with him; indeed, in his early years he had been famous for his beauty and his physical perfections. His dreadful condition came upon him suddenly, and in an extraordinary way. As a young man he was once leading to market the laden donkeys of his rich father, he himself riding ahead on a richly caparisoned ass. Faring along thus, he was hailed by a beggar lying in a ditch. "Give me food," cried the beggar, in a weak voice. Nahum, brought up in righteousness, dismounted from his ass and went very ceremoniously about the meritorious business of feeding the hungry, with "Wait a moment while I do this," and "Just a second while I do that," relishing all the time the spectacle of his own humility and generosity. Meanwhile the beggar died. Whereupon Nahum (whose name was not yet Gimzo) raised his eyes to heaven and said: "May my arms, which were slow to succour this man, wither; may my legs, which delayed to run to his aid, likewise wither; may my eyes, which were slow to see his agony, lose their power of sight." Heaven, taking him at his word, fulfilled the curse against him on the spot. This same Nahum, so punished and so truncated, became a great teacher in Israel and, what is more, a notable optimist. He used to sit, studying and teaching, with the stumps of his legs in a pail of water, so that the ants might not be able to crawl up his body. His name Gimzo came from his favourite slogan: " *Gam zu l'tovah*," which means: " This too is for the best." And if it also came from the fact that he was born in a place called Gimzo it only proves the foresight of Providence, and adds the final proof to the authenticity of the story.

" *Gam zu l'tovah*," the Jews of Kasrielevky and Kozodoievka could say after the reconciliation. And the same could be said by the Jews of Teplik, because of what happened in the case of Sholom Ber, the rich man of the village, and Berel the Red with the lame leg, and Agamemnon Afonegenovich Plisetzky, the anti-Semitic prefect of Teplik.

Agamemnon Afonegenovich Plisetzky, newly appointed prefect of Teplik, was dubbed Haman the Jewhater by the Jews of Teplik almost on the day of his induction; first because his real name was unpronounceable, second because he was the worst kind of anti-Semite, the kind known as "clean-handed." He was not a taker of bribes, a drinker of Jewish brandy, or an eater of Jewish fish. He would not even accept a present for his birthday. Offered one, he refused point-blank, and he said to the astonished Jew: " If you offer me a present it's because you expect something in exchange. I'll keep a special eye on you." In short, a conscientious anti-Semite. No sooner had he taken office than he set about cleaning up the village. He began by driving the horse-

146

thieves out of Teplik; within a month the horse-thieves of Teplik, famous for hundreds of miles around, were scattered to the four winds. Next Haman became busy with the streets and the Jews. " The streets must be kept clean! " was his ukase. No garbage was to be deposited in them, no slops were to be poured out at the doors, back or front. The like of it had never been heard in Teplik. The streets of Teplik had been the repositories of garbage and slops since the days of Rurik — or at any rate since there had been streets in Teplik. This was not all. This Haman, this fantastic and unappeasable enemy of mankind and of Judaism, insisted that no Hebrew teacher be permitted to practise his profession without a licence, and that Jewish shops obey the law and keep closed of a Sunday morning until twelve o'clock. And he meant business! No wheedling, no protests could move him. He made no distinction between rich and poor, prominent and obscure. Offenders were arrested on the spot and sent under convoy to Heissin, the nearest town with a prison and a court. And just to show you the man's inflexibility: sometimes it would happen that the prisoner literally had not a kopeck with which to buy food for himself on the route march to Heissin — Kasrielevky had no monopoly of the more fantastic forms of poverty — in which case Agamemnon Afonegenovich Plisetzky, incredible anti-Semite that he was, rather than balk the law of a Jew, would take a half rouble out of his own pocket and shove it into the hand of the prisoner. An official who *paid* for his anti-Semitism! There's something.

Sholom Ber was not merely a *nogid,* or rich man; he was *the nogid* of Teplik, first, with no second; all of Teplik's Jewish aristocracy, its financial power, its social leadership, its court of final appeals. The position of the banker in a small community, here in America, let us say, is of relative insignificance compared with that of *the nogid* in one of Sholom Aleichem's villages. For nine tenths of Jewish life was self-contained, and you could not escape from the *nogid* except by escaping from the community. If the *nogid* was a decent man, you blessed God for sending you a benevolent tyrant. If he was not, you lived in a double exile. For in the synagogue, at weddings, or circumcision feasts, the *nogid's* place was at the head; ritual privileges were dispensed by him, or with his consent. It was the *nogid* here, there, everywhere.

Sholom Ber, alas, was nothing to bless God for. His pieties were many, his charities few. Public spirit he had none. Only once a year, on Simchas Torah, the Rejoicing for the Law, he kept open house, treated his fellow Jews to tiny drinks of brandy and tiny pieces of cake, and bade them dance. To the vice of parsimony he added an immeasurable pride and a gloomy obstinacy of spirit. When Sholom Ber said " Yes " or " No," all the kings of the East and West could come against him: he would not retract.

The acts and edicts of Agamemnon Afonegenovich, prefect of Teplik, did not touch Sholom Ber at first. The driving out of the horse-thieves had nothing to do with Jews — Jews were not horse-thieves. The restrictions on Hebrew-teachers and shopkeepers certainly touched Jews, but Sholom Ber was neither a Hebrew-teacher nor a shopkeeper. The matter of garbage and slops, however, affected Sholom Ber along with everyone else. When he heard of it, he set his jaws and said: " No." Haman or no Haman, ukase or no ukase, Sholom Ber would stand by the immemorial custom. Let others do as they wished; the garbage and slops of Sholom Ber's household would be disposed of as they had always been disposed of: to wit, most conveniently, on the street.

" Sholom Ber! " said his intimates timidly. " Sholom Ber! This Haman is not like other Hamans. He means business. With him it's one-two, off with the convoy! "

Sholom Ber grunted.

" Sholom Ber! You'll get a summons! "

" Five million summonses! "

Sholom Ber was mistaken. One summons was enough. It was delivered the very next day by Agamemnon Afonegenovich in person, accompanied by two policemen. Sholom Ber, the *nogid,* whom no Jew in Teplik had ever dared to question, let alone contradict, opened up impudently on the prefect. Whereupon the latter told him curtly to shut up. Whereupon Sholom Ber called him Haman to his face. Whereupon Agamemnon Afonegenovich asked for an explanation of the name, was told it was an allusion to Haman the Jew-hater, and added to his protocol: " Insult to the government in the person of the prefect." Sholom Ber the *nogid* was arrested on the spot and ordered held for the day's convoy to Heissin.

Very different from Sholom Ber was Berel the Red, with the lame leg, who was the second prisoner in that morning's convoy. Berel the Red lived in a three-room hovel — to be exact, one room with two alcoves — in the poorest part of Teplik. He made a living by fermenting wine, which he sold to Jews for the Sabbath benediction. Did I say wine? And did I say a living? May the enemies of Israel drink such wine and make such a living! Eight little children, naked and barefoot, subsisted, besides

149

Berel the Red, on the proceeds of his illicit traffic. Yet
Berel the Red was a *Kasriel,* a merry pauper, lame leg
and all; as gay as Sholom Ber was dour, as accommodat-
ing as Sholom Ber was hard.

A few minutes after Sholom Ber was arrested Berel
the Red, squatting among his bottles, heard the door
open, looked up, and beheld the figure of Agamemnon
Afonegenovich Plisetzky towering over him. Two policemen stood behind him. Berel the Red showed neither
defiance nor fear. He finished corking the bottle he held
in his hand and rose. A horde of little children, naked
from the navel down, crowded round the prefect and his
escort, delighted and awed by the shining buttons.

" According to reports I have received," said the prefect, " you are making lots of money."

" It might be worse," answered Berel. " It might also
be better, but there's no limit to better."

" Why, then, are these children naked and barefoot? "

" It's good for their health."

" And what do you do with all the money you make? "
asked the prefect.

" I dispose of it according to the counsel of the Talmud."

" And what does the Talmud counsel? "

" Buy land with one third, put one third in business,
keep one third in ready cash."

" I see you are a cheerful sort of person," observed the
prefect.

" What should I worry about? " answered Berel the
Red. " I need nothing, I have nothing. The account
balances."

" I shall ask my men to make a search," said the prefect. " Who knows what they might find? "

" Certainly, your honor," answered Berel, with alacrity. " And whatever they find, it's fifty-fifty."

What should the men find in the shack of Berel the Red, besides his bottles and his rags? But Berel the Red was a criminal, the law was the law, and Agamemnon Afonegenovich played no favourites. Berel the Red joined Sholom Ber the *nogid* in the convoy.

There was a third prisoner that morning, Henich the loon, who was being taken to Heissin to have his age determined. For if he was over eighteen, his older brother, the sole support of the family, would be called up for military service, and Henich would assume his older brother's economic duties. These three, and Lavre the policeman, made up the convoy which drew forth from Teplik that morning, under the stupefied gaze of the entire Jewish population.

It was a leisurely, pleasant sort of convoy, an outing, almost a picnic. The sun shone brightly overhead, the fields lay green and sweet on either side of the road, the trees shook their heads lazily in the mild wind. Lavre was a dull-witted, good-natured peasant, unspoiled by a little brief authority. The four of them strolled along, and when they were tired they sat down on the grass, sent Henich the loon to the nearest village for a bottle of brandy — Sholom Ber stood treat, chiefly to keep Lavre unspoiled — and unpacked their provisions.

For the first time in his life Berel the Red found himself in sustained and intimate company with proud, snobbish Sholom Ber; for the first time in his life Sholom Ber put up with the proximity and conversation of a tatterdemalion like Berel. For how should these men ever have come together — Sholom Ber in his *nogid's* house, Berel in his shack, Sholom Ber in his seat by the eastern

151

wall of the synagogue, Berel the Red among the paupers near the door? What was there between them, and what had they to say to each other?

To each other, nothing. But there was plenty that Berel the Red had to say to Sholom Ber: the accumulation of a lifetime. By the accident of a common calamity the opportunity was given him, and he took it.

It began in a casual way, with remarks on the weather, and it developed into a monologue on the part of Berel the Red, with occasional interruptions, or rather interjections, on the part of Sholom Ber. No bitterness, no denunciations; only a dreamy, almost kindly evocation of the past. For the sun was warm, the wind tender, and Berel's mood reminiscent. Out of his quiet monologue grows and expands, unintentionally, incidentally, before you are aware of it, altogether by implication, and without a touch of rancour, an unforgettable protest.

Two little boys born, as we would say, on opposite sides of the tracks: Sholom Ber the son of a *nogid,* Berel the Red with the lame foot, son of a nobody. It might have been anywhere and in any age, in Teplik or Weehauken or ancient Babylon; but it happened to be in Teplik, in a Jewish community, and the Jews were steeped in a moral religious tradition, and they were the objects of a common hatred, and they might have been expected to stand together, and they did not. And Berel might have been a revolutionary, but he was not. He might have been embittered, but he was not that either. It is with a queer sort of wonder that he recalls everything, for he is not a thinker or a theorist. He does not know where the blame lies. It was not Sholom Ber's fault that his parents taught him, in his earliest years, that he was, to the exclusion of everyone else, and in the appall-

ing Yiddish phrase, " *a tatens a kind*," " the son of a father," meaning, the son of a somebody. The phrase occurs so often in the world of Sholom Aleichem. He
himself was " *a tatens a kind*," he tells us in his autobiography, and he recalls that even in old Kasrielevky there
was room for a vast gulf between the classes, and there
were people it was not proper for him, the little aristocrat, to associate with. " You weren't allowed to play
with me," says Berel the Red, bearded and elderly, to
Sholom Ber, bearded and elderly. " Not that you wanted
to, either; nor did the other children. In part because I
was barefoot and in rags, in part because I was lame. If
I tried to join your games, you drove me off. You shouted
' Clubfoot ' after me. Sometimes when you happened to
pass close to me, you'd step on my crippled foot, as if by
accident, and when I howled with pain, you laughed."

" Who, me? " Sholom Ber the *nogid* started, his face
reddening. Who — me? These are probably the most
frequently yoked words in any language under the sun.

Yes, he. Berel the Red remembered it all the more
clearly because once his grandfather — Berel was an orphan — had dared to complain to the father of little
Sholom Ber, only to be told: " My Sholom Ber knows
his place. He is the son of a father. See to it that your
Berel knows his place, too." Berel's grandfather had reported the conversation, in Berel's presence, and Berel
never forgot it. *The son of a father*. But what did it
mean? Didn't every son have a father? " Do you know,
Reb Sholom Ber, since that day I've disliked rich men,
and rich men's children, and — to be frank — most of
all I've disliked you."

" Who — me? " Ridiculous! Incredible! Why should
anyone *dislike* Sholom Ber?

153

" Don't be offended, Reb Sholom Ber," continued
Berel, softly. " A foolish thing sticks in the mind. And
there are so many foolish things to remember." There
was, for instance, the wedding invitation which Berel
the nobody had dared to send the great Sholom Ber, and
which the great Sholom Ber had ignored: ignored completely; not so much as a letter in reply. " Who — me? "
And, years later, when Berel was left a widower, with two
tiny children, he humbled himself and sent word to
Sholom Ber, in vain. And again, on the day when his
house burned down, and he was left Adam-naked, more
beggarly, if that was possible, than before, someone went
to interview Reb Sholom Ber on his behalf, and received
the answer that Reb Sholom Ber did not interfere in
public matters.

Why doesn't Berel the Red grow angry, why doesn't
he work himself into a towering rage? Why does he add:
" Don't be offended, Reb Sholom Ber," when he con-
fesses mildly, and without caring too much, that he dislikes rich men? Because it is not his way, or Sholom Aleichem's way. The quietly humorous recital is the more
effective for it, which is perhaps what makes Sholom
Aleichem one of the favourite writers of revolutionary
Russia till this day.

And Berel the Red came to the last and bitterest of
the rebuffs. He had humbled himself again before Sholom Ber, the *nogid*, begging, this time, not for himself,
but for his daughter. There was a match, the chance of
a lifetime, a grand young man from a neighbouring town,
a working lad, of fine character, of some education, too, a
likable young man; Berel's heart went out to him the
moment he saw him. " If I could only get him for my
daughter! God, Father in heaven, help me to get him for

my daughter! " For there was one all but insurmounta-
ble obstacle: the father of the young man insisted on a
dowry. Not a fantastic dowry, just one hundred roubles.
Berel the Red had not a hundred kopecks. Surely in such
a matter, the marrying off of a Jewish daughter, one of
the most meritorious commandments of Israel, Reb Sholom Ber would not turn him away. But Reb Sholom Ber
did turn him away, contemptuously, and with cruel jests.
" And supposing your daughter had fallen in love with
a young Rothschild, would you expect me to provide the
proper dowry? " was what Reb Sholom Ber had said.
" Who — me? " " Yes, you, Reb Sholom Ber." It didn't
matter now, the daughter was dead.

Are there such things as genuine conversions, and can
words alone bring them about? No doubt dealers in
words are inclined to believe it, for their own sake.
And perhaps, in this instance, Sholom Aleichem merely
wanted to crown the life of Berel the Red with one great
action. For as the story is told, under the open sky, among
peaceful fields, Sholom Ber, the arrogant, the obstinate,
looked into the mirror of his loveless life and understood
for the first time that there was reason why he should be
disliked. Another Day of Atonement in the open, this
time not between two communities, but between two
men: an opening of the eyes and heart, an awakening of
regret and shame and of the desire to expiate. It was, it
seemed, Sholom Ber's destiny to become another man,
and for its fulfillment there was needed a Berel the Red,
and a convoy, and a summer's day, and Agamemnon
Afonegenovich Plesitzky, the anti-Semitic prefect who
made no distinction between rich and poor.

CHAPTER XIX

Kasrielevky in Dissolution

❀

THE HABIT of study was always deep in the Jewish folkways. Religion enjoined it: " An ignorant man cannot be pious," said the Ethics of the Fathers; social custom exalted it: " Torah is the best merchandise," says the Yiddish proverb. The pursuit of knowledge under adverse circumstances was a commonplace in Jewish life. Since the days of Babylonian Hillel, who chopped wood to pay his first tuition fees, and the hungry, ill-clad Tanaitic scholars, Jews had looked with approval, but without a sense of the extraordinary, on boys who starved their way through to wisdom. In a hundred old Kasrielevkys the synagogues or study houses — the terms had become interchangeable — housed penniless students of the Torah. A bench for a bed, a tattered overcoat for a blanket, a fist for a cushion, mouldy bread, and water by measure — this was their lot. Happy were those who had an older scholar to guide them; most of the time they stood alone, or in groups of two and three, over a volume of the Talmud, chanting its text and memorizing it.

For such poor students " the eating of days " had been instituted. One had Monday's meals with a certain householder, Tuesday's with a second, Wednesday's with a third. What if there were not householders enough for all the students, as was often the case? Well, then, you did without two, or three, or four " days." In all the old Kasrielevkys, at all times, you might have overheard remarks like these:

" I'm short of a Wednesday, a Thursday, and a Sunday. Do you know where I can get one? "

" How should I? I still haven't got a Thursday and Sunday of my own. My Wednesdays are as good as nothing. Thank God I have a fat Saturday, which carries me over Sunday."

There were well-to-do students, naturally, who were inscribed in regular Talmudical colleges, and who actually received money from home or had all their " days." They were the minority. For the most part the years of study, between boyhood and early manhood, the time of marriage, were years of such privation as often left a permanent mark on the physical constitution. Among the old Kasrielevkys there were always thousands of boys " eating ' days ' and washing them down with tears."

There was, besides the " days," a second institution for the encouragement of study: namely the " kept son-in-law," one of the curiosities of Jewish life, probably without an analogue among other peoples. A well-to-do Jew of old Kasrielevky would marry his daughter to a promising student, and the marriage contract assured the son-in-law a stated number of years of study. During this period the student lived with his in-laws, contributing nothing toward the support of himself, his wife, or his children, of the last of which he was expected to produce as many as possible. His business was to study; not a profession, of course, but the sacred books. At the end of the

stated period he took on the economic duties of a husband and father.

To have a " kept son-in-law " was an honour. The
father-in-law himself might be an unlettered man, which
does not mean an illiterate, of which there were few in
Jewry; but he might be a stranger to " the little letters,"
the successive borders of commentary in which Talmudic text is embedded on the printed page, like a super-
sacred raisin in a sacred tart. In that case his keeping of
the son-in-law was an act of redemption as well as an honour. " If you cannot be a scholar, be the servant of a
scholar," said the tradition. A householder of Kasrielevky once expressed himself thus to Sholom Aleichem:
" I have a son-in-law in keeping — gold, pure gold. It
would be a shame to let him out into the world, to be
spoiled."

A very odd, equivocal figure in the old Kasrielevkys
was the eternal student, the pious and learned husband
who, whether or not he began married life as a " kept
son-in-law," never got round to the business of making a
living. The wife was the provider as well as the undis-
courageable child-bearer. She kept the shop and did all
the buying and selling, or she managed the inn, or she
raised chickens, fed geese, and plucked feathers for pil-
lows; she sat in the market-place and haggled with the
peasants; she cooked and scrubbed and patched; she sent
the boys to *cheder* and married off the daughters. There
were thousands of these valiant women, whose children
were often known by their mother's name, as in a matri-
archate — Braine's Joseph and Lea Dvosse's Chaim. And
he, the student husband, in youth, manhood, and old
age, sat over his books, sundered from the world, exempt
from family duties. But unless he was really a famous and

exceptional scholar, such a man was not genuinely respected. Even in old Kasrielevky he was a slightly ludicrous figure. Certainly the tradition enjoined study; however, it enjoined, with equal emphasis, labour and independence. The wife might be proud of her scholar husband; she might be prepared to forfeit her life for the throne in paradise, and while derisive, in a puzzled way, of her husband's helplessness, might be convinced that her sacrifice was a good bargain. But old Kasrielevky did not take to the " student husband " and the providing wife. Yet this tolerated tradition was only the abuse of the national passion for learning, a degenerate manifestation of an originally high spiritual impulse.

" Study " naturally meant only one thing — the sacred books, with the Talmud as basis and chief substance. It must be remembered, however, that the Talmud is a vast compilation of laws and legal precedents, of legends, aphorisms, moralistic reflections, folklore, history, science, and general information; it is a compendium of life, life regulated and shaped by a religious outlook, an encyclopædia with a theocratic nationalist slant. Unlike the sacred literature of the Christians, it does not confine itself to the theological, moralistic, and contemplative. It is supposed to be, it often was, a detailed preparation for the active life — in short, a complete university course.

Hence the innate contradiction in the picture of the student husband who, unless he was a teacher preparing others for life, became at last an expert *in vacuo,* dealing with symbols and counters, not realities; hence the scarcely veiled disesteem in which he was held. But the special characteristic of Jewish sacred study, its relevance to law, business, trades, marriage, daily behaviour, its point-to-point correspondence with the daily technique of life, made on the whole for an alertness of the intelligence, an eagerness " to know," which could not be confined to the Talmud and other sacred books once the enclosing fence had been broken down. One of the most poignant chapters in the intellectual history of man unfolds in Sholom Aleichem's descriptions of that breakdown. The avidity, the self-sacrificing fury, which once went into the sacred studies was directed, with the coming of the Haskalah, toward modern, " outside " knowledge.

The nearest parallel to the intellectual transformation of the Russian Jewish youth in the later nineteenth century will be found among the scholars of the Italian Renaissance. There were differences. The first was that in Italy modernization began as an indiscriminate acceptance of the forgotten values of antiquity, while among the young men of transitional Kasrielevky it took the form of an indiscriminate rage for the modern. In both cases there was a breaking of moulds; and there is something peculiarly Jewish, something of the Talmud student tradition, in the Italian scholars (the artists have no place in the parallel) of the thirteenth, fourteenth, and fifteenth centuries, in their intellectual single-mindedness, their endurance of poverty for the sake of their ideal, their wanderings over Europe in search of documents and codices.

The second difference was this: An intellectual hunger was born or at least reawakened in the Italian Renaissance. In Russian Jewry it did not have to be born or reawakened; it only had to be switched from one objective to another, from the Talmud to the nineteenth century, from Hebrew to Russian, German, or French, from

Rabbi Akiba to Buckle, from Rashi to Spencer. The insatiable intellectual need was in essence the same as of old; the very technique of starvation was the same.

A third difference went deeper. The Italian Renaissance led, the Jewish followed; the Italian gave, from its beginning; the Jewish had to take before it could give; the Italian was attended by excessive pride, the Jewish by excessive humility. And this humility caused young Jewry to believe that Jewish culture was without any permanent value whatsoever. A concomitant of Jewish modernization was the birth of Jew-shame in the young generation, an affliction which remains widespread among the grandsons and grand-daughters of Kasrielevky in the Western world.

The first recorded case of the break-through in Kasrielevky was that of Benjamin, the son of Israel the beadle. The process was well on in the large cities, in Odessa, Kiev, Warsaw, and St. Petersburg, where Schiller and Goethe and Heine were more frequently mentioned in some well-to-do homes than Ibn Gabirol and Yehudah Halevi, where the daughters in well-to-do homes had piano-teachers and dancing-masters, and the sons were entered in the local Gymnasium. In Kasrielevky the tide was delayed; its onset was therefore the more cataclysmic. While still a child, little Benjamin, attending the *cheder* or one-room Hebrew school of Yerechmiel Moses (he of the lensless spectacles who said they were better than nothing), was the wonder of the town. His happy father deprived himself and the rest of the family of necessities to pay his tuition fees, two roubles a term of six months, plus, of course, the Purim and Channukah gifts. But when Benjamin outgrew the *cheder*, there was no thought of sending him off to a Talmudical college. He studied in the local synagogue instead, fortunate in that he could sleep in a bed of his own, at home. Bibles, Talmudic tractates, commentaries, catechisms, the synagogue had enough of; there were also lecterns at which to stand, and pieces of candle-ends to grow blind by in the nights. So Benjamin studied, with two companions poorer than himself, in the synagogue, and Israel the beadle gloated over his son. " My winning lottery ticket," he called him, and was envied by his neighbours — envied, too, by the rich of Kasrielevky, whose sons were not so gifted. What was the prize for the winning lottery ticket? A great rabbi, a famous scholar, an adept in the wisdom of Israel, and recognition in heaven for the mother who had borne him and the father who had begotten him.

In those days it did not once occur to Israel the beadle that Benjamin might be giving his nights and days to other texts than those of the Codes and Commentaries, and that the books of the heretics had found lodgment in the synagogue of Kasrielevky. The very names of the heretics were only a vague terror in the mind of Israel the beadle: Moses of Dessau, better known to us as Moses Mendelssohn, who had translated the Bible into German for German Jews as a concession and encouragement to ignorance, and had written a modern commentary — modern, that is, for the end of the eighteenth century; and Abraham Mapu, who had debased the Hebrew language for the writing of novels. Worse than these, however, were the Russian grammar books which Benjamin and his two companions conned in secret. This was worldliness, the beginning of apostasy.

It need not be the beginning of apostasy, of course. Often a man could study non-Jewish books without losing the faith; but often he couldn't. Israel the beadle, though he was of old Kasrielevky, was already subtly infected by the spirit of the time. When Benjamin ran away from home and wrote back that he was going over to secular studies, preparing for entrance to the university, Israel the beadle took it badly. But he recovered when letter after letter reassured him that his son was putting on phylacteries every morning and was unshaken in his observance of the ritual. Ah, well, Benjamin was not going to be a great Jewish scholar, a light in the firmament of Jewish learning. There would be no thrones in paradise for father and mother. But Benjamin was going to be a doctor, or an engineer, or a writer, and he was going to remain a good Jew. Let it be so, then. From reconciliation with disappointment, Israel the beadle passed again to pride; and when Benjamin revisited his native Kasrielevky, in the uniform of a Russian Gymnasium student, a sight to stupefy friends and annihilate enemies, Israel the beadle walked again on thin air. His son was still " the winning lottery ticket," and the rich of Kasrielevky were still green with envy. " Wait," thought Israel the beadle, winking inwardly. " All this is nothing. Wait till my Benjamin has finished his courses and made a position for himself, doctor, engineer, or writer, and he will lift up the head of his poor father the beadle, the despised servant, the errand boy of the trustees. *Then* you will have something to envy." And Kasrielevky waited.

Benjamin went back to the distant Russian town and resumed his studies. How did he manage? How did he live? Occasional lessons in well-to-do homes; a bed, too, in exchange for lessons; a highly developed system of starvation, for which he had a hereditary adaptability. On top of that, a highly developed system for dodging the police, also in part hereditary. For Benjamin had no right of sojourn in the Russian town; so it was a continuous changing of names, buying forged papers, bribing officials, changing residence, slipping through cordons.

Benjamin managed. But a change came over the spirit of his letters. Benjamin was learning that starvation, study, and evasion of deportation were not enough. There were restrictions on the education of Jews. The highest marks in the Gymnasium, topped by the golden medal, meant nothing at all when the Jewish quota was closed and there were still Christian applicants, though their marks were poor and they had no medal. Benjamin saw the fateful alternative approaching: baptism or exclusion from the university. He began to write to his father of the new spirit which was spreading in the world, of the decline of the ancient taboos, of the winds of liberty which were blowing across Jewry. Things were not as they used to be, he wrote; there was the emancipation, the Jews must shake off the lethargy of the centuries, occupy an honourable place among the civilized peoples. . . . All this Israel the beadle read with knitted brows, and discussed with his old friend Yerechmiel Moses. What was the boy driving at? What was all this about emancipation, lethargy, civilized peoples, an honourable place? Since when were the Jews uncivilized? Since when had they lacked an honourable place in history? What was " lethargy "? Perhaps if Israel the beadle and Yerechmiel Moses had read such letters objectively, coming from another than their own Benjamin, they would have understood sooner. We are the last to recognize the symptoms of lunacy in a member of the family.

Baptism or failure. Excluded from the university, Benjamin had no hope of a brilliant career. He could, if he chose, go on " studying " and become one of those pitiful unfinished students who went through life giving lessons, writing Russian letters for Jewish patrons, making out official forms for the illiterate. Or he might go back to Kasrielevky, Benjamin the failure. Possibly he might resume his Jewish studies. And then what? A well-to-do Jew might take him as a " kept son-in-law." Or he could find a wife to support him, while he went half crazy over Talmud and Kabbalah, winding up, perhaps, as one of the " end-seekers," dotards whose thoughts wandered among the esoteric books of Messianism and eschatology. He could become a beadle, a pedlar, a shoemaker. Whatever he became, he would always be Benjamin the failure.

But he was tainted. He had tasted of the renaissance, and he was neither of the one world nor of the other. There are two things which cannot be done: replace an appendix and re-establish a tradition. For Benjamin it was forward or nowhere. Very possibly, while he talked of " emancipation," " modernization," " spiritual liberty," and the rest of it, he was obscurely aware of a certain dishonesty. From his early studies he knew that while Jews are permitted to break any but a criminal law where life is endangered, they are forbidden to break the least of the ritual laws at the behest of a tyrant, or for personal advancement. What he proposed to do was to repudiate his people both at the behest of a tyrant and for personal advancement. He would pass from the persecuted minority to the persecuting majority. Of course he would not become one of the active persecutors; he would only accord them a triumph, and this at a time when persecution was on the increase; and all the while he would talk of emancipation and modernization and spiritual liberty. What, after all, did it matter if he passed from a religion which had lost meaning for him to one which had never acquired it for him?

Possibly he hoped to keep the secret of his baptism from his father. Such things happened. Sholom Aleichem tells us of his friend Medvedieff, who apostatized in order to be admitted into the Imperial Opera in St. Petersburg, where he had a notable career. Old Medvedieff never found out, and let himself be supported in his old age by his successful apostate son. But in the case of Israel the beadle there were those who saw to it that the father found out, and all Kasrielevky with him.

Israel the beadle considered his son dead from that day on. He sat the prescribed hour of mourning for him — a son " dead " by apostasy rated only one hour of mourning — and forbade the mention of his name in the home. Israel the beadle had had a son, and the son had embraced the cross — for emancipation. Benjamin, " the winning lottery ticket," was thenceforth of the other world. No Benjamin who said the Jewish prayers, or fasted on the Day of Atonement, or rejoiced in the Passover, or identified himself with the persecuted; no Benjamin to repeat the *Kaddish* after his father's death, no Benjamin to perpetuate the faith, and bring up children in the faith of his fathers. In short, no Benjamin.

We do not know whether Benjamin the son of Israel the beadle was baptized to the same good effect as Medvedieff the singer. There were countless Benjamins who found " emancipation " and made nothing of it. There were, in later days, many fathers who, themselves touched with emancipation, permitted or encouraged their sons to " open the gates " for themselves. By the time old Kasrielevky had become new Kasrielevky, and the days of Chmelnitzky flourished once more, there was a strong tide of apostasy and assimilation in Russian Jewry. At least the assimilation was not always by way of the Church, and not always for the sake of a career.

CHAPTER XX

The Sons-in-Law of Tevyeh

❀

SHOLOM ALEICHEM shows us the "emancipation" not from within, as its participants saw it, but from without, as the alarmed, intensely Jewish world which he loved saw it. He is concerned with Israel the beadle, not with Benjamin; with Tevyeh the dairyman, not with his son-in-law — one of his many sons-in-law — the revolutionary.

Tevyeh is not an old Kasrielevkite. In the matter of time he belongs to transitional Kasrielevky; geographically he is of another world. He lives in a village, mostly among gentiles; his contacts are wider than those of Kasrielevky. He knows the rich Jews of Yehupetz, who come to spend their summers in the *dachas* — cottages — of Boiberik. The modern world, with its changes and scepticisms, is a familiar spectacle to him. For all that, Tevyeh is of the tradition. He is Jewish from the head which he never leaves uncovered to the feet which hasten when he passes a church. But he is tolerant of Jews who are not like him, and this makes him difficult to place. The simplicity of his faith seems to lack consistency. A confusing slyness suddenly appears in his observations, and you are not sure whether this is an excess of naïveté or whether he is deliberately overemphasizing his own simplicity in order to permit you, and himself, a laugh at it.

Tevyeh is for the poor, having known poverty; he believes that a living should be earned by honest labour; he does not understand why the rich Jews who buy his milk and butter and cheese should live on the fat of the land. Yet nothing could be more middle-class than his eternal, and eternally frustrated, efforts to make good matches for his daughters.

" Let it be understood," says Tevyeh, " that the first thing I look for in a man is a little learning. I say that an ignoramus is worse than a hooligan. As for your pieties, do as you like; if you want to leave your head uncovered, like a heathen, or walk on your hands, upside down, like a lunatic, your feet in the air, that's your business. But as long as you can read the little letters, and know what's doing between the covers of a book, you're my kind. If, on top of that, you happen to be a rich man, I consider it a minor defect." Or, as Menachem Mendel's mother-in-law used to say, thoughtfully: " I've always argued it's better to be healthy for two years than sick for one week." Tevyeh was for ever dreaming of rich husbands for his daughters. In these dreams were mingled certain selfish visions, quite at variance with his philosophy of honest labour. How wonderful, he would muse, if Tevyeh the dairyman would be pensioned off by a rich son-in-law, and would spend the rest of his life in works of piety and charity! Sometimes he saw himself riding abroad, not in his ramshackle old cart, drawn by a bony nag as overworked as himself, but in a spanking post-chaise behind two fiery bays — the peer of the Yehupetz *negidim* whom he had served for so many years.

Perhaps he indulged these dreams because he knew deep down that they would never be realized; for Tevyeh on top of the world would have been as misplaced, as contrary to the nature of things, as Puck on Jupiter's throne. The other part of the dreams, relating to the security and happiness of his daughters, was more sincere, but doomed to the same disappointment. For the daughters of Tevyeh may be called the chapters of the tragedy of Tevyeh. We cannot even say that this destiny lay wholly outside of Tevyeh himself. It was not in him to pursue self-advancement; it certainly was not in him to force an advantageous marriage on a reluctant daughter. Yes, he would have liked his daughters to be rich, but he could not get over his affinity with poverty.

Yet when it comes to talk of revolution, world changes, liberty, equality, he lapses into a characteristic over-naïveté which is impenetrable. " Are you going to teach God how to manage the world? If things ought to have been different, wouldn't they have been? " Is Tevyeh saying this with tongue in cheek? Is he pulling Sholom Aleichem's leg or even — God forbid — the Almighty's? It is hard to tell.

With all his love for the people who can " read the little letters," he cannot get over the universal hunger for education which has taken hold of Jewish youngsters like an epidemic. " Look at them! " he cries. " What do they think they're up to? Where will it get them? Nine tenths of them aren't admitted to the schools. This is Russia. Hands off that book, Jew! But there's no holding them back. And who do you think these students are? Sons of the *negidim*? Not a bit of it. Sons of shoemakers, tailors, carpenters, God help us! They leave their homes, they sneak off to Yehupetz, to Odessa; they live in garrets, divide a herring between ten of them, and smell a piece of meat once in six months. Hallelujah! We're students! "

One such student, Pertchik, a little, black, ugly fellow, with bright eyes and a tongue on wheels, became a familiar in Tevyeh's house; and if it was a dangerous thing to introduce a wild student into a houseful of daughters, who was to blame but Tevyeh himself? Driving back one broiling summer day from Boiberik, where he had delivered his shipments of milk and butter and cheese, Tevyeh overtook on the dusty road a lean and hungry-looking young man who was plodding along with a parcel under his arm and leaving behind him the trail of his sweat. " Aha! One of ours! " thought Tevyeh, and sang out: " Hey there! Whoever's son you are, there's room enough in the cart for you." The young man clambered into the cart. " Thank you," he said. " Not at all," answered Tevyeh; " is it not written in our holy book: ' If thou seest thy neighbour's ass astray thou shalt in no wise abandon it '? How much the more, then, thy neighbour's son. Tell me, my lad, where do you come from? " " From Yehupetz." " And what were you doing in Yehupetz? " " Studying." " Studying to be what? " " I haven't the slightest idea." " A good straightforward answer, that, like Eliezer's to Rachel by the well. If you don't know what you're studying to be, why go to all that trouble? " " Leave that to me," answered the young man; " I know what I'm about." " Spoken like a man. And what do you live by? " " By what I eat." " And what do you eat? " " Whatever comes my way." " Very likely. You don't pick and choose, like a son of a Yehupetz *nogid*." To which the young man answered, fierily: " No,

171

thank God. I'm not one of *those*." " Tut, tut! What have
you against the Yehupetz *negidim*? " " Enough to hang
every one of them."

There you were! " Crazy! " reported Tevyeh to Sholom Aleichem. " According to Pertchik, the rich man is
the lowest of the low, and the poor man, especially if
he's a worker, the crown of creation. ' Listen,' I say to
him, ' work is noble, but money's comfortable.' ' Money! '
he snorts. ' It's the world's curse.' ' God smite me with it,'
I answer him, ' as He smote Naaman with leprosy, and
may I never be cured.' "

In spite of which, Tevyeh's heart opened to the young
man at their first encounter. " If you have nothing better to do," he said as he dropped him, " come round this
evening and we'll finish the argument. And maybe my
wife's pancakes will be more to your liking than my
views."

That was really asking for trouble, as Tevyeh himself
admitted when it was too late, when little Pertchik had
found Hodel, the second eldest daughter, even more to
his liking than Goldie's pancakes, and Hodel had been
infected with a mixture of love and revolution. " I'm a
simpleton," admitted Tevyeh to Sholom Aleichem. " I
take everything at face value. I forgot what our sages
said about certain men: ' Honour them — and keep an
eye on them.' "

But Tevyeh was being disingenuous. Only one half of
him, the prudent, worldly, and paternal half, warned
him against Pertchik. The other half was drawn to him.
When Tevyeh poked fun at the wild ideas of the revolutionaries it was, you could see, only to provoke Pertchik
to clearer exposition. And when he pretended that he
could not understand Pertchik's queer habit of disap-

pearing for days at a stretch, and turning up without an explanation, he may have managed to deceive himself, but he does not deceive the reader.

For those were the days when the Russian revolutionaries were " going to the people," working among the masses, upward from below. Those were the days of conspiracy, secret organizations, furtive meetings, underground presses. The air of Russia was quivering with the preparation for the great overthrow. And Tevyeh knew it. But he stood between two worlds. He was rooted in tradition; his habits and affections belonged to the old folkways, to the prayers, the ritual, the Sabbaths and festivals, the sacred books and the sayings of the sages. The justice of the revolution appealed to his instincts, but its technique was utterly foreign to him. What should he be doing among the fierce, irreligious youngsters who flooded the countryside? How could he start talking Marxism at his age? Now, if the revolution had started from his home grounds, as it were, basing itself on Amos the priest-hater and Elijah the king-hater, and conducting itself with due regard for kosher meat and Passover *matzos*, and with a proper respect for the subtle sages of Israel, it might have been another matter. But since he knew that this could not be, and since he saw all that made up his culture disappearing in the change, he put up a sort of fight, half-hearted and confused, in which he betrays a more than passing affection for the " enemy."

Very definitely Tevyeh the religious bourgeois is not a reactionary. He only does not know how to become a revolutionary. When Pertchik and Hodel confront him with their decision to marry, the old ways in him protest. What sort of business is this? Where are the formalities,

173

the proprieties, the negotiations? Have fathers and mothers no more rights? " Why? " he asks, " wasn't I at least invited to the betrothal? "

But the old ways are gone. The betrothal is a private matter between Pertchik and Hodel. And the marriage must take place soon, and quietly.

" But why? " asks Tevyeh.

" Because I'm going away," answers Pertchik.

" When? "

" The quicker the better."

" Where? "

" That's a secret."

" And Hodel? "

" She remains behind till I send for her."

There he stood, Tevyeh, face to face with the implacable new order. He knew now what sort of future his Hodel had chosen for herself; it would be a life of poverty, eternal flight from the police, homelessness, insecurity, occasional prison, perhaps worse. Should he have put his foot down? Would it have helped? Should he have called in the police? Or should he at least have washed his hands of them, accepting no responsibility?

Tevyeh did none of these things. He swallowed his disappointment and entered into the conspiracy to hasten the marriage, telling his wife a fantastic story of an inheritance which Pertchik had to pick up, without delay, in a distant town. And on the day of the marriage — a quiet, private marriage, without guests, without music — he drove the youngsters to the railroad station of Boiberik. " Sitting there with them, in my cart, I keep glancing at them out of the corner of my eyes, and thinking: What a wonderful God we have in heaven! And what a wonderful world, with all sorts of wild creatures in it,

He has created! Here they were, a brand-new husband and wife, fresh out of the box. And he, the husband, is off to God knows where, and she must remain behind. Wouldn't you expect one of them, let's say, to show a little emotion? A tear at least, if only for decency's sake? Not the slightest sign! Tell me, can you make such people out? ''

Many weeks passed before the message came for Hodel. Pertchik was in prison, expecting to be sent to Siberia. As soon as he knew the place of his exile, she was to join him.

That, as far as Tevyeh was concerned, was the end of Hodel. She disappeared from his life as completely as Benjamin from the life of Israel the beadle, but by a more honourable route. From Tevyeh's own recital peers through a mixture of bewilderment, resentment, and pride. Mad those youngsters undoubtedly were, heedless of their parents, indifferent to tradition — but what characters!

It was the second time that Tevyeh, the religious bourgeois, had seen his hopes of good marriages for his daughters disappointed; the second time that he himself had co-operated in the disappointment. It was also the second time that he had pulled the wool over his wife's eyes. We shall see that there was something phony about Tevyeh's worldly-wise dissertations on money and social position. He was at heart not only a revolutionary, but a romantic.

Zeitel was Tevyeh's oldest daugher, first on the list for marriage, with six more waiting to be disposed of. One does not have to be a Russian Jew of the late nineteenth century, one does not have to belong to Sholom Aleichem's world, to understand what it means to have seven daughters to marry off, or to sympathize with the joy which filled the heart of Goldie, Tevyeh's wife, when Leizer Wolf, the butcher, asked for the hand of Zeitel. Leizer Wolf, a widower, was no longer young, but he was a man of substance; he was not a learned man, but he was still a man of substance; he was not even kind-hearted, but he was still, and ever, and always, a man of substance: with a house of his own, solid furniture, piles of linen, innumerable pots and pans, and fistfuls of money. Leizer Wolf did not ask for Zeitel's hand: he bellowed for it. Leizer Wolf was on fire for Zeitel; he did not ask for dowry; he did not expect Tevyeh to stand the cost of the wedding; he did not ask Tevyeh to provide Zeitel's trousseau. Leizer Wolf would pay for everything, and he even hinted grossly that Tevyeh himself would lose nothing by the match. No wonder Goldie, the practical mother, could hardly believe her ears. A rich man like Leizer Wolf had the pick of the poor girls of Boiberik, and it was Zeitel's incredible good fortune, and Goldie's and Tevyeh's, and all the family's, that he should have chosen Zeitel.

"Father in heaven!" exclaimed Goldie when she heard the news. "I thank Thee for Thy grace and mercy. Tevyeh! Didn't I tell you you were a fool to worry? Sit down, my husband, and draw up a list of the things our Zeitel needs: a silk dress for the wedding, a summer dress, a winter dress, a mantle, underwear — wait, two mantles, one with fur — shoes, corsets, handkerchiefs, gloves — he can pay, our Leizer Wolf, he wants to pay." And the tears ran down Goldie's cheeks for her daughter's good fortune.

Assuredly if it had been in Goldie's hands, Zeitel would have married Leizer Wolf the widower, and would

176

have kept a grand house, and begotten many children, and seen them well fed, well clothed, and known as " sons of a father." What if she was in love with Mottie the tailor, and he with her? Was that any reason why her children should shiver in winter and go hungry the year round? So Goldie would have argued, had she known of the love of Zeitel and Mottie. So, in fact, Tevyeh did argue, knowing of it. He was a great hand at arguing one way and acting another; the more convincing his arguments, the more likely was he to ignore them; Jew-wise, he was content with the intellectual victory, leaving the material triumphs of the world to others.

So it was Tevyeh who came to the rescue of Zeitel and Mottie and found a way to unite them in wedlock over his wife's opposition without breaking up the peace of his house. It was a puerile stratagem he hit upon, one unworthy of a philosophic dairyman, but it worked perfectly, and it sheds much light on the kind of world his Goldie, and thousands upon thousands like her, lived in.

Late in the night, when Goldie and the children were fast asleep, Tevyeh set up a horrible screaming, like that of a man being done to death. Goldie started up with a cry of terror.

" Tevyeh! Tevyeh! God be with you! What is it? "

" Where is she? " gasped Tevyeh, rolling his eyes. " Where is she? "

" Who? "

" Frume Sarah, Leizer Wolf's wife."

" Tevyeh, God help you! Frume Sarah's been in the true world this many a year."

" I tell you she was here a moment ago, Goldie."

" Tevyeh! "

" She had me by the throat, do you hear? And she

177

screamed at me. ' What? Your daughter inherit my place, wear my clothes, sport my jewelry, carry my keys? And I remain sleeping peacefully in the Eternal House? Never! Three weeks your daughter will live with Leizer Wolf the butcher, a curse in his bones, three weeks, no more — and after that she'll sleep with me.' "

" Spit out three times, Tevyeh," cried Goldie. " Let that evil spirit sink into the waters and be swallowed by the earth, let it crawl on the roof-top and be lost in the forest, but may it never come near me and mine. As for Leizer Wolf the butcher, let him so much as dare to show himself here! "

" But it was only a dream, Goldie," protested Tevyeh. " And our sages say — "

" What do I care for you and your sages! Pfui on Leizer Wolf the butcher, and his wife who can't rest in her grave, and on Leizer Wolf's money and trousseau and promises. I won't have it! "

Thus it was that Tevyeh let himself lose an argument, though it went painfully against the grain; and thus it was that Zeitel married not Leizer Wolf, the rich butcher, but Mottie, the penniless tailor. She bore him many children, and they went about half naked though their father was a tailor, and undernourished, because he was a tailor. And Zeitel worked herself to the bone, and was happy.

What is our impression of Tevyeh so far? An indulgent and understanding father, something of a weakling, too. For he could not pretend to himself that he had acted in the best interests of his daughters. Who was to guarantee that either Zeitel or Hodel had character enough to justify their decisions? Love dies, revolutionary ardour cools, the bitter pressure of the world remains.

178

It is so easy to play the tolerant friend: " She has her own life to live; who am I to interfere? " Tevyeh was not happy in the recollection of what he had done for his two oldest daughters. And now the third took her place in the queue. " I tell you, Reb Sholom Aleichem, I thought I had known suffering and disappointment till then. But we have a loving and merciful Father in heaven, have we not? He said to me: ' Wait, Tevyeh, my son; I will do that with you which will make everything that has happened till now look like purest happiness.' "

This time the calamity had to do neither with poverty nor with revolution, which are trifles in the eyes of God, but with apostasy, which is the sin beyond forgiveness. On this point Tevyeh the tolerant suddenly reveals a hardness which an outsider would never have believed him capable of. We reach the core of obstinacy which has sustained his people for so many centuries. Disagreement on principle only amused Tevyeh; indeed, he liked it; it gave you something to talk about. But apostasy with a purpose, betrayal, hypocrisy, cowardice, and selfishness wrapped in fine words — no! When Pertchik railed against the accepted order, Tevyeh respected him; for Pertchik was honest. But when Eve, his third daughter, fell in love with Chvedka, the village clerk, and turned equalitarian, with " God created all men equal," and " Isn't it the stupidest thing in the world that human beings should be divided into Jews and Christians, masters and servants, rich and poor? " Tevyeh heard, not the authentic voice of protest, but the abject misuse of principle for a concealed motive. Very possibly Hodel's revolutionary passion had been two thirds love of Pertchik. But Hodel paid the price. She identified herself with the persecuted. Not so

Eve. Eve pleaded nobly for the levelling of the Jew-Christian barrier, but she contributed nothing toward it. She did not ask her Chvedka to defy *his* world, while she defied hers. Like Benjamin, the son of Israel the beadle, of Kasrielevky, she made common cause with the persecutor. What she wanted from her father was at least his tacit permission to help perpetuate the barrier which she was pretending to weaken. She did not run off with Chvedka, in defiance of Christian and Jewish obscurantists alike; she fled to the village priest, sought sanctuary in a convent, and had herself baptized.

From that day on Eve, the daughter of Tevyeh, was as dead to her father and her family as Benjamin was to his. " The Lord gave, the Lord has taken away." The words conjure up a simple picture of unwavering fanaticism; but that picture is false. The true picture is another one. It is Tevyeh standing up in his cart, in the forest by Boiberik, on a certain afternoon when his daughter came to seek reconciliation before she had repudiated her betrayal of her oppressed people.

" I was homeward bound from Boiberik, as usual," tells Tevyeh, " and my heart was heavy, my mind full of a thousand thoughts. Life, and death, and this world, and the world beyond the grave — what are they? And what is man, and why these struggles between men? And I'm doing my best not to think of her — of Eve, that is. But the harder I try, the less I succeed. I remember her as a baby, a weak little thing, an ailing chick, and how I used to carry her in my arms through the nights, her hot head on my shoulder. And I forget what she's done, and my heart longs for her, the way a tree must long for a branch that's been lopped off. And then, all of a sudden, the cart stops rolling, and I look up. Eve! My Eve, my daughter, unchanged, as if she's left us but an hour ago. And my instinct was to jump down, throw my arms round her, and take her to me. Then right behind this impulse came memory, and I said to myself: ' Tevyeh! Remember! ' So I stood up in the cart and pulled the horse to the right. But she, my daughter, sprang in the same direction. I pulled to the left, and she sprang left, too, and lifted her arms to me. I felt as if half my heart were being torn out. The sweat broke out on me, my legs trembled. What was I to do? ' Tevyeh! ' I said to myself. ' Remember! ' And just then my daughter grabbed the reins wildly, and cried: ' Father, Father, let me die if you won't speak to me.' ' Is that the way it is? ' I asked myself. ' Is it force you'd use? Oh no, my little one, you don't know Tevyeh.' And with that I brought the lash down on the horse. And the horse sprang forward, turning his head back, as if to look at her. ' Don't look back,' I said to him, and lashed him again. And I myself kept my face turned forward. Do you know how much of my life that moment cost me? Do you know what I suffered the rest of the way home, with her voice ringing in my ears: ' Father, Father, let me die if you won't speak to me.' ' Tevyeh,' I thought, ' are you sure you're not taking too much on yourself? Tevyeh, is this the way of a father? ' And it seemed to me, at that moment, that I had less right to live than a worm. And all sorts of ideas came into my head. What *is* all this business of Jew and Christian? Why did God have to create two kinds of people, and if He did create two kinds, why do we let it remain that way? And I was angry with myself because I couldn't find the answer, and because I hadn't read the books which give the answer. So, to drive these thoughts out of my mind, I began to sing the afternoon prayer:

'Blessed are those that dwell in Thy house, they shall praise Thee for ever.' I sang loudly, at the top of my voice, but another voice inside me sang louder: ' Eve! Eve! Eve! ' And still another voice, louder than mine: ' Father! Father! ' And when I came home that evening I said not a word about the meeting. And I don't speak about her to anyone, though I know only too well where she is, together with him. But my enemies will not live to hear me utter a word of complaint.

" Only sometimes I have a queer impulse — don't laugh if I tell you about it. In the middle of the week I put on my Sabbath coat, and drive over to the railroad station in Boiberik, and I go up to the window, and say to the man behind the window: ' Give me a ticket to Yehupetz ' — that's where they're living. ' Yehupetz? ' says the man behind the window. ' Never heard of the place.' ' That isn't my fault,' I answer him, and go out of the station, and drive home, and take off my Sabbath coat, and get down to work on my butter and cheese. . . . Didn't I say you'd laugh at me? "

CHAPTER XXI

The Humour of Kasrielevky

❀

JEWISH humour, or, rather, Yiddish humour, of which Sholom Aleichem is the supreme exponent, has fared as badly at the hands of its translators as the Jewish people itself at the hands of its apologists; and for the same reason. The apologists exert themselves to prove that the Jewish people is in reality indistinguishable from every other people, the so-called differences being the result of an optical illusion; the characteristics of Jews, they tell us, are such as will be found everywhere among non-Jews, and therefore are not Jewish characteristics at all. The translators of Jewish humour, whether they exert themselves or not, make it appear that Jewish humour is like every other type of humour, the proof being that it makes some people laugh; and the Jewish joke is one that happens to have originated or to be current among Jews. To make it Jewish, however, they put in a few words in italics, like *gefillte* fish and *Shema Yisroel,* and invert the order of subject and verb. The result is not a translation but a pogrom.

Undoubtedly humour cannot easily be transmitted from one language into another, for very often, where it is not a play upon words, it is a play upon the spirit of the language — that is to say, upon the spirit of a people. A prerequisite to transmission — or to such transmission as is possible — is, then, the re-creation of the background or sounding-board. That, however, is a laborious and mostly a humourless business. An honest translator understands that where the humour is hopelessly intramural, it must be left where it is, and it must perish when the walls crumble. But sometimes there are examples which can be given foreign currency without falsification, though rarely without some sort of introduction. It is true that talking around a joke will blunt its point, but perhaps enough of it will remain to justify the effort. Occasionally the reader should (to use a phrase of Sholom Aleichem's) laugh on credit; he may see the joke later; and perhaps he will never see it, in which case he is so much to the good.

There is a humour of situations and incidents and characters which is universal, and there is enough of that in Sholom Aleichem to establish him in any language without much difficulty. But peculiarly Jewish, and peculiarly of Sholom Aleichem, is a humour neither of situations nor of incidents nor of characters, but of the mental twist. Not what happens to people is funny, but what they themselves say about it. There is nothing funny about Tevyeh the dairyman as a character, and nothing funny ever happens to him. What Tevyeh does is to turn the tables on tragedy by a verbal ingenuity; life gets the better of him, but he gets the better of the argument. Then we laugh with him to encourage him — and ourselves.

This is, of course, the difference between the humorist and the satirist — the laughing " with " or " at." When Sholom Aleichem becomes the satirist, as in his descriptions of new Kasrielevky, he invites us to look down on others, and he is the less Sholom Aleichem. When he is the humorist, and identifies us with his characters, he is himself, and incomparable.

At its extreme the Jewish joke is purely cerebral, being part of the intellectualist tradition. We have already seen the place occupied by scholarship in the popular mind of the Jews. Here was a folk which for two thousand years had given to the scholar the place of honour reserved by other peoples for the warrior and ruler. Jewish mothers rocking their cradles in Kasrielevky sang to their babies of high careers in the sacred studies; and even the popular songs of grown-ups celebrated the delights of learning. Such songs are quite grotesque in English. As, for instance:

> See the peasant run into the inn,
> To snatch a drop of brandy;
> See the Jew run to the study house,
> To snatch a page of Talmud.

The outlandish effect is heightened by the rollicking melody. We shall understand the untranslatability of the song if we try to imagine a group of English bargees making the welkin ring with:

Come, landlord, bring us a page of Shakespeare. . . .

The Jews were no more a nation of scholars than they were a nation of priests; but among no other people was there such universal interest in scholarship, or such an interpenetration of the masses with the slang of scholarship. The logical technique of the Talmud, the phraseology of its ratiocination, belonged to the conversation of the market-place, and was parodied in popular jokes. One

185

of these tells of a Talmud student running about the city frienziedly and crying out in despair: " Help! Help! I have a wonderful answer. For God's sake someone tell me the question." Another is a take-off on " the method of induction " (odd stuff, this, for popular humour) : " What verse in the Bible tells us specifically that Jews are forbidden to go about with uncovered heads? " Answer: " Genesis xii, 1: ' And the Lord said unto Abraham, Get thee out of thy country.' Can you imagine Abraham going about with bared head, like a heathen? " This is the father of Zangwill's story: Said one Chassidic enthusiast to another: " Do you know that my Rabbi converses daily with God Himself? " " How do you know it? " " My Rabbi told me so." " And suppose he told you a lie? " " Idiot! Will a man who converses daily with God tell a lie? " And again in the field of pure logic is the conversation between two Jews. " Tell me, why does the prayer *Yekum Purkon* appear in two places in the Sabbath book? " " That's insurance — in case one of them gets lost." " Then why does the prayer *Mi sheberach* appear only in one place? " " Silly! That's exactly what proves my point. There *were* two *Mi sheberachs* and one of them got lost! "

These witticisms are admittedly a trifle thin in English; they are offered without apology by way of clarification, instances of the specifically mental in Jewish humour. They are also an introduction to the humour of verbal retrieval, the word triumphant over the situation. Let the world be unjust, we shall always have at least the *mot juste*. There is a Yiddish proverb: " When does a poor man rejoice? When he loses something and finds it again." The intimation is that this is the best he can hope for. Jewish humour is to a large extent the humour of

186

the *schlimihl*, who is a central figure in the folklore. This word is, again, only approximately translatable. To say that a *schlimihl* is a luckless person, one born under an evil star, or with a wooden spoon in his mouth, is to touch only the negative side. It is the *schlimihl's* avocation and profession to miss out on things, to muff opportunities, to be persistently, organically, preposterously, and ingeniously out of place. A hungry *schlimihl* dreams of a plate of hot soup, and hasn't a spoon.

The only dangers a *schlimihl* manages to escape from are those that do not exist. There is a story of a pestilence which was laying waste a town. The symptom of the disease was the turning red of the hands. A doctor, called into a house to examine a child, turned in sudden alarm on the father and said: " Look! You've called me in for your child and have forgotten yourself. Your hands are as red as blood." " That's nothing," answered the father, " I'm a dyer by trade." " Run to the synagogue, man, and give thanks to God! " exclaimed the doctor. " You've had a narrow escape."

A group of Jews were gathered round a synagogue stove, recounting miraculous adventures, and instances of divine intervention in extremity. Said one: " Last winter my wife, my children, and I were travelling by sleigh to a neighbouring village. Suddenly, as we were passing through the forest, we heard the howling of wolves. And such a howling! Hundreds of wolves, thousands! I lashed my horses and we sped toward the river, the howling wolves drawing nearer every moment. We reached the river, and the wolves were already in sight. The river was frozen over and we flew on to the ice. It was a question, you understand, of getting to the farther bank, where our cries would be heard in the village, and so it

187

was a race between us and the wolves. But right in the middle, when it looked as though we'd make it, the ice cracked wide open, the sled went down, with myself, my wife, my children — and in an instant the wolves were on top of us. *Now* what do you think God did for us? " " What? " asked the listeners, their eyes bulging. " Why," answered the narrator, complacently, " thanks be to Him who reigns in heaven, the whole story is a lie from beginning to end."

It is only a step from the non-existent danger from which the happy *schlimihl* escapes by the skin of his teeth, to the actual calamities with which he has an uncontrollable affinity. In the first case he laughs, thinking of the terrible things that can happen to him and don't. In the second case, when they do happen, he laughs because he can think of the right thing to say, the thing which, as it were, puts calamity in its place and shows it where it gets off. Sholom Aleichem's tenderest and most amusing passages conform to the second spirit, which is most specifically Jewish. We have read some of his reports on Tevyeh the dairyman. The technique occurs over and over again, not invented by Sholom Aleichem, but by the Jewish people, the *schlimihl* of peoples, and merely invoked by Sholom Aleichem.

Probably the outsider must find a touch of perversity in one who looks for laughter amid the flames of a burning city. Yet there is humour, without any abatement of compassion, in the story of the great fire of Kasrielevky, and in the picture of old Reb Yozifel on that day. He, while others were saving life and property, was concerned only with the sacred Scrolls and books in the synagogue. He dashed — figuratively speaking, for Reb Yozifel was close to eighty, and his dashing days were over

— into the blazing building, and brought out two of the Scrolls before the flames drove him out for good. He sat down on a bench at a little distance from the synagogue and addressed himself thus to the Almighty:

" Look you, Lord of the world. I have done what I could. I have saved two of the Scrolls. I wash my hands of all further responsibility. But don't for a moment imagine that I am leaving this spot. I shall stay here and see if you actually intend to burn the Torah which you gave us on Mount Sinai through your servant Moses." And there old Reb Yozifel stayed until Adam of the baths came and literally carried him away.

Galgenhumor, the laughter of the gallows, sounds in the letter which Yisrolik of Kishinev writes, after the famous pogrom, to his friend Jacob in America: " Dear Yankel: You ask me to write you at length, and I'd like to oblige, but there's really nothing to write about. The rich are still rich, and the poor are dying of hunger, as they always do. What's new about that? And as far as the pogroms are concerned, thank God we have nothing more to fear, as we've already had ours — two of them, in fact, and a third wouldn't be worth while. All I can tell you is that I'm alive, though the Angel of Death had me by the throat three times. I'm only sorry for my wife and children; they had to hide out three days and three nights in the garret of a friendly gentile: nothing to eat, nothing to drink, three days and three nights. All our family got through it safely, except for Lippi, who was killed with his two sons, Noah and Mordecai; first-class artisans, all three of them. Oh yes, and except Hersh. Perel was found dead in the cellar, together with the baby at her breast. But as Getzi used to say: ' It might have been worse; don't think of the better, because

189

there's no limit to that.' You ask about Heshel. He's been out of work now for over half a year. The fact is they won't let him work in prison. What's he in prison for? Eating pork on Yom Kippur, of course. They're arranging great things for him, I hear: the rope, or a firing squad. It's all a matter of luck. Some people have it, some don't, as Getzi used to say. Look at Yossel Henish, for example; he died before they even had a chance to put him in prison. Talking about luck — do you remember Leib, the son of Nehemiah the carpenter? We always said he'd come to nothing. Well, he's fooled everybody; he lives like a lord in the Peter-Paul Prison. But I really don't know what there is to write about. If you happen to see Abraham Moshe's son, tell him his father is a *schlimihl*. He died before we got the Constitution. Leizer's in prison for travelling outside the Pale without a passport. Serve him right! Who told him to be a teacher and look for pupils where he oughtn't to? Mendel did a clever thing, though; he up and died. Some say of hunger, others of consumption. Personally I think he died of both. I really don't know what else there is to write about, except the cholera, which is going great guns. . . ."

One of the best-beloved characters in Sholom Aleichem's world is the little boy Mottel, the son of Peissi, the cantor. There is a whole sub-world in Sholom Aleichem, that of the children, to which we shall make a special journey; Peissi's Mottel must be mentioned here because he is the author of a phrase now famous wherever Yiddish is spoken: " Hurray, I'm an orphan! " and because he is a perfect device for the presentation of the tragic under the aspect of the playful. Grown-ups are always queer to children; they are queer, in particular, because of their dependence on things, their inelastic submission to the law of " having " instead of the law of " being." Mottel is the perfect little *Kasriel,* for he knows by instinct that you only have to see the world in the proper way and all is well.

Peissi the cantor lies dying, and one by one his household possessions must be sold to buy food and medicine. Mother weeps and big brother Ellie is gloomy. But why? What fun it is, what an adventure, keeping the sales secret from Father, who stays in his bed in the alcove and does not know what is going on! Michel the pedlar comes in to buy Father's sets of the Talmud and Mishnah. What a sight he is, this Michel, as he plucks his beard and pulls faces, and argues with Mother and Ellie in an undertone! What is it that prevents Mother and Ellie from having as good a time as Mottel? Yossel the goldsmith is persuaded to buy what is left of the silverware. You could talk for years about Yossel the goldsmith, such a suspicious man, such a bargainer! As for the selling of the big sideboard with the glass window, that is perhaps the grandest adventure of all. For the sideboard has been part of the room ever since the world existed. It has never been moved from its place. And here, all of a sudden, four men, puffing and panting, detach it from its eternal abode, and the mystery of the wall is exposed. And nobody understands but Mottel. After the sideboard, the bed is sold, and Mottel must sleep on the floor, which he has always wanted to do. You can't compare sleeping on the floor with sleeping on a bed. A bed is a little thing; the floor is boundless; you can roll over and over, you can go anywhere you like, you are still " in bed." What do people want beds for anyway?

This child, too, is father to the man; Kasrielevky's hu-

191

mour is in Mottel's bones; Kasrielevky is a grown-up Mottel, not as adept as he in the creative transvaluation of values, but still native to the practice. " Let's look at the thing upside down, maybe that's the right way up." This will help to explain why Kasrielevkites who could grin wryly at a pogrom insisted on shedding tears at a wedding. Ostensibly Jews are forbidden to know perfect joy as long as the Jewish homeland is in ruins and the Glory in exile; the breaking of dishes at betrothals and weddings is a memorial of the Destruction. But the Kasrielevkites were not content with this formal acknowledgment. They had a custom which is one of the world's curiosities, the " keening " at the wedding. The *badchan,* or professional jester, without whom a marriage ceremony would have been as incomplete as without musicians, had to make the guests cry as well as laugh. The bride was seated in state, and the *badchan* walked to and fro wailing over her as if she were about to be buried. He mourned her lost childhood, and dwelt on the burdens and sorrows of the life on which she was entering. " Weep, little bride, weep, think of the years to come, the pain of motherhood, the separation from your beloved parents, the sadness of old age. . . ." And he kept it up until bride and bridegroom, relatives and guests, were dissolved in tears. This, too, was part of Kasrielevky's humour.

CHAPTER XXII

The Language of Kasrielevky

❀

USING the word "humour" in its old sense of "mood," we may say that the humour of Yiddish is peculiarly that of an exiled and landless people. Not just of any landless and exiled people, of course, but of a people with the religious and intellectual history of the Jews. The Jewish intellect has been called practical; so has its religion. They are both practical in that they are concerned with man on this earth, with human relations here below. But the oddity of the situation, as we have seen, was precisely that this practical people was compelled to carry on a make-believe of rural tradition while it was denied access to the soil.

Yiddish, the language of Sholom Aleichem's world, is a folk language; but unlike all other folk languages it has not a base in nature. It is poor, almost bankrupt, by comparison with other languages, in the vocabulary of field and forest and stream. Again unlike all other folk languages, it is heavily loaded with intellectual and literary allusions.

Yiddish has almost no flowers. That is not merely to say that Sholom Aleichem's Jews could not tell a cowslip from a harebell, for a typical Londoner or New Yorker is no better off. The very words for the common flowers, which are familiar to city dwellers everywhere, are lacking in Yiddish. The rose, the violet, the lily and the daisy are recognizable to Sholom Aleichem's Jews, both as objects and as words; a few other flowers are recognizable as words — tulip, jasmine, acacia, and poppy. But when it comes to harebell, clover, gardenia, dahlia, gladiolus, rhododendron, broom, clematis, fuchsia, cowslip, hyacinth, the word itself does not exist in Yiddish, except as a violent transliteration out of German or Russian.

Yiddish is a world almost devoid of trees — that is, if we exclude the fruit trees, apple, pear, cherry, peach, and the like. The oak, the willow, the pine, and the fir have definitely Yiddish names; that is, names to be encountered in conversation and in non-technical books. But the ash, the sycamore, the maple, the hickory, the larch, the alder might as well be *Fraxinus, Ficus sycomorus, Acer saccharum* and the rest of it, as far as Yiddish is concerned. And this is not to speak of subdivisions familiar at least to the ear of the city dweller, like silver maple, scarlet maple, sugar maple, etc. Shadings and synonyms in nature descriptions, like knoll, clump, grove, copse, coppice and thicket, prairie and moor, meadow and lawn, are absent. River and lake are translated by one word, and you must guess from the context whether it is standing or flowing water; stream, brook, rill, rivulet, runnel — Yiddish knows them not.

The animal world is almost depopulated in Yiddish. It knows the horse, the dog, the lion, the tiger, the rabbit, the squirrel, the mouse, the bear, the donkey, the elephant, and of course the kosher and therefore edible animals, which both chew the cud and have cloven hoofs. But it has no names for familiar creatures like the mole,

194

the badger, the otter, the ground-hog, the reindeer, the mink, the raccoon. There are two generic names for monkeys, but nothing corresponding to gorilla, chimpanzee, orang utan, baboon, as there is nothing corresponding to the ordinary subdivisions of dog, like mastiff, harrier, beagle, spaniel. All you can do is give the Russian or German word, and add: " a kind of dog."

The skies above Kasrielevky are practically empty of birds, to judge by the absence of names for them. A nightingale, a swallow, a dove, a peacock, a parrot, a crow, a sparrow, an eagle, a duck, a hen, and a turkey would have made a fairly complete aviary for Kasrielevky. Not that the Kasrielevkite would necessarily recognize a nightingale when he saw it, but he knew that a man with a sweet voice sang like a nightingale; neither would he recognize a swallow, but he knew that it did not make a summer (the proverb is current in Yiddish, too). He had never heard of the blackbird, the wren, the bluebird, the robin, the pheasant, the magpie, the chaffinch, the buzzard, the egret, the falcon: this, again, apart from the birds which are slightly unfamiliar by name even in English, like the nightjar, the chaffinch, the toucan, the bittern, and so on.

There is, likewise, an astounding dearth of fish, hardly compensated for by the ubiquity of the herring, which among the Kasrielevkites was less a fish than a national institution. The pike, the carp, and one or two other edible fish (that is, such as have both fins and scales, according to Biblical prescription) everyone knew, and there it ended; the perch, the trout, the turbot, the eel, the gudgeon, the tarpon, the minnow, and, ironically enough, the jewfish did not exist. Yiddish purists will, of course, find words for perch and trout in the dictionary. The point is that only the exceptional Yiddish scholar, never the ordinary, intelligent, Yiddish-speaking Kasrielevkite, would know about it.

There are no detailed and intimate nature descriptions in Sholom Aleichem, for there was no nature knowledge among his Jews; nor will sustained nature descriptions be found anywhere in Yiddish prose or poetry. There was a love of nature but no familiarity with the variety of her charms. The woods are fresh, the fields are green and odorous, the grass is soft, the birds sing, the insects hum, the flowers bloom, the clouds chase one another, the sun goes down in fire (or blood), and that is about all there is to it.

All these experiences and perceptions were lacking because their material was withheld from the Jews. There were large areas of what we generally call " folk " self-expression to which the Jews were for ever strangers. They lived in townlets and villages, but they had never danced or wrestled on the village green, they had never competed at quarterstaff or with bow and arrow. They had never tripped round a Maypole, or greeted the spring with any of the nature rites of the surrounding peoples. They did not worship, as others did, prehistoric local gods disguised as respectable saints. They did not march in great religious processions. Much of their religious ceremonial was domestic and private. They had never gone hunting and snaring and fishing for the fun of it, and hardly ever in the way of business. They had no continuous and active cult of arms and armies, of rulership, courts, royalty, nobility, and worldly pomp; no ranks, commands, generals, conquests; no racing, on foot or horseback, in sleigh or on skates; no tournaments, heralds, and knights-errant.

They were in the world, and in many ways not of it. Its fun and gamesomeness was not for them. In part their tradition forbade them to enjoy themselves unrestrictedly; for they were in exile, and they would outlive the exile, and merit the great repatriation, by cultivating the moral and intellectual faculties. But in part they were making a virtue of necessity; for they were the uninvited. Whatever access they had had to the land in the early Middle Ages was cut off from the time of the Crusades on. The best they could hope for was to have their usefulness, the incidental result of their high standard of education, recognized; so they set their wits against the brute force which surrounded them.

This blend of privation, makeshift, and ingenuity is mirrored in the Yiddish language, and its " humour " must be understood against the background of centuries of history. Alien to Sholom Aleichem's people and language is the riotous laughter of sheer physical well-being, of high animal spirits. Horseplay, slapstick comedy, and the practical joke they would have regarded as infantilism. They did not guffaw when a man slipped on the ice and came down with a crack; they winced. The boozy and boisterous jocundity of a Falstaff would have disgusted them. They were not squeamish about broad stories, but the *Decameron*, with its innumerable and monotonous variants on the strategy of deception, would have struck them as trivial. Their laughter was not earthy because, in the literal sense, their life was not earthy.

Yiddish is a language of refuge, intimacy, domesticity, and affection. It has a warm religious colouring, but it is free from cant. It is also a knowing language, full of hints, allusions, and interjections which take their meaning from tone and context. It is rich in " portmanteau

197

words." Because of its high emotional charge it passes easily into the maudlin; on the other hand, it does not lend itself to pomposity, and it has no professional and academic jargons — that is, if we except the jargon of sacred learning, which is of the stuff of the language. Its vulgarities are not repulsive, but comical. Pure, simple Yiddish has a tenderness which can only be reproduced in English by a careful use of Anglo-Saxon words; but there is no way of conveying the atmosphere of this language, with its uniquely private history.

I have already mentioned the break in spirit between Yiddish and the Middle High German which is its verbal base. The transformation wrought upon the original material is not reflected in the words themselves. As words they are easily recognizable; but their connotations and associations are so remote from those of their German analogues that they might just as well have been taken from the Latin or the Sanskrit. In any case, it is just as hard to translate Sholom Aleichem into German as into English or French.

The passing of Kasrielevky and of Sholom Aleichem has been attended by the passing of the Yiddish which was their language. For Yiddish has undergone many changes since those days. The experiences in which it was steeped, and upon which it depended for its effectiveness, were those of other generations. The Yiddish of Soviet Russia has another tone; so has that of the modern Yiddish writers generally. It is much easier to translate because it is much nearer to international journalese; it has moved away from the separatisms of a dying world. Which is all to the good, except so far as the quality of the Yiddish is concerned.

CHAPTER XXIII

Kasrielevky Billingsgate

❀

T HE YIDDISH curse, particularly as developed by the Kasrielevky market-woman, must be classified as a branch of Yiddish humour. It was a pastime and a form of self-expression rather than an implement — even theoretical — of war. A people physically disarmed takes refuge in dreams and words; where resentment cannot issue in action, it makes shift with the imagination, and in the course of time the purely imaginative element triumphs over the emotion; the curse became a dreamy exercise practised for its own sake. The Yiddish curse was the domain of women. They had not the man's learning to serve them as escape; they had not so many prayers and other religious duties. In a sense, then, the curse was a substitute: there is a close etymological relationship between " prayer " and " imprecation."

The nearest approach to the Yiddish curse for ingenuity, variety, volume, complication, and completeness is to be found in the mediæval Church anathema. But there is this difference; the Church curse makes your blood run cold, the Yiddish curse is downright funny. And it is funny because unlike the Church curse it does not believe, or pretend to believe, in its own potency. The greater its exuberance, the more striking its bathos. It is the *reductio ad absurdum* of the curse.

The simplest curses in Yiddish are mere expletives, equivalents of the English " To hell with you! " " Blast you! " or " Curse you! " In Yiddish it is " Into the earth with you! " " A cholera on you! " " May you be slaughtered! " or " A black year on you! " But these expressions can be contracted and expanded. They can become " Into the earth! " or " A cholera! " or " Slaughtered! " or " A black year! " — launched without any particular direction, a mere mention of evil to darken the air with a hint. This is the lowest currency. A little warmth transforms them into: " Nine ells deep into the earth with you! " " A black, desolate year on you, on your hands and legs, your body and life! " " May an unusual death snatch you away! " " A cholera in your bones! " — which for some reason, probably unscientific, is considered more uncomfortable than the ordinary variety of cholera. The phrase " unusual death " is of Hebrew origin, and the Kasrielevky pronunciation is " *meeseh meshineh.*" It has been suggested that the word " sheeny," for Jew, comes from the second half of the phrase, but this does not explain why only the English should have taken it up. Actually the market-women could not have said what " *meeseh meshineh* " meant, literally. A variant of this curse is: " May you take a *meeseh meshineh*" — the word " take " being used here in the same way as we use it in English for " taking " medicine. There is a story attached to " taking a *meeseh meshineh.*" A Jew sitting opposite a Prussian officer in a train was forced to listen to a long recital of the military triumphs of Germany. The officer would exclaim, whenever they were passing a fortress or a fortified city: " You see this? We, the Prussians, have taken it! " Between cities and fortresses he would recall, in a kind of chant, all the foreign places where the arms of Germany had been victorious. " We have taken Przemysl! We have taken Kamenetz-Podolsk! We have taken Radomysl! " At last the Jew asked, timidly: " Pardon me, sir, have you also taken Ameesehmeshineh? " " No," answered the officer, haughtily, " but we intend to take that too."

From the extended or decorative curse we move on to the abstract curse, which becomes the more imaginative as it diminishes in specificity. " A wild dream on you! " It is difficult to fasten this down. Does it mean: " May you have a wild nightmare "? Or does it mean: " May a wild dream become a waking reality for you "? It probably means neither, for the phrase, like so many others of its kind, has become stereotyped; it is a sort of hieroglyphic of horrendous connotation but without an intelligible message. More involved, and more metaphysical, is this: " May all the evil dreams I have ever had, may the dreams I had yesterday, and the day before, and last year, unload their interpretation on your head! " Connected with this curse is the belief that the effect of a dream varies with the interpretation put upon it. Hence a woman of Kasrielevky would tell her dream to a friend in order to have it favourably " pointed." If we attend to the literal content of " May all the evil dreams," and so on, we shall find it hard to understand what emotional satisfaction could be derived from such an unsubstantial malediction. Or from: " May his name and his memory be wiped out " — a phrase which, like " *meeseh meshineh*," has been naturalized from the Hebrew into the Yiddish. " *Yimach shemoy* " — " May his name be wiped out! " Probably " from the book of life " was implied originally. Now the phrase has been cut loose and has become more of an insult than an imprecation. A man may be referred to as a *" yimach shemoy "* or, with the addition of a Russian suffix, a *" yimach shemoynik "* — one who deserves, presumably, to have his name wiped out. The range of insult in this phrase is wide, varying with the context and the warmth of the tone: it covers anything from " rascal " to " villain." In this sense it is occasionally equivalent to *" mamzer,"* the Hebrew-Yiddish word for bastard. But *" mamzer "* is a portmanteau word. Often it is used affectionately, as a term of admiration: a *" mamzer "* means an especially clever person; it also means a pest of a person; and it can also mean something worse. It is as hard to convey these shadings as it is to explain why a man is usually flattered when he is called " a sly dog " but insulted if he is called by its synonym, " a cunning hound."

Quite unreal is the organized, constructive, or architectural curse, of which the classic instance follows: " May you have a hundred estates, and on every estate a hundred mansions, and in every mansion a hundred rooms, and in every room a hundred beds: and may a malarial fever toss you from bed to bed." This compound of magnificence and misery leaves us contemplative rather than horrified; it suggests achievement, not discomfort. There are frequent instances of the kind of overemphasis which results in self-contradiction. Our old friend Tevyeh the dairyman curses, with good enough cause, Ephraim, the marriage broker: " May a pestilence come upon him." This should not be taken to mean: " May there be a pestilence and may Ephraim, the marriage broker, be carried off by it." For in addition to waste of pestilence intended for Ephraim, innocent people would be involved. The form of the curse indicates that Tevyeh wants a pestilence to be concentrated exclusively, and without overflow, on Ephraim, the marriage broker; may Ephraim, the marriage broker, become in his single person the closed operative area of a pestilence. Tevyeh likewise says, meditatively: " May a barracks collapse on Ephraim." He was referring, of course, to a Russian barracks, or armoury, a building of exceptional size and weight. As far as the lethal effect was concerned, an ordinary house, or at most an apartment building, would have served the purpose; but Tevyeh insisted on the demonstrative superfluity of a building large enough to bury a regiment concentrating its collapse on little Ephraim, the marriage broker. Tevyeh's apparent vindictiveness was proportionate to the distress which Ephraim had brought upon him and on his youngest daughter by the promotion of an unfortunate match: the only rich man to take a daughter of Tevyeh's turned out to be a *yimach-shemoynik,* who soon lost all his money. But that Tevyeh's vindictiveness is only apparent we learn from his next words: " Come to think of it, what have I against Ephraim, the marriage broker? A poor devil like myself, struggling to make a living." And when he meets Ephraim on the streets of Boiberik he offers him a pinch of snuff.

Certain of the standard curses are perfectly horrifying in their vividness and ingenuity, if they are seen in their lost freshness. " May you crawl up perpendicular walls! " calls up a dreadful picture of mental and physical torment, a man clawing at space in the extremity of his agony. But it comes lightly off the tongue in Yiddish. " May he have a searing pain in his seventh liver," while anatomically unsound (the furthest one can go, to be literal,

would be the abomasum, or fourth stomach of a rumi-
nant), conveys the idea of an intolerable penetration of
visceral pain: the seventh liver being the essence, or inmost privacy, of the liver. Yet these brutal phrases are
uttered with a certain vulgar good humour, and there is
no relation at all between the content of the curse and
the emotion accompanying its delivery. For that matter,
the simpler or less cultivated Kasrielevkite woman maintained no proportion at all between the degree of a disaster and the resulting lamentation. You might pass her
door and hear her wail, suddenly: " A blackness has come
upon me! My only child is dead! " Or " A blackness has
come upon me! The soup has run over! "

While there was an accepted body of standardized
curses for ordinary use and commonplace persons, the
more gifted beldame was an improviser. Tzipeh Beileh,
the wife of Shimon Eli the tailor, was among the female
troubadours of Yiddish imprecation. When she let herself go she was lyrically murderous; she became in her
one person a chamber of horrors, an arsenal of diversi-
fied destruction. " May the grave throw up your father
and swallow you! Let nothing be left of you but a stone
and bone! A bullet from a gun into you! Be hanged and
drowned, fried and roasted, chopped and minced! Thief!
Murderer! Robber! Apostate! A desolate, black dream
on you, on your head, on your limbs — dear God, loving
Father in heaven! " The closing discharge sounds like a
sudden and uncalled-for piece of blasphemy. But there is
a break in the sentence, a sudden shift in the mood of
utterance: the first half is aimed at the person being
cursed; the last five words drag in the Almighty in an unexpected vocative of supplication. God is merely remembered as a witness and ever present help. This kind of

break — " You robber! I hope you never rise from your bed — dear God! " — is open to grave misunderstanding.

Besides the architectural or cumulative curse, there are the rhyming curse and the apposite or apropos curse. " (May there come upon you) a weeping and a creeping, a bawling and a crawling, a plague and an ague, a drying and a frying and a dying " is one example of the rhyming curse. There is a traditional chant for this sort of expression, so that you could tell what was being said in your neighbour's house by the inflection, even if you did not hear the words. The apposite or apropos curse is a sort of " catch," or linked phrase: it is hooked on to the last word uttered by the object of the curse. Thus, if he wanted to eat, and said so, the response would be: " Eat? May worms eat you, dear God! " Or: " Drink? May leeches drink your blood! " " Sew a button on for you? I'll sew cerements for you!" If the person addressed does not supply the lead, the curser does it for herself. " There runs Chaim Shemeral! May the life run out of him! " A servant girl complains: " She wanted me to pluck the chicken this afternoon — God pluck her eyes out! " " Are you still sitting? May you sit on open sores! Are you silent? May you be silent forever! Are you yelling? May you yell for your teeth! Are you playing? May the Angel of Death play with you! Are you going? May you go on crutches! " " Eight hundred roubles he stole from me! " a woman tells, weeping. " May eight hundred boils break out on his tongue! " Then, fearing that the tongue would be overloaded, or the boils too small, she adds, thoughtfully: " And on his face and body."

Sometimes the curse is merely picturesque, not apropos or with rhyme. " May he swell like a mountain! May he wither like a worm! May the soul be wrung out of him! "

A queer, friendly use of the curse is its direction toward the enemies of the person you are addressing — but this is not peculiar to Yiddish. " Sarah Beileh, bless you, may your enemies shrivel before such a thing happens." Friendlier still is the negated or inverted curse: " May the black year not come on you! May you not be swallowed up by the earth! " This is often used by mothers toward their children. It must not be confused with the blessing, for it is a reminder that the child has merited punishment, which is being averted. It is an affectionate reproach and warning. Sometimes the basic material of the curse is given such tortured and attenuated form that the original intention can be recaptured only by long explanation. Thus, a loving mother will deliver an inverted curse at her child: " May I suffer whatever evil is intended for you! " But since she does not want any evil to befall her, she puts it this way: " May I not suffer whatever is intended for you! " That does not mean that she withdraws her protection from the child. She still interposes herself, and offers to serve as lightning-conductor, but in the same breath she abjures the evil. It means, then: " May the evil intended for you be directed toward me, but may it fail to reach me! " An instance of this elliptical talk, outside the field of the curse, is the emphatic promise to do something, which is made with the phrase: " Without vowing it! " The vow is frowned upon (it will be remembered that the *Kol Nidre* of the Yom Kippur service is a recantation of religious vows) ; in effect, then, one says: " I promise to do this, without a vow, only because the vow is forbidden."

In Kasrielevky, as anywhere else in the world, the use

of curses was largely confined to the poor and the ignorant; but the folk quality of the Yiddish curse, its cultural rather than its personal character, gives it a peculiar place in the language. There is no substitute for it in English, French, or German; and that is something of a pity, for when people can make such use of curses, they are less liable to put them into effect.

CHAPTER XXIV

The Superstitions of Kasrielevky

❀

AKEN as a group, the Jews of Sholom Aleichem's world were probably less given to superstitious beliefs and practices than their gentile neighbours. This does not mean, necessarily, that there were fewer superstitions current among the Jews, but rather that a smaller proportion of the population accepted them. There was a strain of practicality, scepticism, and rationalism even in the common folk; and on the whole the tradition had been weighted against the magical and the supernatural. The Judaism of our time is the Judaism of the Pharisaic scholars of the Second Jewish Commonwealth. They, in their struggle with the official priesthood of the Temple, had weakened the belief in the human intermediary between man and God. The rabbi, following the Pharisaic tradition, was not a medicine-man, but a teacher of religion, law, ethics, and history. Until the degeneration of Chassidism into Tzaddikism (which is described below) the superstition of sacerdotalism was absent from Jewish life. Sholom Aleichem's old Kasrielevky is thoroughly mediæval; religion and the synagogue play a far larger role in it than even the priesthood and the Church in mediæval Europe. But you do not meet with anything like the equivalent of the Christian priestly power, based on the intercessionary function of the clergy; that is, not until you touch on the Chassidic episode in Jewish life, concerning which I shall have to say a good deal.

The ordinary superstitions of Kasrielevky are of no particular interest except to the specialist. They differ somewhat from the superstitions of the Russian peasants in their comparative emphasis on the personal; that is to say, gentile superstition had more to do with things, with cows and horses, with wheat and corn, with weather, with the chase, with the hills and rivers and lakes. Jewish superstitions inclined more to matters of the spirit.

The transmigration of souls was accepted by many; not as a definite article of faith, but vaguely, without very close scrutiny. The word " gilgul " (connected with galgal, a wheel) means both transmigration of souls and a transmigrated soul. It was current among the plain folk (among Christians metempsychosis is an esoteric faith) . A " gilgul " must be distinguished from a " dibbuk " — a demon, or evil spirit, who has taken possession of a person, and who, unlike a " gilgul," does not belong where he is, having no claim to occupancy, and can or should be driven out.

There was a belief in the letz, a mischievous poltergeist, and in nisht gute, malevolent demons at large. The evil eye was almost as widely feared among Kasrielevkites as among southern Italians. Expectant mothers surrounded themselves with precautions against it, and the bed of the new mother was decorated with amulets and prayer-sheets against demons and the evil eye. But a much larger proportion of the people than among the gentiles ridiculed these terrors and the measures taken

against them; and occasionally there were quarrels between husbands and wives on the score of scepticism, usually, of course, on the male side.

The sickness of a child would inspire a mother to send
a handkerchief to the Chassidic rabbi (the non-Chassidic
rabbi would have no truck with this sort of thing) and
have him say a certain prayer over it, the handkerchief
thereby acquiring curative or defensive properties. A
child recovering from a dangerous sickness was often
given a new name, to make it difficult for the Angel of
Death to find him again. Of recourse to the intercession
of the dead and " measuring of graves " — to be distinguished, of course, from memorial and sentimental visits
to the cemetery — I have already spoken.

Far more interesting than these, and hundreds of other
individual superstitions, is the general body of belief
which grew up with the spiritual decline of the Chassidic
movement; for we have here a social and intellectual
phenomenon which deserves a special place in the general history of religion.

About two hundred years ago there appeared among
the Jews of Podolia and Volhynia — not far from the
heart of Sholom Aleichem's country — a religious genius
by the name of Israel, better known by the title he acquired among his followers, the Besht — from the first
letters of the three Hebrew words *Baal Shem Tov*, Master of the Good Name. He taught the immanence of
God, the continuous interaction between heaven and
earth, the joy and cheerfulness of life, the precedence of
feeling over intelligence and of simple goodness over
learning. None of this was new, and warrant will be
found for almost every doctrine of the Baal Shem in ancient Hebrew literature, going back as far as the Bible.

His genius lay in his manner of teaching and in his ability to raise up followers worthy of himself. Chassidism has been described as a popular reaction against the dry, scholastic rabbinism which dominated Russian-Polish Jewry in the early eighteenth century. It was that, among other things. But the usual implication, that such a movement was bound to occur simply because it was needed, ignores the element of chance. It chanced that the Baal Shem and a group of gifted spiritual leaders emerged at about that time. Without them there would have been no Chassidic movement.

This is not the place for a history of Chassidism; but it is quite impossible to describe the world of Sholom Aleichem without devoting considerable space to the spirit introduced into Jewish life by the Chassidic movement. For this was not simply the introduction of certain doctrinal innovations; it was a change in the tone of life of hundreds of thousands of Jews; it was the creation of a variety of social forms, of a special literature, and of a new tradition.

We must try to recapture the first freshness of Chassidism in order to acquire an insight into its effects. The Baal Shem and his disciples were essentially men of the people. They were concerned with the poor, the ignorant, the despised, whom they conceived to be children of God as dear to their Creator as the learned and distinguished. They inspired the lowly with a sense of their closeness to the Almighty; they created an intimacy, a familiarity, between man and God, which restored to the downtrodden masses a feeling of personal worth. And the Baal Shem and his disciples were adepts in the transmission of their views by means of parables. From the beginning the stories of the Chassidim, circulated first by word of mouth and later in little, ill-printed pamphlets which pack-carriers distributed in the villages together with needles, combs, socks, mirrors, prayer-shawls and phylacteries, delighted thousands of readers and listeners.

The defence of the downtrodden, even against God Himself, was a favourite theme of the Chassidic leaders. Of Reb Levi Isaac, of Berditchev, called the Compassionate One, it was told that on a certain Day of Atonement, hearing the Jews confess their sins to the Almighty, he became tired of this one-sided demonstration of humility; he suddenly closed the doors of the Ark, turned to the congregation, and cried: " That's enough now. It's God's turn to confess *His* sins! " Reb Levi Isaac had certainly not read Omar Khayyám:

> *For all the sins wherewith the face of man*
> *Is blackened, man's forgiveness give — and take.*

There once came to Berditchev a wandering preacher who asked Reb Levi Isaac for permission to address the congregation, so that he could make a collection for himself afterwards. At first Reb Levi Isaac, " the Compassionate One," refused, because he knew the habits of the *magidim,* or preachers, and how they loved to rant about the sins of the Jews. But this one pleaded hard, and said: " I promise not to upbraid the Jews. Only let me preach, because I am collecting a dowry for my daughter." So the Compassionate One let him mount the pulpit, and the preacher started off softly enough, but after a few minutes his nature got the better of him and before he knew it he was calling down fire and brimstone on the Jewish people for its hard-heartedness and uncharitableness. Thereupon the Compassionate One rushed forward, smote the pulpit with his fist, and cried: " Don't believe him, God! He's only trying to collect money for his daughter's dowry! "

Reb Levi Isaac of Berditchev, " He of Berditchev " — so one called the various great rabbis, " He of Tolne," " He of Liade," " He of Sadagora," the implication being that the town in question had acquired significance only by virtue of this man — Reb Levi Isaac of Berditchev had a charming saying: " Nowadays Jews tell lies in the street and the truth in the synagogue! Alas for the good old days when they used to tell the truth in the street and lies in the synagogue! " The Compassionate One was referring to the confessions: Jews came to the synagogue, beat their bosoms, and cried: " O God, we have lied, we have sinned, we have robbed." And alas, they were telling the truth! How much better it would be if all this were a lie because they had been honest outside the synagogue. But generally the Compassionate One was more concerned with the defence of the Jews against accusations of sin. Another story is told of Reb Levi Isaac in this connection: he rose early one morning to say his prayers and, looking out of the window, saw a drayman so eager to be through with his devotions and go about his business, that even while he had the phylacteries on his head and the prayer-shawl on his shoulders, even while he was saying the *Shachris,* he was smearing his wagon-wheels with grease. Reb Levi Isaac, afraid that some evil angel would carry the report of this desecration to heaven, lifted up his arms ecstatically and cried: " Look down, O God, and see what a wonderful people thou hast! Even when they are occupied with their daily tasks, Thy Jews address Thee in prayer! " By putting this false but generous interpretation on the impiety, Reb

Levi Isaac hoped to intercept the more honest one before it was delivered in heaven.

The excessive merit attached to scholarship and the Holy Books found its corrective in the sermons and stories of the Chassidic rabbis.

It was told of him of Gridung, Reb Yudele, that one day a young wife came to him, weeping bitterly. Her husband, she said, an ignorant and sinful man, lay dying, and wanted the rabbi to come to him. Reb Yudele gathered some of the men of the city and went to the woman's house; but when he opened the door of the room where the dying man lay, he sprang back, turned whiter than the wall, and shut the door in terror. He let a few minutes pass, opened the door a second time, entered, and sat down on the bed.

The dying man, seeing the rabbi, began to weep.

" Rabbi, I am about to pass into the next world, and I have neither learning of any kind, nor a single good deed, to plead for me there."

The rabbi asked him to think well; but still the man could recall nothing in his own favour.

" I am a very ignorant man," he said. " I despised learning. My trade was that of a skinner. I went from slaughter-house to slaughter-house, I bought the skins of the slaughtered animals, I cut them from the flesh and sold them."

" Bethink yourself carefully," the rabbi urged. " Is there not a single good deed in your life to plead for you before the Throne? "

" No," the man answered, still weeping. " Not one."

" I conjure you," cried the rabbi, " to remember a good deed out of your life. Let it seem trivial in your eyes; recall and recount it."

Then the man, unsure of himself, and afraid of being rebuked, said: "There was something, once, scarcely worth mentioning. One morning, while I was on my way to the slaughter-house, I saw a wagonload of men and women coming toward me down the hill. The driver was drunk and could not control the horses. On either side of the road was a deep and rocky valley. Now, as the road descended, it became steeper; and what with the weight of the wagon and the drunkenness of the driver, the horses began to run faster and faster, till it seemed they would all be dashed over one of the edges. When I saw this, and heard the screaming of the men and women in the wagon, I, who was going uphill, ran out into the middle of the road and threw myself against the horses, and slowed them down for a minute or two, so that the men and women could scramble out. Then, having no more strength, I let go, and the wagon and horses were dashed into the rocky valley. That is the only kindness I can remember ever having done a human being in my life."

Then the rabbi said to the dying man: "Hear me! I charge you, by the Ineffable Name, that when you are dead you come back to me from the next world and report to me how they dealt with you." Then Rabbi Yudele withdrew from the room, and his companions with him.

In the street his companions asked the rabbi timidly why, when he had first opened the door of the dying man's room, he had started back and turned pale. Whereupon Reb Yudele answered:

"According to what the woman told me, I thought I was paying a visit to the deathbed of an ignorant and sinful man. But when I opened the door I saw at the man's head a divine candelabrum with seven candles, such as is suspended by the heavenly powers only over the deathbed of a dying saint. Therefore I was filled with terror. And for that reason, too, I asked the dying man so insistently a second and a third time to recall his good deeds, for I knew I was in the presence of one of the concealed saints, one of the Thirty-six, in whose merit the world is sustained."

Now, shortly after this, it is told, the dead man obeyed the command of Rabbi Yudele and visited him in a dream, to tell him how he had fared on his arrival in the other world.

He said: " When I came before the judgment throne, the recorders had assembled my bad deeds and my defects, which were many — the greatest of them being my failure to learn the Holy Books — and my good deeds, which were very few. The good and bad deeds being placed in the respective scales of heaven, the bad deeds of course weighed down the good. Then suddenly there arrived, I do not know from where, a wagonload of men and women, and the order was given that this too should be placed in the scale of the good deeds. And what with the men and women, and the horses and the harness and the mud on the wheels, the scale of the good weighed down the scale of the bad. Then the verdict was issued that I was to be admitted at once into paradise — whither I shall now, with your permission, return."

Again, in illustration of God's love of simple though uninstructed goodness, the Chassidim told a story which they attached to the time of the *Ari*, the great mediæval Kabbalist of Palestine. There was a drought in the Holy Land, and the congregation offered up prayer for rain, but without avail. One scholar after another, one saint after another, led the congregation in prayer, but the skies remained hot and cloudless. Then there came up to the pulpit a simple shopkeeper and prayed with words of his own, not with words from the books of the learned; and at once the skies darkened, and rain fell abundantly. Awed and astounded, the Jews asked of this man what pious acts he had performed, what virtues perfected, that he should so command the ear of Him who lives for ever. The man had no answer. Only in the course of random conversation he told them that in his ignorance of the right forms of prayer, he had fashioned for himself his own link with God. He had persuaded himself that the four parts of his shopkeeper's balance — namely, the upright, the crossbeam, and the two scales — were the four letters of the Ineffable Name, and that therefore to deal dishonestly, and to give false weight, was desecration of the name of God. The Ari, who was listening to the conversation, at once declared that if a man had made God so intimate a part of his daily life, he had achieved sainthood; hence the power of his prayer.

And still another story the Chassidim told (there are literally thousands of Chassidic stories) to illustrate the power of simple goodness, even when linked with illiteracy. A drayman was driving his wagon through the forest one Friday afternoon in the rainy season. His progress was so slow that he feared that the Sabbath would begin before he could reach the village. And while he was urging his horses on, an axle broke, and the wheel sank into a deep hole in the ground. " God, help me! " the man cried; and suddenly a number of peasants appeared as it were from nowhere, lifted the wagon out of the mud, mended the wheel, and sent the drayman rejoicing on his way. The man's heart was full, but he had never learned how to formulate a prayer; so, in sheer dumb gratitude, he lifted up his whip and cracked it to the glory of God, but with such force that a spark flew out of it and ascended toward heaven. Now, at that moment, the story goes on to tell, God was weighing in His mind the merit of the world, and it seemed to Him that mankind had become so cold and heartless that the race was not worth preserving; better, He was thinking, to destroy the world and begin all over again. And when He had almost reached the decision, the spark came up from the drayman's whip and so delighted Him that he was suddenly convinced of the merit of humanity.

These Chassidic stories are an index of the attitude of the early teachers toward the simple people. But there was something more. The first Chassidic masters were not only men of genius in the religious field; they were saints of the type of St. Francis. They were tender, thoughtful, and imaginative. They lived in poverty, and were always cheerful. Of the founder of Chassidism it was told that he could not sleep if there was money in the house. It is hardly to be wondered that the masses of Jewry in the vicinity of the masters were won over to them.

There was, as I have recalled earlier, a bitter struggle between the old, entrenched rabbinate and this new force which challenged it for the leadership. The feud between Kasrielevky and Kozodoievka, as Sholom Aleichem records it, must have had some connection with the fight for control between the Chassidim and the Misnagdim (a *Misnaged* means literally an opponent, or protestant) . But we must not confuse the Chassidism of Sholom Aleichem's day, in the second half of the nine-teenth century, with the Chassidism of a century earlier. The old purity and freshness of the movement was gone. The childlike simplicity and the appealing genius of its leaders had been replaced by a great organization or series of organizations. The descendants of the original " saints " had set up a hereditary priesthood — the famous dynasties of wonder-working rabbis. The cult of the *Tzaddik* had replaced the simple relationship between man and God. The very reverse of the Besht's teaching was now the watchword of Chassidism. The *Rebbi*, the " good Jew," occupied a position in Jewish life which has not had its parallel among the Jews before or since. The Rebbi was perfection itself; he was the key to the next world; he was the only approach to the heavenly powers; he not only had God's ear, but in certain instances it was claimed that he could *compel* God to do his will. To contribute to the comfort and greatness of the Rebbi was the first and highest virtue.

The Chassidic rabbis set up great courts; entire towns, with thousands of inhabitants, sprang up about them; Chassidic followers left wife and children for months at a time, and in some cases permanently, in order to be near the beloved rabbi, to listen to the words that fell from his lips, to sit at table with him and snatch the food his hands had touched. The sick flocked to him for comfort, the barren for children, the perplexed for advice. A rabbinic court was a mixture of a miracle centre, a political headquarters, a ducal palace, and a fair.

Of course this did not apply to all the Chassidic leaders. Many remained poor, some remained simple lovers of humanity. But Chassidism by the end of the nineteenth century had unquestionably lost its spiritual driving force; and in many instances it was a destructive feature in Jewish life.

There were furious rivalries between various dynas-

219

ties, each competing for the others' following. Chassidic zealots were jealous of the reputations of their rabbis. Fantastic stories were told of the intercessory influence of the rabbis and of their miraculous powers. And it may be said that the superstitions attaching to the Chassidic leaders outweighed in Sholom Aleichem's world the total volume of superstition attaching to every other aspect of Jewish life.

Sholom Aleichem's father, Nohum Vevik Rabinovitch, was himself a follower of the famous Rebbi of Tolne. And yet Nohum Vevik was, by the standards of that time, an enlightened man. We may recall that he ridiculed his relative Lifschitz for believing in a poltergeist. He was a man of considerable reading, a chess-player, and a convert to modern education.

The great Chassidic rabbis of Europe, their courts and organizations, their following and their political power, are no more. They existed, down to the beginning of the Second World War, in Poland and in certain parts of Austria and Rumania. Their hold on Sholom Aleichem's world, in Russia, was destroyed by the Bolshevik revolution. Today, with the crushing of Jewish life in Poland, the last of their European citadels have crumbled; and even if some sort of Jewish life is restored in a liberated Europe, it is altogether improbable that the Chassidic courts will be part of it.

But it is one of the curiosities of Jewish history that the last remnants of the Chassidic organism should survive in — of all places — the United States. In the Jewish sections of New York and Chicago, and perhaps of one or two other towns, the vestigial forms of the Chassidic courts still maintain an obscure and disintegrating existence. Mighty names of dynasties which once made millions of Jews tremble now attach to queer little groups of fanatics, or sentimentalists, in delapidated apartment houses in the slums. In the mass migration to America, the transference of half of Sholom Aleichem's world across three thousand miles of ocean, there were involved fragments of *Weltanschauungen*. There came to America the worker, the labour-leader, the pietist, the Zionist, and the Chassid.

You may, with a little effort, find your way, even now, into esoteric coteries of Chassidic enthusiasts which are reminiscent of stage productions of *The Dybbuk* or of *Yosche Kalb*. Less than a year ago there came to me, here in New York, an elderly Jew who was in need — for reasons he would not disclose — of a Chassidic rabbi, a saint; and he had been told that I could direct him to one.

I conducted this Jew — let us call him Reb Leibel — to a certain small synagogue on the East Side of New York, and there, on that particular afternoon, we found the beadle, one Reb Yossel of Tulcea, and three other men. I introduced Reb Leibel to Reb Yossel, and said that Reb Leibel was looking for a " good Jew " — a Chassidic Rebbi.

" But the highest," said Reb Leibel. " The very best in America! "

" The highest! " exclaimed one of the men, under his breath. " A trifle like that! The highest saint is, of course, unknown, for he remains hidden."

Reb Yossel of Tulcea, annoyed by the interjection, tugged at his beard and said: " Maybe he is hidden, and maybe I know the name of the street and the number of the house." Then addressing himself to Reb Leibel: " If you were discussing saints at large, there is quite a handful here on the East Side. But if it's the real thing, the master of them all, the one in his generation, there's only Reb Isrulikl Kortzer, may his days be many and prosperous."

" Ha! " another of the men interrupted. " Naturally! Reb Isrulikl Kortzer! "

Reb Yossel Tulcea turned on this second man with sudden fury.

" And what is the matter with Reb Isrulikl Kortzer? He doesn't please you? "

" Not please me? " answered the other, unintimidated. " And why shouldn't he please me? A fine Jew, Reb Isrulikl Kortzer. But how can he be mentioned in the same breath with — "

" With Reb Chaim Tolner, naturally," snorted Reb Yossel.

" Exactly," said the other, blandly.

The man who had muttered: " The highest," made a face as if a peeled lemon had been thrust into his mouth.

" Have you both been robbed of your wits? " he asked. " You, Reb Yossel, and you, Reb Mendel? *Neither* Reb Isrulikl *nor* Reb Chaiml. I repeat that the highest saint is of necessity unknown to us and to all his generation, while all heaven is thunderous with his name and the angels tremble when he thrusts past them and approaches the Throne as a son approaches his father. But if you are talking of the revealed saints, then it is laughable to compare any man of flesh and blood with Reb Itzikl Sloiker."

" Aha! " crowed Reb Yossel, and turned to the third man. " And now let us hear from you, my good, dear Reb Moishe. Whom would *you* thus elevate to the first place among the saints of our day? No doubt it is your village which has enriched the world with the light of our generation."

The third man was the least aggressive although, as I remember, he was the tallest. He pointed to the second: " I, for my part, take my stand with Reb Gershon. I think the world and its fullness of Reb Itzikl Sloiker. Do you know what is said of him? It is said — "

" It is said of him! " cried Reb Mendel, in an ecstasy of irritation. " It is said! It is said! " And his eyes bulged with anger. " Do you know, I ask you, the connections and the glory of Reb Chaiml Tolner? Of *the* Tolners, you understand. A descendant in direct line of *the* Tolner of the Tolners, his merit be our shield. He sees the Prophet Elijah whenever he wants to, Sabbaths and Holy Days and week-days. Not it is *said* of him. He actually sees him, and talks with him as friend to friend. When he was a boy of seven Reb Chaiml had already reached the stage of the unveiling of Elijah. Who are your Reb Isrulikls and Reb Itzikls, may God not punish me for my talk? "

A triple trumpet-peal of derision burst from the pursed lips of Reb Yossel Tulcea.

" P-p-pa! P-p-pa! P-p-pa! So there's nobody but your Chaiml Tolner! And what would you say if I told you that your Reb Chaiml does not reach to the shins — God! What am I saying! — not even to the heels of Reb Isrulikl? And secondly, this Jew came for *my* advice, Reb Mendel, and not for yours."

" What if he did? " asked Reb Mendel hotly. " Shall I take a mouthful of water and be dumb while you mislead an innocent Jew? "

The man called Gershon seized my friend, Reb Leibel, by the arm, and said beseechingly:

" Mr. Jew, I do not know who you are; but two of us here, respectable Jews without an axe to grind — ask the

223

whole world, you will not hear a bad word against us —
bear witness to the incomparable greatness of Reb Itzikl
Sloiker. Do you know who his grandfather was? I will not
insult you by informing you that this grandfather of his
was none other than Reb Lezerel Sloiker himself, whose
fiery breath burned up the wicked if they approached
within ten miles of him. Do you know what they tell of
Reb Lezerel Sloiker? This: that but for him the Messiah
would have come sixty years ago. For when the persecutions began in Russia under Alexander III — may his
name and his memory be blotted out for ever — the Messiah made up his mind to anticipate himself by a thousand years, for he could not bear to look upon the miseries
of the Jews, the Merciful One save us. Therefore the
Messiah came before the Holy One, Blessed be He, and
said: ' Merciful One, I feel that the hour has struck for
my appearance on earth, and for the redemption of Thy
people.' And the Holy One, Blessed be He, answered:
' Wait, for my beloved son, Lezerel Sloiker, is in the
midst of his sacred studies, and a sweet singing comes
to My ears. Moreover, he is about to reveal a piece of
exegesis which I have kept hidden from Myself since the
first six days of the creation! ' Whereupon the Messiah
(may he come speedily and in our day, amen and amen!)
fell upon his face and said: ' Merciful Father, surely I
will not presume to interrupt the studies of your son,
Lezerel Sloiker. But now I shall have to wait another
thousand years, for these moments come but once in
many ages.' Mr. Jew, as I stand here, and as it is day all
over the world, I had these facts from my father, who
knew Reb Lezerel Sloiker all the days of his life."

At this point the other men tried to interrupt, but Reb
Gershon raised his voice and continued feverishly:

"Now listen to this. Reb Lezerel Sloiker once said:
'I shall not withdraw from the world, and the Angel of
Death will have no power over me, until my son Nachman will beget a son who will be as great as Reb Yocha-
nan ben Zakkai, his memory be our blessing, and Simon
ben Yochai, the merit of the righteous be our shield, and
Moses our Teacher, combined, and whose light will shine
on the other side of the world.' Now mark the words:
'On the other side of the world.' And this grandson, this
Reb Itzikl, the son of Reb Nachman, who lives only three
blocks from here — I am ready to conduct you to him
this very minute, and it will cost you the merest trifle —
was born on the evening of the withdrawal of Reb Lezerel
from our world. For Reb Lezerel said: 'He is here! I
hear his voice, and in his wailing, as he issues from the
womb, are the inmost secrets of the Torah,' and forth-
with became no more. That was how Reb Itzikl was
born — and not like an ordinary human being, but in a
shirt, do you understand? And if you want further proof
that Reb Lezerel Sloiker, when dying, referred to none
other than Reb Itzikl, who lives only three blocks from
here, consider those last words: 'His light shall shine on
the other side of the world.' What can he have meant but
America?"

Hereupon Yossel Tulcea, who had been hopping from
one leg to the other, burst out: "Stop bewildering this
Jew with your ridiculous stories. If Reb Lezerel Sloiker
was a great saint — and I do not deny it, bright be his
portion in paradise, and let his light shine there like a
sun — that does not mean that his grandson is his equal!
Do you know — " Yossel Tulcea appropriated Reb Leibel's lapel, dispossessing Reb Gershon — " do you know
what happened to Reb Isrulikl Kortzer? Yes, to Reb

Isrulikl Kortzer, himself, not to his grandfather, or his grandmother, or his grandmother's grandfather? Listen, and gasp! Last year Reb Isrulikl was going to visit his son, Reb Zechariah, in Chicago. And suddenly, when the train was twenty miles from Chicago, it stopped and would not go any farther. Nor could they find anything wrong with the train, or the engine, or the rails. They sent in haste for the greatest engineers and the highest specialists; and all of them sought in vain for the cause of the stoppage. Everything seemed to be in perfect order; the fire burned, the whistle whistled, the wheels went round, but the train would not budge. And while the people were rushing about in great excitement, Reb Isrulikl sat talking to himself. Finally Reb Isrulikl's beadle, who was of course accompanying him, gathered courage and, most respectfully, said to Reb Isrulikl: ' Rebbi, the train refuses to go.' To which Reb Isrulikl said: ' I know, I know.' Thereupon the beadle said: ' Reb Isrulikl, will you not give the word for the train to go? It is a great pity that so many people should suffer.' But Reb Isrulikl answered: ' The train will not go until *he* is removed from the rails.'

" Then wonder and fright and astonishment, and a quaking of the limbs, fell upon the beadle, who said: ' So! There is someone upon the rails! And all the engineers and specialists cannot see him! And behold, my Rebbi, who sits in the train, and does not stir out, and has not even looked out of the window, sees him! ' So the beadle too stepped out of the train and walked up to the engine and looked at the rails and saw — nothing!

" Then the beadle came back to Reb Isrulikl, who was still talking to himself, and by now the train was several hours late. But as evening drew on, Reb Isrulikl came to a decision, for he finally stepped out of the train and walked to a spot in front of the engine and stood there conversing, it would seem, with the empty air. First he talked sternly, then he talked pityingly, then at last he became very angry, bent down, picked up an invisible thing, threw it away, clapped his hands several times to clean them, and returned to his car. The same moment the train began to move and it arrived at its destination in peace.

" Now the beadle was afraid to ask what had happened. But that evening, in the house of Reb Zechariah, after the meal and the benediction, Reb Isrulikl said to his son, Reb Zechariah: ' My son, you have not reproached me for having come late, though you knew that I could have come on time, train or no train. And this restraint is a great virtue in you, and has already released ten thousand souls from the torments of the Evil One. Now I will tell you the reason for my lateness. Give ear, and let your heart likewise listen:

" ' The train was in perfect order, but it could not go forward because a Jewish soul was lying across the rails. I could, indeed, have proceeded hither without the train, by the Overleaping of Distance, which is the prerogative of saints. But I was advised from on high that I was implicated in this matter. Thereupon I debated with myself whether I ought to go forth and enter into conversation with the soul, and hesitated, being afraid of the outcome. Finally, on consulting the Heavenly Academy, I received direct advice from Rabbi Akiba himself — he left a disputation with the Baal Shem Tov in order to talk to me — to delay no longer. So, going forth, I spoke to the soul lying across the rails and inquired sternly: " Soul! Why do you lie across the rails and prevent this train from

taking all these good people to their destination, where
their relatives wait for them, perturbed by the delay?
And why do you cause so many engineers and specialists
to rack their brains in vain to discover what is wrong
with the train? This is cruelty to the living. Why, also,
do you prevent me from proceeding forward to my son
Zechariah, in Chicago, thus holding up the converse of
the two greatest sages of the generation, and thereby
diminishing the wisdom of the world? " And the soul
answered: " The fault is yours. I wander about the world
and I find no rest; nor shall I find rest until you have
given me a healing." " Speak," I said. And the soul answered: " I have sinned against you. I have spoken evil
of you. Until you forgive me there will be no rest for
me." Thereupon I answered, pityingly: " Soul, I forgive
you." But the soul continued to lie there, and I became
angry. " Begone! " I cried. " Lie there no more, and delay me no more. For the train will not move and Rabbi
Akiba has forbidden me to proceed by the Overleaping
of Distance. Fifteen different illuminations of the third
verse of the second chapetr of Habbakuk have been lost
for ever from the eternal stores of wisdom by this delay
in the meeting between myself and my son Zechariah! "
But the soul said: " I have sinned also against your daughter. About her, too, I have spread evil reports." Then I
cried: " No, for that I will not forgive you." And as the
soul refused to budge from the rails, I bent down, lifted
it up, and flung it from me, beyond the Hills of Darkness,
on the other side of the Sambattyon. Then the train could
move forward and I am here.'

" When Reb Isrulikl had finished telling this horrifying story — and the hair stood upside down on the heads
of the listeners — Reb Zechariah, his son, said: ' My fa-

ther, my father, thank you in the name of Him who lives for ever for having given me the opportunity to perform a good deed; for now I shall persuade you to come with me and find that soul, and you and I together will forgive it, and it will find peace.' That very night they went by the Overleaping of Distance to the place where the soul had lain on the rails, and with the use of the Ineffable Name they recalled it from beyond the Hills of Darkness on the other side of the Sambattyon, whither it had been cast by Reb Isrulikl in his anger. And together they forgave it for the sin of spreading evil reports concerning the daughter of Reb Isrulikl and the sister of Reb Zechariah. And that, Reb Leibel, happened right here in America, in the presence of thousands of witnesses."

The eyes of the beadle, Reb Yossel Tulcea, were shining. " To that man," he wound up triumphantly, tugging at the lapel of my friend Reb Leibel, " I will take you, since you seek the highest saint in America. A five-minute walk from here."

" A marvellous story," sneered the man called Reb Mendel. " It has only two little defects: namely, that it happened, not here in America, but in the old country, and that the saint who cast the soul beyond the Hills of Darkness was not your Reb Isrulikl, but the famous and Holy Reb Nuhum of Tchernobl, his memory be our blessing."

" And I tell you," cried Reb Gershon, " that the wonders of Reb Itzikl Sloiker are such that when you hear them your heart stands still and the nails on your fingers and toes stand upside down."

Reb Yossel Tulcea was speechless with resentment. When he found his voice, he shrieked at Reb Mendel:

" Sinner! Unbeliever and son of Epicurus! Apostate! You have called Reb Isrulikl a liar, for he told me of the incident with his own lips. *Your* soul will lie across the rails some day, and *you* will be flung beyond the Hills of Darkness. But there will be none to recall you thence and give you peace."

The competition became more furious, so that my friend Reb Leibel and I were forgotten in the midst of it; and as the recitals mounted from marvel to marvel, the air became thicker and thicker with mysterious figures: Asmodeus, the evil familiar of King Solomon, emperors ancient and modern, from Hadrian of Rome to Nicholas Romanov of Russia, tyrants who had been made to eat the parchment scrolls bearing their own wicked decrees, the Not-Good-One himself in a terrifying variety of guises, such as a two-headed cat and a six-legged dog, a raging river and a sack of wheat, an alluring wanton with seven breasts and a coiled tongue eight ells long, archangels benevolent and malevolent, Gabriel, Raphael, and Samael, the demon whose name is as the sound of the blowing out of a candle (for which reason prudent men do not blow out a candle, but snuff it out with their fingers), Korah, who had been swallowed up by the earth with his rebellious tribe, yes, the Patriarchs themselves, Abraham, Isaac, and Jacob — all these came and went at the bidding of the saints of the East Side of New York. My friend Reb Leibel and I listened, forgetful of our mission. The flies hummed in the dusty room, the tattered volumes of the Talmud looked down from the single bookcase with the cracked, unwashed glass. Where was I? In New York or in old Kasrielevky? In New York, I said to myself, because old Kasrielevky has been utterly destroyed, and all the places which harboured the saints have passed under the flaming harrow. This alone is left — this, and the record in Sholom Aleichem.

Sholom Aleichem, who speaks with such tenderness and affection of old Reb Yozifel, the " regular " rabbi of Kasrielevky, assumes a very different tone when he describes, as he does in a sketch called *Pancakes for Hannukah,* the court of a Chassidic dynasty in a mythical townlet which he calls Kopelishel, in the vicinity of Mazeppavka, itself a mystical townlet in the region of Kiev.

On the eve of the feast of the Maccabees Nosy the beadle (his real name is Israel, but the adenoidal sing-song of his speech is responsible for his nickname) , carrying a lantern through the snow, makes the rounds of Kopelishel, announcing with great dignity that the " court " (the *Hoif,* from the German *Hof,* which is, literally, the court) invites all and sundry to appear that evening to eat of the pancakes traditionally associated with the festival. " All and sundry " means, of course, only the men, who in any case need no invitation, for this display of graciousness and hospitality on the part of the court is an ancient institution in Kopelishel. The women stay at home and envy their husbands.

Kopelishel consists of a rich court and a poverty-stricken townlet. The court is Kopelishel's industry. From a hundred towns and villages the followers of the Kopelishel Chassidic dynasty bring in their contributions in exchange for the spiritual protection of the Rebbi and his family. One should perhaps say the Rebbi and his tribe, for it is a tribe, or at least a clan, that is installed in the group of buildings called the court: the Rebbi and his wife; the sons of the Rebbi and their wives; the daughters of the Rebbi and their husbands; the grandsons and granddaughters with *their* wives and husbands, if they are old enough to be married, which means, generally, if they are above the age of seventeen. Sacred personages, all of them, strangers to want or work, an aristocracy differing from every other aristocracy in the world in that it has no physical instrument for the maintenance of its privileged position. The link between Church and State which everywhere else constitutes the classic combination, is absent here: a unique instance of voluntary servitude on the part of the masses. The " followers " of the court pour in their contributions without expectation of earthly reward; the " court " has no influence with the government of Russia; it is incapable of diminishing by a jot or tittle the terms of an anti-Jewish decree; its promises relate exclusively to the government of heaven.

Nussi is the major-domo of the Kopelishel court, the master intrigant, the go-between, the chief flatterer, and the court's messenger to the townlet. Nussi knows the ins and outs of the townlet and court; Nussi brings the favours of the Rebbi to the townspeople, and the labour of the townspeople to the Rebbi. Nussi knows how to cajole a donation out of the court; Nussi knows which of the Kopelishel paupers to bully, which to bribe. Wherever there is an oligarchy there is always a class of skilful and useful toadies. Nussi concentrates in his person that class for the religious oligarchy of Kopelishel.

It is a picture worth seeing, the pancake banquet of the eve of Channukah. There is a peculiar disparity between the festival, with its memories of men of valour and independence, the Hasmoneans, and the pitiful little folk of Kopelishel, gathered to do honour to the court. They eat downstairs, in the yard, swallowing the hot pancakes dipped in goose-fat, while upstairs, at the windows, the Rebbi and the clan, the sons and sons-in-law, the grandsons and grandsons-in-law beam down upon the townsfolk and meditate on their own generosity. Downstairs it is a rabble of beggars, tattered gaberdines, down-at-heel shoes, skullcaps open at the seams; upstairs it is silk and velvet, pearl necklaces round the white throats of the buxom women, gaberdines of costly satin, rich carpets, massive furniture.

They sit at the windows, they beam upon the Chassidim, and it seems to them that something is amiss. The eaters of the pancakes lack the appropriate enthusiasm. There should be a little more gaiety: Channukah is a gay festival; pancakes, especially when supplied free of charge, are a dainty dish; the presence of the Rebbi is an inspiration: why are the townsfolk so down in the mouth? Nussi is sent down to stir them up a little. More spirit, Chassidim! The Rebbi wants to see you happy.

So the whisky is passed around, and Nussi goes from Chassid to Chassid, poking this one in the ribs, pinching the other. " A little life! The Rebbi is watching! A dance! A dance! "

They take the hint. A ring is formed in the yard; the Chassidim join hands; a pious dance begins. Voices are raised in the traditional chant of the Kopelishel Chassidim:

> *Ai! Ai!*
> *Bim! Bom!*
> *Ai! Ai!*
> *Bim! Bom!*

That's better! The Court smiles, the Rebbi hums the melody, the daughters-in-law tap out the rhythm with

233

their daintily shod feet. Great is the Chassidic court of Kopelishel!

" Foot it! Faster! Louder! " cried Nussi the toady; and the hungry Chassidim put their last energies into the dance. God forbid that the court should find them ungrateful or lacking in respect.

Late in the night the Chassidim of Kopelishel, the pancakes danced out of them, stream out of the yard and set off across the snowy fields to their scattered homes. It is past midnight. The court is asleep. The wives are waiting at home. And as they crawl through the snow, which crunches under their feet, a voice is raised suddenly, in a wail of impotent rage:

" May a hundred thousand devils rip into him and into his ancestors all the way back to Adam! "

" Into whom? " ask several voices.

" Into whom? Into Nussi the toady, who is a hundred times worse than all the others! "

" Leave him alone," says someone. " He's a miserable pauper like ourselves."

" A pauper! If I could only earn in one year what he makes in a month! "

" Is that as far as your imagination will go? "

" Let me get that far first; I'll bargain for more later."

Silence falls again. The figures scatter, vanish into the tiny, snow-covered huts. Only the snow remains, and the moon looking down.

CHAPTER XXV

Rabbis and Rabbis

❁

THE ENGLISH word " Rabbi " is compelled to do service for at least three words current in the world of Sholom
Aleichem: *Rav, Rebbi,* and *Rabbiner.* The *Rav* was the
traditional spiritual head of the community. Strictly
speaking, his was not a paid position, though in practice
it almost always was. The *Rav* was not a prayer-leader; he
was not — as we have seen — the intermediary between
the community and God. The *Chazan* or cantor was the
sheliach tzibur, the messenger of the community, the
leader in prayer. Intermediary there was none. The *Rav*
was the authority on ritual questions, the leading scholar,
the spiritual guide, the crown of the community, the
personification of the best traditions. Reb Yozifel is the
type of *Rav* at its best.

The word *Rebbi,* though it might be used loosely in
addressing a Rav (since the word means " teacher " and
is also used for the ordinary Hebrew-teacher, the keeper
of the *cheder,* or one-room Hebrew school) , was specifically applied to the Chassidic leaders. It is quite impossible to say, in Yiddish, the *Rav* of Sadagorah, or the *Rav*
of Tolne, in speaking of those famous Chassidic personages. It is the Sadagorah *Rebbi,* the Tolne *Rebbi,* the

Rebbi of Ger. " *Rebbi* " in this sense is interchangeable with a special phrase, " a good Jew," which, again, does not simply mean a good Jew: it means, in this context, a Chassidic leader. These are oddities of Yiddish which would not be worth dwelling on if they did not lead to certain wider social aspects of our study.

Now, a *Rabbiner* (which is nothing more than the German word for " rabbi ") was neither a *Rav* nor a *Rebbi*. He had not the scholarship and standing of the former; he had not the popular following of the latter. He was not a Jewish phenomenon; he was what we call in Yiddish a " lung and liver hung on your nose," a nuisance thrust upon you from the outside, something you are compelled to put up with simply because you are unable to get rid of it.

About the middle of the nineteenth century the Russian authorities were making sporadic efforts to " modernize " the Jews — that is, bring them down to the moral and spiritual level of the Russian masses under the Romanovs. One of the instruments of Russification was a new and special type of rabbi — the *Kazionne,* or Crown Rabbi, the *Rabbiner,* whom the Jewish communities were compelled to elect of their own free will. Compelling someone to do out of his own free will something he dislikes is an old trick with tyrants. The *Rabbiner* was the official Rabbi vis-à-vis the government. He kept the records of the community. He spoke for the community, represented it to *natchalstva,* or officialdom. But he was no more a spiritual leader than a president of a university is an educator. No Jew ever went to the *Rabbiner* for advice either on religious or personal problems, certainly not for spiritual edification. His Jewish learning was exiguous, his standing nil, his function despised.

236

It should not be inferred that the *Rabbiner* was personally an ignominious type. Quite often he meant well, or at least thought he meant well. In this he resembled the Jewish notables of Russia (*Shtadtlanim*, they were called, from the Hebrew word *l'hishtadel*, to try, to exert yourself — and they were called *Shtadtlanim* because they *tried* to do something for the Jews of Russia), who stood in a peculiar relationship to the government. The *Shtadtlanim* (and they too meant well, or thought they meant well) promised the authorities that, in exchange for relief from certain anti-Semitic measures, they, the *Shtadtlanim*, would guarantee the good behaviour of the Jewish masses. To the Jewish masses the *Shtadtlanim* guaranteed that in exchange for their good behaviour they would obtain from the government mitigation of anti-Semitic measures. It occurred to no one that a bargain of this kind between the government and the masses was automatic and needed no intermediaries. The *Shtadtlan* was as superfluous — and therefore as dishonest — as a salesman placing orders with a government in war-time. But the *Shtadtlan* was the rich Jew. He needed prestige. He was concerned with the general condition of the country, for every disturbance of the *status quo*, every manifestation of social instability, alarmed him as a member of the propertied classes. He was also, let us concede, concerned with the welfare of his people. But his position was morally repulsive. He was, or in some measure pretended to be, the defender of the Russian autocracy. In actual fact he was often by no means that. The rich Jews of Russia were at least liberals. But in their negotiations with the government they had to play the game; and often their liberalism was superficial. They had to discourage not only the spread of revolu-

237

tionary principles among Jews, but the rise of Zionist sentiment. In Sholom Aleichem's Russia there already existed the complex of forces which are part of the American Jewish scene. There are American-Jewish *Shtadtlanim* who play the same game, in a different setting: calling upon Jews to do this or that, to withdraw their support from liberal candidates at elections, to refrain from putting forward (or from permitting to be put forward) a liberal Jew as a Supreme Court justice, in order to placate the anti-Semites.

The *Kazionne* Rabbi, the *Rabbiner,* was a *Shtadtlan in petto.* His salary was paid out of a special tax levied on the Jewish community. And since he was, for spiritual and religious purposes, quite useless, the Jews nearly everywhere found themselves supporting two rabbis, the *Kazionne* and the *Rav.* With all this, the *Rabbiner* was often a decent sort; he was not *forbidden* to possess Jewish learning, and occasionally he took advantage of this laxity of the Russian law. Here and there Jews realized that, after all, the *Kazionne* Rabbi was in the same boat with themselves. But on the whole the relationship was a painful one; the *Rabbiner* was looked upon with distaste, and he in turn regarded his " charges " as uncivilized, recalcitrant, and ungrateful.

To illustrate the relationship at its worst, I have chosen from the records of Sholom Aleichem a story none the less charming in itself because it happens to be highly instructive.

In a certain little town in Poltava — that is to say, in the heart of the Sholom Aleichem country — a young man who possessed the necessary civic qualifications and more than the necessary Jewish equipment was " elected " to the position of *Rabbiner.* As it happened, this young man was of the decenter sort of *Rabbiner*, less concerned with the whims of officialdom than the needs of the Jewish community. Handicapped though he was by his status, he did his best to win the community over by interesting himself in the Hebrew school, the charities, and communal affairs generally. Above all, he aspired to establish himself as the " arbitrator," the position peculiarly enjoyed by the *Rav* of the old school.

On a certain day there came to him four of the leading Jewish citizens, the cream of the community, the trustees of the synagogue, and the richest men in the townlet. They came on a matter of business, a dispute which they were reluctant to take to court, but which they were willing to submit to the *Rabbiner*. Very flattering indeed. The *Rabbiner* thanked them heartily for their expression of confidence: this was exactly what he had been waiting for. Unfortunately, his opinion of the four trustees mitigated considerably the pleasure of the compliment. Three of them were known as the " troika " — the threesome. They had been partners in business for many years. They had quarrelled more than once, but they had remained together on the basis of a simple argument: " If the next piece of business happens to be successful, why should I be out of it? And if it happens to be a failure, why should the others be out of it? " The fourth man was new to the combination, but the *Rabbiner* surmised that his principles, too, were of the same order.

Suspecting in advance that his verdict would be unpalatable to all four, the *Rabbiner* demanded, in advance, a fee of twenty-five roubles from each of the disputants; not for himself, God forbid, but for the poor children of the Hebrew school. With the money paid,

239

he sat down and listened with the closest attention to
the details of the dispute, a highly involved one, full
of charges and counter-charges, juggleries, confidence
tricks, evasions, flim-flam, fraud — in fact, everything
short of downright forgery and pocket-picking. When the
four men had delivered themselves at great length of
their claims, the *Rabbiner* quietly stated his opinion:

" Gentlemen, having considered carefully your state-
ments, I find myself compelled, in all honesty, to issue
the following verdict: not only is each one of you in the
wrong, but I have never in all my life listened to such a
story of mutual roguery, thievery, and deception. It is
an intolerable shame that Jews should be capable of
dealing in this fashion with each other. I therefore throw
the case out of court, and declare your fees confiscated
for the purposes I have mentioned."

The four trustees looked at each other, stunned. This
was not the sort of verdict they had expected, and it was
not the kind of language they were accustomed to from
a *Kazionne* Rabbi. They were about to withdraw when
one of them, the outsider to the partnership, asked if he
might reward the *Rabbiner* with a story, in payment for
his services.

A story? By all means! Who in Sholom Aleichem's
world ever turns down a story? The men reseated themselves, and the fourth of the disputants began:

" Years ago, when I was still a young man, I was liv-
ing in a little town which was blessed with a total of nine
Jewish families. How did I make a living? I kept a hotel.
I bought and sold wheat. I picked up odd lots of any
kind of merchandise. Between one thing and another,
I just about managed. One fine day, right in the midst

of the wheat season, my wife takes it into her mind to be delivered of a child — a boy! *Mazel tov!* But a boy means a circumcision ceremony on the eighth day, doesn't he? And a circumcision ceremony means a quorum of ten Jews, doesn't it? And there are only nine adult Jews in town, including myself. What's to be done? Where am I to get a tenth Jew in that Godforsaken townlet?

" On the eighth day after my son's birth I went down to the railroad station, hoping against hope that a Jewish traveller would get off the train and I could invite him to the house for the ceremony. It was a Friday afternoon. Sure enough, when our one daily train drew in, there steps off a respectable-looking Jew, carrying his valise. He rushes over to the lunch-counter and looks hungrily at the collection of cakes, sandwiches, beer-bottles — you know the kind of stuff they keep on those counters: half of it ham, all of it uneatable. I go up to him: ' Mr. Jew, how would you like to earn yourself a portion in paradise, and at the same time eat a good solid meal, a plate of golden-yellow soup, a steaming goulash that melts in your mouth, and white Sabbath bread fresh out of the oven? ' The man looks at me as if I'd taken leave of my senses. ' Listen, man,' I say to him, ' it's a question of life and death, or pretty near it: a question of inducting a little Jew into the congregation of Israel ' — and I explain the whole business to him.

" ' But I've got to catch that train! ' he says. ' I've got to be in Yehupetz before nightfall.' ' Yehupetz, shmehupetz,' I answer him. ' Do you or don't you want to earn yourself a portion in paradise? Do you or don't you want to eat a good solid meal, Jewish cooking, a goulash that melts in your mouth, golden-yellow soup, white Sab-

241

bath bread fresh out of the oven? ' And without waiting
for his answer, I grab his valise and run off with it. What
could the poor man do? He followed!

" Well, we had our tenth man, and the circumcision
ceremony was performed according to the law and tradition. And my traveller, my life-saver, got a meal that
evening that would have made a king's mouth water.
My woman was already on her feet, and cooking, and,
without boasting, I can say that my woman's cooking
hasn't its equal in Poltava or even in the rest of Russia.

" That was a Friday evening, you understand. No
question of my guest moving for twenty-four hours. And
on the next day, on the Sabbath, I say to him: ' You've
saved a Jewish soul, do you understand? I can't speak of
a reward — there's no reward big enough. But today
you're going to eat a piece of roast chicken that you'll
remember the rest of your life. An hors d'œuvre of
chopped onion and goose-fat, with a couple of glasses of
brandy, and a roast chicken — my wife's work, that'll
leave you homesick for this town. You understand? ' Sure
he understood. But when Sunday morning came, and he
made ready to resume the journey, I say to him: ' Are
you out of your mind? Do you think I'm going to let you
go just like that? A man who saved a Jewish soul, so to
speak, a man sent to me from heaven? No, sir. You're
going to stay here and taste my wife's borsht, because
unless you come this way again you'll never taste borsht
like that as long as you live.' And let me tell you, *Rabbiner,* that was borsht out of borsht-land: with a couple
of crisp potato pancakes, and a glass or two of red wine —
what's the use of talking! My man grumbled, but
smacked his lips.

" And then, on Monday morning, he *must* be leaving

of course. ' Not on your life! ' I tell him. ' This is the
third day after the circumcision. Don't you know that
on the third day after the circumcision it's usual to hold
a special feast? And do you think after all this I'll let
you walk off like a stranger? Wait! You're going to
eat dairy *varnishkes* this evening that'll open your eyes!
I wouldn't let you miss those *varnishkes* for anything
in the world.' My man begins to yell: ' Murder! Is
there no pity in your bosom? I've business to attend
to.' ' Business-shmizzness,' I tell him. ' A plateful of my
wife's dairy *varnishkes,* with a couple of bottles of beer,
is the best business in the world.' And sure enough, I
made him stay. I made him stay four days with me, and
only on the fifth day did I let him pack his valise. And
just as he was about to leave, I handed him a bill.

" He looked at me, sort of dazed. ' What's this? ' ' The
bill,' I said; ' thirty-seven roubles and fifteen kopecks.
It's itemized.' ' The bill,' he repeated in a whisper, then
let out a yell. ' The bill? Isn't it enough that you killed
four days for me, held me by the throat, after I'd done
you the service of attending the circumcision ceremony
of your new-born son. What is this? A joke? Or a
hold-up? ' ' It isn't a joke, mister,' I tell him, ' and it isn't
a hold-up. It's just a simple reckoning. I'm not charging
you for the first afternoon — that was your good deed
for the day. But there was no good deed involved in your
staying here, eating your head off, drinking my best
cognac and wine and beer, for four days.' ' Then why
did you plead with me to stay? ' ' Salesmanship,' I
answered.

" Well, Rabbi, the poor man was a sight! He couldn't
get it into his head that bed and board cost money. At
last I said to him: ' Listen. Do we have to quarrel? There's

243

a *Rabbiner* in the next townlet, an honorable gentleman, a scholar and a sage. Suppose we put it up to him?
I pledge myself in advance to accept his decision.'

" Done! We get into the train, proceed to the next
townlet, and go to the Rabbi — the *Rabbiner*, that is.
My ' guest ' lets loose, dishes up the story from beginning to end, omitting not a detail. The *Rabbiner* listens,
patiently, just as you did, to the very end, then turns to
me and asks: ' Well, what have you to say? ' ' Me? ' I
answer, ' I've nothing at all to say. This gentleman has
told you nothing but the truth.' With that the *Rabbiner*
turns back to my guest, asks him again how long he had
stayed with me, what he had eaten, what he drank,
whether he was satisfied with the cooking, did he enjoy
the cognac — and when the second recital is over, the
Rabbiner shrugs his shoulders, looks at me knowingly,
and says to my guest: ' Sorry! You'll have to pay! '

" The man turned green, yellow, and purple. But he
pulled out a fifty-rouble note and flung it in my face.
' Here,' he said. ' Give me the change.' ' Change? ' I said.
' What are you talking about? Who wants your money?
Take back your fifty-rouble note, man. What do you take
me for? Isn't it enough that you saved a Jewish soul,
helped me to induct my son into the congregation of
Israel, gave me the pleasure of your company for four
days? Do you expect me to charge you for it? Is this
Sodom and Gomorrah? '

" Well, the man was absolutely flabbergasted. ' For
God's sake! ' he gasped. ' What is this? What did you
want the whole comedy for? Why did you drag me here? '

" ' Just like that,' I answered. ' I wanted to show you
what a clever Rabbi we've got.' "

244

Therewith the fourth of the trustees ended his story, and was about to retreat with the others. But the *Rabbiner,* smiling good-naturedly, stopped them with a gesture.

" Just a minute, gentlemen. One good story deserves another. Do you mind? "

And when they had seated themselves again he began:

" This didn't happen to me, but to a friend of mine, a businessman, not too well off — just about manages to make a living. A year or two ago, on the day before Yom Kippur, he was on the road, carrying with him a pretty big sum of money — several thousand roubles. Not his own, of course, but the firm's. Yom Kippur — the most sacred day in our Jewish calendar. I needn't remind you, gentlemen, that it's forbidden to carry money about on that day. What was my friend to do? Leave the money in the inn while he attended services? How could he? His mind wouldn't be on his prayers. At last he hit on an excellent idea. He asked the innkeeper where he could find the Rabbi of the town, and, hugging his package of money, betook himself to the Rabbi's house.

" There he explained his problem. ' Rabbi, I'm carrying a big sum of money with me. Not mine — it's God's first and then the firm's. Tomorrow's Yom Kippur, I daren't have money on my person. I'm afraid to leave it with the innkeeper. Would you perhaps be kind enough to put it away for me till tomorrow night? '

" ' But you don't know me from Adam,' said the Rabbi. ' How can you trust me with such a sum of money? ' ' Rabbi! ' said my friend, shocked. ' Aren't you a Rabbi in Israel? ' ' But you still don't know me,' answered the Rabbi. ' What's more, I don't know you! ' So it went,

245

back and forth: 'Aren't you a Rabbi in Israel?' and
'You don't know me and I don't know you' — till they
hit on a plan, which was, to bring in the four leading
trustees of the synagogue as witnesses.

" And so the four leading trustees were sent for, and in
their presence the Rabbi counted over the money, note
by note, put it in a handkerchief, sealed the four corners,
placed the handkerchief in his safe, gave the key to his
good wife — and that was that.

" My friend, vastly relieved, returned to the inn,
washed, ate a good supper, attended the evening services,
attended the services all next day, fasted like a good Jew,
wept his heart out to the Almighty, and when the last
shofar blast had sounded, went back to the inn to break
his fast. After which, at peace with God and man, he re-
paired to the Rabbi's house to recover his money.

" ' Good evening, Rabbi. God send you a good year.'

" ' Good evening to you, friend. God send you a good
year, likewise. And who may you be? '

" Whereupon my friend smiled at the absent-minded-
ness of the Rabbi and answered: ' Why, Rabbi, bless
you, I'm the man that was here yesterday afternoon and
left a big sum of money with you — not mine, either,
but God's first and then my firm's.'

" The Rabbi looked at him bewildered.

" ' You were here yesterday and left a big sum of
money with me? '

" ' Why, yes, Rabbi, of course. You counted it out and
put it in a handkerchief, and sealed the handkerchief
and put it in the safe and gave the key to your good wife
— don't you remember? '

" The Rabbi still looked blank, and my friend began
to have a queer feeling at the pit of his stomach.

" ' Rabbi! In God's name! There were four witnesses. The leading trustees of your synagogue.'

" With that the Rabbi became stern. ' I see you're taking it seriously,' he said to my friend. ' Send at once for the trustees.'

" The beadle ran out, and in a few minutes came back with the trustees. The moment they entered, the Rabbi addressed them in a warning tone of voice:

" ' Gentlemen, this stranger, this man you see before you, this new-comer to our town, has entered my house and has made the statement that yesterday, in your presence, he delivered to me, for safe-keeping over Yom Kippur, a large sum of money. He now claims that sum of money and cites you as witnesses.'

" That was enough for the trustees. They looked at the Rabbi, they looked at each other, and a sly grin flickered on their lips. Ho-ho! A stranger! A large sum of money! The Rabbi was no fool!

" ' Never seen the man! ' said the first trustee, frowning.

" ' Never seen the man,' said the second trustee — and so the third, and the fourth.

" Well, what do you think my friend did? He just fainted. Passed out. Collapsed on the floor. You get the situation, gentlemen? An honest man, carrying thousands of roubles, not his own — who was going to believe that he had entrusted it to a Rabbi in the presence of witnesses, and that they denied everything? He was ruined. Done for.

" When he came to, which was fully half an hour later, after several glasses of water had been dashed in his face, he got up looking ten years older. Then the Rabbi went to the safe, opened it, took out the handker-

247

chief, unfolded it, and returned the man his money —
every single rouble.

"'Rabbi! In God's name!' croaked my friend, more
dead than alive. 'What did you have to do that for?'

"'Just so,' said the Rabbi. 'I wanted to show you
what kind of trustees I've got.'"

CHAPTER XXVI

The Two Extremes

❀

THE QUALITY of Sholom Aleichem's writing makes it hard to remember which of his characters are " fictional " and which — as in his autobiography — " real." There is about all of them an intensity and symbolism by which they transcend the distinction between the invented and the factual. Early in this account I said that Tevyeh the dairyman and his distant relative Menachem Mendel, the *luftmensch,* were the diametrically opposite types of Sholom Aleichem's world: the first with his simple, substantial relation to the earning of a livelihood, the second with his complete lack of relation to reality, the first with his matter-of-fact daily labour, the second with his insanely laborious pursuit of the labourless livelihood. Tevyeh and Menachem Mendel (the latter comes in for a fuller description in the second half of this chapter) are, I shall not say fictional figures, but reconstructed persons. But if we treat all the men and women in Sholom Aleichem as living personalities, there is an even more instructive contrast to illuminate the extreme tendencies in Sholom Aleichem's world: that between Menachem Mendel and old Loiev, Sholom Aleichem's father-in-law.

As a youngster just out of the Gymnasium, Sholom
Aleichem became, like thousands of his kind, a tutor;
for those were the days — the late seventies of the last
century — when the fever of modern education was taking its first good grip on Russian Jewry, and every family
that was infected with the fever and could afford the
luxury took a household tutor. There was usually a difference in economic status between the family which
hired the tutor and the family to which he belonged;
but they had a common setting — the setting of urban
Jewish life. It was altogether different in this case. Old
Loiev, who hired young Sholom as tutor for his daughter Olga — the girl who later became Sholom Aleichem's
wife, and who died but a few months ago in New York —
was a variety of Jew that the gymnasiast from Voronka
and Pereyeslav had never seen before.

" He looked," reports Sholom Aleichem, " like a Russian general or field-marshal; and his voice was like that
of a lion. When his son presented me to him, he took out
a pair of silver-rimmed spectacles, saddled them on his
nose, and studied me long and earnestly, quite without
affectation, as if he were examining a fish. Then he put
out his hand, pressed mine warmly, and asked, in the
familiar second person singular: ' What's your name? '

" Hearing that the name was Sholom, old Loiev, sof-
tening, as far as he could, the leonine roar of his voice,
said: ' Well, youngster, be kind enough to step into the
next room while I talk the matter over with my son.' "

The interview took place at a hotel in the town of
Bohslav, at a distance of several miles from old Loiev's
home; and while father and son were settling the tutor's
fate in the next room, the latter was dreaming, he tells
us, sweet dreams of a pleasant, well-paid job, of a charm-

ing pupil, of an irresistible mutual love, of a father's consent and blessing — he was dreaming, in fact, what actually came to pass in the course of time. What he could not dream of, however, was the reality of the life into which he was about to be inducted.

For old Loiev's home was a genuine country estate, and old Loiev was a genuine farmer on a grand scale, a patriarchal tiller of the soil, an aristocratic figure out of an utterly non-Jewish world. The vast house was simply and solidly furnished; the servants went about quietly, in felt slippers; the awe and authority of old Loiev brooded over the establishment. And not only over the establishment, but over the village, where he was loved and respected by the peasants as perhaps no Russian landowner had ever been loved and respected.

Apart from his two or three hours of daily duty as a tutor, young Sholom was free to do as he liked. There was an excellent library downstairs, mostly Hebrew, with all the authors of the Haskalah represented — for Hebrew was the only language old Loiev read. Not that he played the " gentleman farmer." By no means. All day long he was out in the fields, supervising the sowing, the reaping, the threshing, the care of the cattle; and in every branch of farming he used the newest, most scientific methods, so that the Russian farmers of that district used to say of him: " If you want to learn how to manage a farm, go to the Jew Loiev." Evenings, dinner was served in state: young Sholom, who had been brought up in the friendly formlessness of a Jewish middle-class family, beheld with mingled terror and astonishment the dishes brought in by a uniformed lackey in white gloves; true, the lackey was just an ordinary village lad, little Ivan, but he had been trained by old Loiev to play to perfection the role of butler. Knives and forks and spoons of all sizes flanked the plate, so that Sholom had to go through the familiar comedy of watching what the others did before he ventured to touch any of the implements.

This is a very far cry indeed from Kasrielevky; and the wonder lies not in the contrast as such, for the same contrast existed, *mutatis mutandis,* between the Russian nobleman and the recently liberated Russian serf. The extraordinary feature in this situation was the complete Jewishness of the Loiev home, the Hebrew books which the father read, the Hebrew education he gave his children, and his simple assumption that the combination of Judaism and the soil was just as natural as the combination of Judaism and the ghetto — or even more so.

Sholom Aleichem goes on to say: " It is difficult to imagine what turn might have been taken by the history of the Jewish people, and by its role in the economic and political life of Russia, if the laws of Ignatev had not driven the Jews out of the villages and forbidden them to till the soil. Such farmer owners as old Loiev were not a rarity in that district, or in other parts of the blessed ' Pale of Settlement.' There was, in fact, a rush for the soil, and Jews performed marvels in places that had been neglected and given up as barren." And he quotes, in support of his views, a Russian writer of those days, Vassili Feodorovich Simerenko.

Yet the expression he uses argues against his implied thesis. He says: " Such farmer owners as old Loiev were not a rarity." He does not even permit himself the expression: " They were fairly common." For though it is true that the impulse to the land has remained embedded in the Jewish people, and though it is true that — especially in Palestine — they have demonstrated a high degree of ability as farmers, it is also true that a people cannot be switched from soil to city, from city to soil, four or five times over in the course of centuries. Ninety per cent or more of the Russians tilled the land in those days; but even before the laws of Ignatev there were not five per cent of the Jews on the land. An agricultural tradition calls primarily for stability, which was precisely what the Jews were denied. Moreover, they had been forced into a certain economic function — also, they had done their best to adapt themselves to this function — which urbanized their minds.

The history of the Jews of Russia is a hopeless tangle of economic and psychological (religious being, in the connection, included in the psychological) interactions. The Jews were an indispensable part of the economic machinery. Over and over again the psychological hostility which they aroused ran up against the needs of the economic organism. One impulse, or one section of the population, thrust them out; another impulse, or another section of the population, called them back. Emperors and empresses were at loggerheads with the nobility, merchants with peasants, on the Jewish problem. While everybody disliked Jews, some thought them useful. others harmful; the best that could be said of them was that they were a hateful necessity: and even where this was admitted, there were some who were ready to forgo the necessity. Administrative instruments of the nobility and the landowners, the Jews, as managers, tax-collectors, innkeepers, whisky-manufacturers, did the dirty work of society because no one else had the brains for it. Throughout the centuries one can trace, in wavering but inexorable lines, the steady disintegration of the function of the Jews. Attached to the nobility, serving as a nascent middle class, they lost their usefulness as the position of the nobility declined. And as a gentile middle class emerged, the Jews, denied access to the soil, excluded from the guilds, distrusted as competitors even by the working class — except where the latter was revolutionary — found themselves suspended over the abyss. The predominance of the *luftmensch,* the man-who-starves-by-his-wits, in the Jewish picture is a result of this complex of forces. The process was not at an end when the First World War ended; and it will have to be evaluated and countered when the Second World War is over.

Menachem Mendel is Sholom Aleichem's marvellous delineation of the *luftmensch.* We know Menachem Mendel through one series of letters which he addresses to his wife, Sheineh Sheindel, and through another which she addresses to him. How does Menachem Mendel make a living? How does he maintain his family, or how is the family maintained? We do not know. We read his extraordinary letters, filled with accounts of innumerable activities, and we never discover a trace of income.

We meet him first as a speculator on the exchange. These are the days of Russia's primitive industrial development, in the latter part of the nineteenth century. Menachem Mendel sets out for Yehupetz (Kiev) with his wife's dowry. Fortunes are being made daily by people he hears about but never meets. His letters glow with enthusiasm and hope and explanations of the mysteries of the stock market: *hausse* and *baisse* (bulls and bears), buying on margin, pyramiding, selling short — a perfect anticipation of the American frenzy of 1929. Nothing is missing — not even the bucket-shop. Menachem Mendel emerges from his first flurry of speculation a shorn lamb.

Menachem Mendel, left penniless, suddenly bethinks himself that a speculator is a sucker. It's the broker who collects the money, let the market rise or fall, let Putilov shares make or break, let London lend or refuse to lend (all of which he explains in homely Yiddish to his sceptical Sheineh Sheindel) ; the broker gets it coming and going. So he becomes a broker. Unfortunately, the same brilliant idea has occurred to five hundred other Menachem Mendels in Yehupetz, so, after " clawing perpendicular walls " for a season, Menachem Mendel learns another profession.

He becomes a commission merchant on the sugar market. He writes home to Sheineh Sheindel to ask how the beets are coming up locally, and whether insects are much in evidence. By the time he gets her bewildered reply, he is no longer a sugar broker: he is a discount man. That's the business. You buy up debts at a discount. But since debts you have bought up show a tendency to remain uncollectable, Menachem Mendel becomes, in rapid succession, a real-estate agent, a building promoter, and a buyer of farms.

From none of these professions, all of them described with much enthusiasm to Sheineh Sheindel, does he derive any income. He turns, therefore, to timber. Timber failing, he goes in for factories. Factories yielding no profit, he tries mines; and from mines he shifts to oil — the Caucasian oil fields were in their first blossom.

And all this time, we must remember, Menachem Mendel, in Kiev, or in Odessa, is without a residential permit. He must dodge the police. He must change lodgings frequently. He must do business on the run. And it is amazing what an amount of business he manages to transact without attracting the attention of the police or a rouble of income.

Having failed in all of the above-mentioned lines, Menachem Mendel becomes a writer. He has heard that the journals pay a kopeck a line for articles and stories. A thousand lines a day is nothing to Menachem Mendel — and a thousand lines a day means ten roubles a day — a very handsome income. Others besides Menachem Mendel have calculated similarly, and the calculations always look so reasonable. But Menachem Mendel the writer ends up as Menachem Mendel the marriage broker. And Menachem Mendel the marriage broker fades from the scene when, arranging a promising marriage, he forgets to determine the sex of the other party, and finds himself trying to mate two young men.

Menachem Mendel is the apotheosis of Jewish rootlessness. He lives in the midst of shadows, and of the rumour of reality. He rotates at the centre of a whirlwind of telegrams, combinations, commissions, quotations, fees, and cuts. He talks of sterling, of bonds, of international loans, of wars, of threats of war. And his wife keeps writing to him, in a crescendo of despair, quoting always the wise words of her mother: " A dumb man told how a deaf man had heard that a blind man saw a legless man running for his life." Or, again: " A sick man can become well, a drunken man sober, a black man white, but a fool will remain a fool."

But Menachem Mendel is not a fool. He is, if we want to go behind the humour of the presentation, a sick man. He has lost the tactile sense. He has been kept so long — he and thousands like him — from earth, from labour, from substance, that he has taken to dealing in pure terminology or counters. Unfortunately the nature of the economic system is such that more than one dealer in terminology has ended up the possessor of a great fortune.

Sick men like Menachem Mendel by the thousand, by the tens of thousands, haunted the market-places of Ye-hupetz and Boiberick and Kasrielevky and Heissin and Bohopolie and Kozodoievka. They were always looking for what the English call a spot of business. Perhaps a rich gentile was selling a house, or buying a horse; per-haps a stranger was in search of an investment. Perhaps somebody wanted a loan. Perhaps a load of wheat could be sold. Perhaps somebody was on the verge of bank-ruptcy. Menachem Mendels haunted the railroad sta-tions and the hotels, accosted new-comers, offered every kind of service under the sun, competed with one an-other for the possession of a rumoured prospect; Mena-chem Mendels came home in the evening dry-throated, aching in every limb; Menachim Mendels rose in the morning, said their prayers, snatched up their canes, and issued forth again, in the eternal, imbecilic quest for the accidental windfall, for the leavings and scrapings of transactions. And what is most mysterious about the Menachem Mendels is that they did not become stark, raving lunatics, they did not become criminals, they did not even become neurotics. Menachem Mendels are not exclusively Jewish, of course; but the Jewish quota of Menachem Mendels has been altogether too high, and the tragedy of their lives has not received the sympa-thetic attention which is its due. Some day an analyst of the evils of capitalism will turn for a moment from the dark saga of the exploited toilers and find a word to spare for the wretched Menachem Mendels of the world.

CHAPTER XXVII

The Open World

❀

S HOLOM ALEICHEM's picture of Russian Jewry is in a sense one-sided; not because he omitted to treat of certain areas which remain in shadow, but because his genius kindled most naturally in contact with the old tradition. He is irresistibly charming and supremely compassionate among the Tevyehs and Menachem Mendels, in Kasrielevky and Mazeppavka. This son of a middle-class family, who married into Jewish landed gentry, who had a modern education as well as a thoroughly traditional Jewish one, and was all marked out for complete assimilation, was drawn nostalgically to the Yiddish-speaking poor. But the Yiddish-speaking poor, while numerically the largest section of Russian Jewry, and spiritually its most cohesive and most consistent element, were by no means all of Russian Jewry. There was a powerful middle class in the larger cities; there was a movement into the open world in days when Kasrielevky still dreamed its dream of the Middle Ages. Even when the great flood of Westernization set in, round the eighties and nineties, there were already considerable numbers of Jewish pioneers, doctors, lawyers, dentists, engineers, journalists, mathematicians, merchants, revolutionaries, who formed a vital part of awakening Russia. There were mighty Jewish families with financial and industrial interests throughout the Empire, the Guinzburgs, the Poliakovs, the Wissotzkys, which ranked, financially, with the Rothschilds of western Europe.

But this section of Jewry Sholom Aleichem treated peripherally, even when he devoted special treatises to it. It was not his spiritual stamping-ground. You feel him, there, an uncomfortable giant, a genius reduced to immense talent.

He might have done better to follow his instinct completely. After all, novels about the European middle class, whether Russian or Russian Jewish, or English or American, are plentiful enough. So are novels about revolutionaries. But novels and stories which reproduce a distinct and exotic civilization which is embedded in an alien and uncomprehending world are rarities.

Two novels of Sholom Aleichem devoted to " the open world " of Jewry represent the payment of his debt to " completeness." He wrote the first, *Sender Blank,* at the age of twenty-eight. It is a bitter study in egotism. Sender Blank, a well-to-do Jew, a parvenu, who has worked his way up from small-time usury to big business, lies dying; and his family is assembled for the event. In the two days between his resignation to death — the Burial Brotherhood is in fact already sent for — and his inconsiderate recovery, we are treated to as unsavoury an exposition of human meanness, greed, callousness, and snobbery as ever darkened the pages of Balzac. It is, in fact, of Balzac that this young writer, Sholom Aleichem in 1887, reminds us: there is the same relentless analysis of the

springs of human selfishness; the same vividness of por-
trayal; the same aloofness; the same swiftness of delineation.

A Jewish Hebrew teacher of Kasrielevky, day-dreaming, said that if he had Rothschild's money, the first thing
he would do would be to whitewash his Hebrew school.
He was undoubtedly the brother of the mendicant who
said that if *he* had Rothschild's money, he would be
richer than Rothschild, because he could still go begging. Very far from this subworld of the tiny folk is the
world of Sender Blank. Here we meet with fortunes and
inheritances in the hundreds of thousands of roubles;
with heavy speculation in wheat and coal; with large industrial enterprises: not, of course, in the class of the
Poliakovs and Guinzburgs, but definitely of the provincial moneyed aristocracy.

In this bleak and ruthless exposé of personal types and
a type of life, we no longer find the cultural setting
which imparted a certain warmth, or at least human ac-
ceptability, to the rich men of old Kasrielevky. These
sons and daughters, these sons-in-law and daughters-in-
law, are not susceptible to the spiritual pressure of a tradition. We feel that a Sholom Ber of Teplik could be
reached by a moral force, that his conversion in the
fields, on the day when he marched with the convoy to
Heissin, is possible; but a Sender Blank, gross, cunning,
fleshy, caught in the money-stampede of the bourgeoisie,
is irretrievable; nor have his sons and daughters (with
one exception, who is introduced merely as a foil) any
roots in moral and cultural folkways through which they
could be nourished humanly. This is " economic man,"
the essentially characterless internationalized type. The
fragments of Jewish lore strewn here and there among

their lives are irrelevant to their essential nature.

Are these people real? Yes, they are real, but not representative; and they do not serve a true artistic purpose. Sholom Aleichem was not a great hater, like Swift or Voltaire. Instead of infecting his reader with indignation, he moves him, in such a novel as *Sender Blank*, to uneasiness and disgust. For either one must write with magnificent destructiveness, in the vein of *Gulliver's Travels*, or of *Candide*, or else choose representative material. *Sender Blank* is middle-class gone mad; he is therefore real, but pathological, and like many young writers Sholom Aleichem fell into the error (in his case only temporary) of confusing the novel with the social casebook. Besides, it is an understatement to say that he was not a great hater; he could not hate at all. He could be unhappy, but he could not hate. Typical of the spirit of Sholom Aleichem is, for instance, his report of a conversation with a Jew which takes place on the boat carrying both of them to America. Says the immigrant to Sholom Aleichem (this was in the early days of the First World War) : " What we Jews of the village of Yanov went through under the Poles, and then afterwards under the Russians, when they chased out the Germans, can't be described. Because you know how it is with Ivan: wherever he appears, there has to be a pogrom against the Jews! It's not that he's a bad fellow, this Ivan of ours. On the contrary, he's a very decent sort. *It's just his damn bad luck!* "

When a man has the gift of seeing human misbehaviour under this double aspect of pity and irony, he wrongs himself in yielding to the impulse of hatred. He should leave that to the adepts. And for the right orchestral accompaniment to his own melodic manner,

Sholom Aleichem had to have the world of Yiddish humour — that is, the world of Yiddish tradition.

That is why, even when he writes affectionately and
affirmatively, but outside his intimate world, he misses
fire again, despite his superb craftsmanship.

The twenty-fourth volume of Sholom Aleichem's collected works is a novel of the 1904 revolution; not as seen
by outsiders — that is, through a narrow window of Kasrielevky — but chiefly as lived by the participants, young
Jews and Jewesses in the current of modern thought.
Certainly the narrative holds our interest; certainly the
people in it are three-dimensional; and very few writers
have surpassed Sholom Aleichem in re-creating that atmosphere of radiant hope and idealism which preceded
the granting of the 1905 Constitution, or the ghastly psychological let-down which followed the treacherous retraction. This much conceded as a matter of honesty, we
must add that the intellectual statement of the struggles,
the expositions of principle, the descriptions of conspiratorial technique and secret organization, have been done
as well by others. It may be that Sholom Aleichem was
impelled by a sense of duty to add the Jewish record to
the general record, to set down, even if it was repetitious
and superfluous from the general point of view, the Jewish contribution to the revolution; and it may be that
this was a necessary chore (although, to be sure, the Jewish role in the Russian Revolution has probably been exaggerated in the Western world). But Masha Bashkevich
and Tamara Shostepal and Sasha Safranovich and the
other young revolutionaries tell us nothing that we cannot learn from the Russian novels. Even the discussions
between Sasha (who is none the less a revolutionary because his revolution is within Jewish life, and directed

toward Zionism) and Tamara, who is absorbed entirely by the Russian struggle, are familiar and stereotyped: Sasha thinks of Jewish freedom and Jewish regeneration; Tamara thinks of world freedom as the automatic guarantee of Jewish freedom. Tamara cannot understand how Sasha can focus his attention on the particular problem of a handful of human beings — the Jews — when a hundred million Russians are crying: " Bread and freedom! " Sasha cannot understand how Tamara can ignore the double problem of the Jew, who suffers everything that the Russian masses suffer plus the additional burden of his Jewishness. Forty years have passed since those arguments were recorded by Sholom Aleichem; but they are staples in American Jewish life today.

" Monsieur Safranovich," asks Tamara, " which weighs more heavily on you, the general suffering of humanity or the particular suffering of the Jews? "

And Sasha answers:

" There is no standard by which to measure. It's just as if you were to ask a doctor: Which hurts more, having a finger cut off your hand or having a toe cut off your foot. My only answer is it's bad to have a finger cut off, and it's twice as bad to have both a finger and a toe cut off. And if you want to know, I'll tell you a secret. I suffer more from my Jewish burden than from my general human burden. Because on top of the general pain there's a special torment and misery and heart-ache: why should we Jews be the persecuted of the persecuted, the slaves of slaves? "

To which the answer comes that the complaint is a false one: it is not the Russian masses who enslave the Jews, it is the bureaucracy; which was the standard answer in those days — as it is for some, today, the standard

263

answer to the Nazi persecutions of the Jews. We know by now that the problem is not so simple. There *is* a folk anti-Semitism, as well as a bureaucratic exploitation of anti-Semitism. In any case, why should Sholom Aleichem take time out from his unique specialty to contribute nothing new to these dialectics?

One of the most charming passages in this book — *The Storm* — is the description of the little revolutionary commune, consisting entirely of Jews, which has its living-quarters in the apartment of the printer and poet Malkin. We are given a list of the members:

Meyer Friedel, twenty-two years of age, a member of the *Bund,* the Jewish revolutionary labour organization; he has failed in three Gymnasiums, because he regards mathematics as a bourgeois study; he takes courses at the St. Petersburg University; he has " rights of residence " by virtue of his " employment " as a linotyper.

Chaim Braudo, thirty-four. He was once a Hebrew teacher, but studied Russian by himself. A passionate anti-nationalist and anti-Zionist, but in secret reads the Hebrew periodicals. He is entered on the records as a tailor. Probably consumptive.

Moses Berezniak (real name Moses Fidler), about forty; escaped from Siberia. Graduated from two universities. Sought by the police. A giant of a man, hot-tempered. Makes a living by singing in a Sunday choir. Does not look Jewish.

Ethel Veirauch, twenty-four. Originally of Bobruisk. Entered on the records as a wig-maker. Finished Gymnasium; now studying dentistry.

Eva Wohl, twenty-one. Comes of a distinguished family, her father boasting that he is descended from Samuel Wohl, the famous Jewish King of Poland. Jilted a rich suitor. Took courses in massage. Entered in the records as a milliner. A passionate revolutionary.

Then there were Malkin, the landlord, his wife, and the baby — the last of whom is killed, in the course of the story, in the famous and infamous Gapon affair in St. Petersburg.

It is a mixture of Murger and Tolstoy, of bohemia and the barricades. It is hard to believe, reading this description, written in 1907, that from such groups was forged the steely leadership of the Russian Revolution.

When Sholom Aleichem wrote *The Storm,* in 1907, the tide of revolution had receded, and it seemed as though reaction was firmly enthroned for decades to come. Many young Jews gave up hope and turned from revolution in Russian life to revolution in Jewish life: the first large stream of Russian-Jewish workers, youngsters then, today the labour-leaders in the Jewish homeland, turned Zionist and made their way to Palestine. The westward tide of emigration set in with renewed force. *The Storm,* then, is a book of disillusionment. It closes with a picture of disintegrating revolutionary forces, and a happy reconciliation of persons, with hints of marriage between Sasha and Tamara. Basha the revolutionary is dead. Hundreds like her have been killed in the Russian prisons or have committed suicide. There is no hint in Sholom Aleichem of the activities of certain obscure individuals by the names of Nikolai Lenin, Leon Trotsky, Josef Stalin; or of a periodical called *Iskra.* Sholom Aleichem died, in America, in 1916; neither he nor anyone else outside the élite corps of revolutionaries believed that the day was at hand. Certainly he did not foresee that in a Russia reborn in revolution he would be one of the best-loved writers.

There was a lower Jewish middle class in Russia which was neither of the " open world " nor yet of the closed world of Kasrielevky. It was a Yiddish-speaking class, still bound to the tradition, but already in contact with provincial modernity. The curious position which these Jews occupied may best be described as that of immigrants in the land of their birth. They spoke the language poorly; they were second-class citizens; their children were drifting away from them; and their spiritual life was rooted in a world which, though it had been on Russian soil for centuries, was understood by none but themselves.

These men and women were the children of Kasrielevky, already middle-aged; the grandchildren were destined for revolution, or America, or Palestine. They were what I have called Kasrielevky in transition; and among them Sholom Aleichem is at home again, as he was in old Kasrielevky.

By this time the railroad ran through Bohopolie, Heissin, Teplik, Nemirov, Chashchevatte, and a dozen other forlorn places. Perhaps it is an exaggeration to say " ran." There was one train a day, and the Jews, who had refused to believe in trains, were quick to make fun of the one they got. They called it " the Loafer." And since it sauntered through the heart of the Pale, it was always packed with Jews: commercial travellers (travelling salesmen, to us Americans), merchants, pleasure-seekers — Jews with beards, Jews in gaberdines, Jews who carried their prayer-shawl and phylacteries with them, and were not ashamed to put them on for morning prayers, Jews who spoke a voluble Yiddish, and felt at home. Yes, they felt at home, in spite of repressions and pogroms, as the villagers who live in the shadow of Vesuvius feel at home; for pogroms were a natural phenomenon, a " God-thing," and on the whole it is doubtful whether throughout the year more Jews were killed or crippled in pogroms, pro rata, than Americans by automobiles.

" The Loafer " was fullest in the autumn time, round the high holy days, when Jews made journeys to their native towns and villages to visit " the graves of the fathers." You could always tell who was " going " and who was " coming ": those who were going still looked fresh, those who were returning were red-eyed with weeping. And if you travelled a few days on " the Loafer," during the penitential season or at any other time, you could get a fair picture of the life of this middle class.

For Jews are a talkative lot; and when Sholom Aleichem uses the device of " the story told on a train," it is not as artificial as among English or American writers. A whole volume consists of these " railroad stories," and it is one of the warmest and most illuminating of his works.

Here the revolution, the May Laws, the " privilege of residence," the opening up of Jewry to modernity, are seen half from the inside, half from the outside. The talkers are not moderns, they are not revolutionaries; but neither are they Reb Melechs or Reb Yozifels. Their children learn Russian. The Gymnasium is no longer anathema. On the contrary, everyone tries to get his son in, and many are the stories told concerning the bribes, the dodges, the use of influence (" protektzie " — our American equivalent is " pull ") connected with getting a bright boy into a Gymnasium, or keeping him out of the army. For these Jews, without being revolutionaries, made use of a revolutionary technique against a government they despised. It was a matter of principle with them not to strengthen the rule of the Romanovs if they could help it.

And stories are told, too, of children lost in or to the revolution; if the Jews fell short of their quota for the army, they " went over the top " in their quota for the revolution. One father gave a daughter to Artzibasheff: perhaps even some Americans will remember the furore which *Sanine* created at the beginning of this century, and the wave of suicides which it set in motion among the Russian intelligentsia. One gave a son to the revolution proper; he tells of it neither with pride nor with shame. A third describes the fantastic efforts he made to get his gifted son into a Gymnasium, how he uprooted himself from his native town, how he succeeded, at infinite cost, in finding a school which would take the boy — only to have the boy join, shortly after his admission, in a political strike against the principal.

But something else has come into transitional Kasrielevky: a type of worldliness alien to the old Kasrielevky. Card-playing has become a popular pastime: in certain sections of Jewry it has become a disease, as we shall see further on. There are cardsharps on the trains. There are con men. There are baggage-snatchers. This too is of the new world. But as yet " the Loafer " is well freighted with the ancient culture. You will not be stared at if you quote a verse from the Talmud, or an opinion of the Rambam (Maimonides). You need not hesitate to send round to other cars for an extra man or two to make up the congregational quorum of ten, in case you have to say the afternoon prayer with a *Kaddish* in memory of a parent or child. Or if you happen to have forgotten your prayer-shawl and phylacteries at home, it is perfectly proper to ask a random neighbour for the loan of his. And if he too has forgotten those necessary appurtenances, or is only making a journey of a few hours, you apply to a third man. Perhaps one of the cardsharps will oblige, and perhaps one of the con men will cap your quotation from the Rambam with one from Rashi.

CHAPTER XXVIII

Fringe Types

❀

HEN games become an obsession, when they are played not for relaxation but under the pressure of a compulsion neurosis, we know that we are in the presence of a disintegrating society or group. There was a section of middle-class Jewry in Sholom Aleichem's world — the later world, that is — which was pathologically addicted to card-playing; and where card-playing takes on the form of a disease, there emerges the social fringe type of the cardsharp and the professional gambler.

Sholom Aleichem lived during the period which saw the disease pass from the " outside world " of Sender Blank's children to the " inside world " of the children of Kasrielevky.

" Today," he wrote in 1912, " cards are an everyday matter. In the old days, if you remember, we used to play cards once a year — during the Maccabee festival of Channukah. Of course, if you want to be absolutely truthful, we did use to play at other times too. But how? And where? In absolute secrecy, behind locked doors! "

Children in the *cheder* used to play cards when the Rebbi was called away. Not real cards — where were they to lay hands on a pack of real cards? Just pieces of paper marked like cards. Sometimes the young " kept " sons-in-law would sneak into the women's section of the synagogue during a week-day — who would look for them there? — and snatch a hot little session of *préférence, okke,* or sixty-six. Particularly sixty-six, which became in time a Jewish game, as pinochle is today in America. But cards were a folly, a sin, and a device of the heathen.

Sholom Aleichem tells how, one day, Ribah Leah, the wife of one of the trustees, came running out from the women's section of the synagogue, pale as death, and screaming: " Help! Help! We're lost! We're done for! They'll get us! "

A terrified crowd, headed by a few leading householders, including the cantor and the cantor's son-in-law, made for the synagogue. They expected to find there either a dead body hanging from a rope, or a planted Christian child, or some other forerunner of calamity — those were the pogrom days. Herself more dead than alive, Ribah Leah led the multitude up into the women's gallery, pointed to her lectern, and said, before she fainted away: " In there! "

They looked " in there " and saw a most sinister object: not, indeed, a severed limb, or a blood-stain, but a picture of a black priest; or rather of two black priests, each upside down to the other, and marked by two black and bulbous crosses. The *Rav* looked, the cantor looked, the *Shochet* looked — but they did not dare to touch it. Finally Velvel Ramshevich, the cantor's son-in-law, looked, and cried out joyously:

" Why it's nothing! It's a joke! It's a King of Clubs! "

" What do you mean a King of Clubs? "

" It's a card. You know — cards that you play with! "

271

The *Shochet* fastened his gaze on Velvel Ramshevich and asked:

" If that's a card, of the cards you play with, what's it doing here, in the women's gallery? That's question number one. And secondly, how do you, the cantor's son-in-law, come to know what a card is, so that you can tell at once that this is a — a King of Clubs? "

Poor Velvel had some tall explaining to do; and how he got out of the mess Sholom Aleichem does not tell us, for that is not the point of the incident, which is intended merely to illustrate the innocence of the old Kasrielevkites.

This same Velvel Ramshevich later became the centre of the infection in his particular Kasrielevky. His wife, Chayaleh, the cantor's daughter, threw off the wig which every married woman wore in Kasrielevky and went about in her own hair. Their house was known as " the little Talmud circle." Here a man could get a forbidden book to read, here he could smoke a cigarette on the Sabbath, here he could get a slice of sausage — and not necessarily kosher, either — on a fast-day. But all these little conveniences were come-ons. The house of Velvel and Chayaleh Ramshevich was, to put it quite bluntly, a gambling joint. And not even an honest gambling joint. The Ramsheviches, and Chayaleh with the red hair and black teeth even more than Velvel, were altogether too consistently lucky. It came to such a pass that young husbands gambled away their wives' dowries, jewelry, and even plate. The place became a stink in the nostrils of the town, but there was nothing to be done about it.

It was open house day and night. Velvel and Chayaleh took turns sleeping and playing. The beds were never made, meals were never cooked. On the sideboard there was always a supply of cold cuts and bread. You came when you wanted, you left when you had to. It was the real thing.

Except in one respect: old Kasrielevky was dying in these people, but it was not dead. On Channukah the regulation candles were lit, one on the first night, two on the second, up to the eighth, and the benediction uttered; not by Velvel or Chayaleh, but by one of the guests. Velvel and Chayaleh were broad-minded: if you wanted to say your evening prayers, or if you had sat through an all night session and wanted to put on shawl and phylacteries for the morning prayers, it was perfectly all right with them. Most of the frequenters of the house came from pious homes and had been brought up in the ways of God. Cards were cards, *okke* was *okke*, but a Jew was a Jew.

The habits of childhood were still strong here; the understanding, if not the practice, of the Jewish virtues still prevailed. No poor man was turned away from the door; no Jewish appeal went unheeded. You had, then, a queer mixture of vitality and decay in this house of the Ramsheviches. What was destroying Jewish life was not an inherent failure of cultural strength, but outside circumstance: the majority of the gamblers were those unemployed, untrained, unplaced "kept" sons-in-laws, who might be described as Menachem Mendels in the making.

There was something touching in the struggle which went on in these people between corruption and tradition. They knew what was worthy of respect, but they were incapable of living up to the perception. There came once into the Ramshevich house — this was in the

midst of a Channukah when, card-playing being permitted even by tradition, the living-room was so crowded
that the players sat at table in shifts — there came once
into the house two queer old figures out of the Jewish
past, two bearded wanderers such as were already becoming rare even in those days. Beggars? No, not exactly.
Collectors, rather. " Grandsons of the Baal Shem Tov,"
the founder of Chassidism, who were travelling through
the cities of the Jewish Diaspora raising funds for the
Talmudical colleges of the Holy Land.

" Grandsons of the Baal Shem " were at one time ex-
traordinarily numerous, and therefore the term should
not be taken literally. Grandsons of the first disciples of
the Baal Shem, great-grandsons of the Baal Shem himself, and pious old Chassidim with a Chassidic family
background — any of these might be represented as
" Grandsons of the Baal Shem." It was, in fact, a loose
term, and nobody dreamed of examining the genealogy
of a claimant to the title.

It may be safely said that two old men like these would
never have been admitted to the house of any of the sons
or daughters of a Sender Blank; and if they had managed to get in, they would have been turned out in short
order. Not so in the house of the Ramsheviches. They
were permitted to sit down — though not at a table —
and asked the object of their visit; they looked at the
warm Channukah candles, then at the players, and explained themselves in old-fashioned Yiddish, with many
quotations from the sages, and asked humbly for contributions. There was not a single person in the room
who either laughed or refused: cards are cards, *okke* is
okke, but a Talmudical college in Palestine is still —
well — it is still something.

So far the story is rather touching; what follows is distinctly less than edifying. The two old wanderers accepted the donations — here a rouble, there a half rouble — unfolded a huge handkerchief containing a mass of silver coins, and remained seated. The glimpse of that heap of coins had an electrifying effect on the Ramsheviches and their clientele. Meaningful glances were exchanged. If someone — the idea was really absurd, but the gambling habit demoralizes judgment as well as decency — if someone could draw the old fellows into a game — it was, after all, Channukah — if they could be persuaded, for the fun of it, to take a hand — if —

Very slowly, in the most persuasive detail, Sholom Aleichem describes the progress of the unpleasant incident. It need hardly be added that the Grandsons of the Baal Shem were stripped to all but the last rouble; and that, just when they were about to be edged out of the game, the luck turned, and by morning every rouble in the pocketbooks of the Ramsheviches and their guests had been deposited in the huge handkerchief of the wanderers. Nor need it be added that the wanderers turned out to be, not Grandsons of the Baal Shem, but a couple of super con men. The real interest of the story lies in its description of manners, and in its introduction of fringe types symptomatic of the state of a certain social stratum.

Sholom Aleichem tells us elsewhere of an experience in the outer circle, among Jewish card-players of the assimilated middle class. This was in the house of the *nouveau riche* Platon Pantalonovich Lokshentopov — probably Peshach Pessi's in his youth — to which Sholom Aleichem was formally invited for " a card party in honour of Channukah." Platon Pantalonovich was a one-day-a-year Jew, a Yom Kippur Jew. Yiddish had been banished from his house, not because he was ignorant of the language, but because it might offend the ears of the French *gouvernante*. Beside his vestigial superstitious Yom Kippur habit, Platon Pantalonovich had retained a weakness for Jewish dishes. His special contempt was for the Zionists, with their modern insistence on Jewish values.

" Zionists! " he would snort. " Don't talk to me about them. I can't stand the sight of them. And don't think it's because I dislike Jews. On the contrary, I honour a Jew — though between you and me, you know what they're like. Still, my house is Jewish, I want you to know. On the Passover we have *matzos,* on Booths we have *pirozhkes* with honey, on Purim we have *hamentasches,* yes, sir, and even *teiglach,* and poppyseed cakes, and all those good things."

And on Channukah he had a card party. Not that he and his circle were short of card parties at any other time of the year, but Channukah added zest to the games. But why?

This was what Sholom Aleichem was asking himself when he entered the house. And he addressed himself first to Platon Pantalonovich.

" Please tell me, my dear Platon Pantalonovich, what made you have a card party ' in honour of Channukah '? "

" Ask me another," answered the host, guiding his guest toward one of the tables, and disappeared.

Sholom Aleichem turned next to the hostess, Pantomina Pantelemonovna Lokshentopov, a solid lady shimmering in silk and coruscating with precious stones.

" Do tell me, dear lady, what *is* Channukah? "

" Isn't it a sort of holiday or something? Yes, I'm sure it is. Oh, excuse me. Let me introduce you to — "

It was a cousin of hers, Fanfaron Faaronovich Yom-tovson, who, curiously, was puzzled by the same question as Sholom Aleichem, but on different grounds. He really wanted to know what on earth this Channukah, in honour of which he had been invited, could be.

" Perfectly astonishing," he complained to Sholom Aleichem. " I'm just dying to know what sort of holiday this Channukah is, and I've been asking up and down the room — nobody knows."

" Well, frankly," replied Sholom Aleichem, " I'm quite a bit astonished that a man with the name of Yom-tovson shouldn't know the answer himself."

" Are you, indeed? " retorted Fanfaron Faaronovich. " I'll bet you my head that among the fifty or sixty Jews here, you won't find one who can give it to you."

" Man! What would I be doing with your head? I'll bet you twenty-five roubles instead."

So they went from table to table, inserting the question wherever they could, and Yomtovson described each person before they approached him. " Channukah? Channukah? " answered the first. " Pass! " " Channu-kah? " answered the second. " One spade! " " I know," said a third. " Channukah is a festival when you play cards." " And eat pancakes dipped in goose-fat," added another. A fifth begged Sholom Aleichem to visit him at the hotel, he might be able to tell him; just now he was busy. And so from end to end of the room. It was Sholom Aleichem who lost the bet.

The demoralized card-playing classes of Jewry — I am speaking of the genuinely diseased element, for such it was, and not of occasional players — represented Jewry in

decay. From among them came neither the active bourgeois liberal leadership, nor the revolutionary groups,
nor the creative Zionist and Jewish nationalist leaven.

The description of the " What is Channukah? " experience of Sholom Aleichem is something of a digression
here, apropos of card-playing. Platon Pantalonovich and
his guest were not fringe types; they were a class. But
the Ramsheviches and, still more, the nameless " Grandsons of the Baal Shem " were genuine fringe types.

We are introduced to another fringe type in *The
Storm* — a product of social conflicts and shifting foundations, a symbol of a general process of decay — Yashka
Vorona, the spy and stool-pigeon. His passport bears the
name Yakov Vladimirovich Voronin. His original name
was Yenkel Voroner — that is, Yenkel of Voronne, a
little town in Lithuania. Here is a brief biography of him:

" His father was a *melammed*, a Hebrew teacher; his
mother a baker. Till the age of five he was undernourished. At five he found employment carrying lunches to
the better-off children in *cheder*, earned a groschen now
and again, and bought *beigels* with it from his mother.
On Purim he delivered *shalachmonus*. Went barefoot in
the summers, till the age of thirteen. Refused to put on
phylacteries after his *bar mitzvah*. Was beaten by his
father; had a hand broken. Ran away to Grodno. Slept
in the open. Became acquainted with a lunatic, who
taught him Russian and mathematics. Stole a volume of
the Talmud from the synagogue, pawned it to buy half
a loaf of bread. Ran away to the Talmudical College of
Mir. Pretended to be very pious, prayed and studied from
morning till night. Ate ' days.' Stole pieces of bread from
the tables of his hosts. Was caught one Saturday smoking
in the toilet. Was beaten. Ran away to Byalystok. Be-

came a teacher. Was paid a gulden (half a rouble) a week for two hours' work a day. Starved. Became engaged to a girl who was stone-deaf. Got fifty roubles dowry and bought himself a pair of boots (the first new pair of boots in his life!). Ran away to Vilna. Took his examinations there, passed the sixth class. Became acquainted with Bundist revolutionaries. Wrote several Yiddish dramas. Took them to a publisher who offered to buy them by weight, two gulden a pound. Tore up the dramas, wrote a satire on publishers. Showed it to his friends, who were tremendously impressed. Sent it to a Yiddish periodical, which neither answered nor sent back the satire. Fell in love with a girl. Was shown the door. Tried to drown himself in the Vileika. Received word that his father was dead, his mother starving. Vowed to study seriously and become a lawyer. Entered the employ of a druggist. Worked two years. Sent his mother a rouble a week, regularly; two roubles for every festival. The druggist, prompted by his wife, accused him of handing out perfumes free of charge to poor girls. Ran away to St. Petersburg. Wanted to study medicine. Starved. Tried to get an interview with Baron Guinzburg. Stood several hours in the snow. Attracted the attention of the police. Was arrested. Threatened with being sent under convoy to Grodno. Baptized. Lost all hope of help from Baron Guinzburg. Could not send money to his mother. Managed to get employment in the arsenal. Attended lectures at the university. Hung around at meetings. Became acquainted with students and workers. Concealed his apostasy. Was implicated in an affair of stolen dynamite. Almost sent to Siberia. Gave way to pressure and betrayed two of his comrades. Was released. Thought of hanging himself. Received an invitation to police headquarters, was offered the job of spy. Overjoyed to receive his first hundred roubles. Fell in love with a young gentile washerwoman. Married. Had two children by her. Serves his masters faithfully. Officialdom completely satisfied with him. Has his own house now. Receives regular promotion. Suspected by some workers, was threatened with death. Was given the honour of reporting personally before a high official. Sent on a delicate mission to Warsaw. Fulfilled it satisfactorily. Received a handsome bonus, and right of permanent residence in Petersburg. Would be quite content if the workers didn't put the fear of God in him."

This was the man who was responsible for the arrest and the death of Masha Bashkevich.

Another fringe type to whom Sholom Aleichem introduces us is " Auntie Dobrich," the seventy-year-old sister of Sender Blank, the only creature in the household who has a genuine attachment to the " dying " man. She is " in the household " only for the occasion; she does not belong in the rich establishment of her brother. The butt of the younger generation, even in those days of impending death, she answers everyone patiently and sweetly. " It is hard to understand," says Sholom Aleichem " the simplicity and gentleness of this old woman. Is she really a good soul? Or is there something behind it? ' Auntie Dobrish ' had buried three husbands by the time she was fifty, and is known, therefore, according to our tradition, as a ' killer.' She has no children."

He continues: " It seems she foresaw that in her old age she would be left utterly alone in the world. So she managed to save up a nest-egg of a few hundred roubles. She also has a little house of her own and a grocery store. Out there in the village the Jews all call her ' Auntie

Dobrish ' and the gentiles ' the Dobrukha.' Besides selling groceries she acts as a ' healer.' Sells all sorts of herbs.
She is a specialist in exorcizing the evil eye, toothache,
and demons. She also makes wax figures, tells fortunes
from cards. Everyone is a little afraid of her, and the
Christians hold her in honour. Summer mornings she
goes out before sunrise to collect her herbs by the light
of the moon, whispering charms as she does so. Certain
ugly stories are told about ' Auntie Dobrish ' in the village, and the police keep an eye on her."

Other strange, almost unnatural figures flit in and out
of Sholom Aleichem's world; some of them are given in
detail, others are mentioned in passing. They occur
mostly in the transitional period. But one of his most
fascinating peripheral characters belongs within the very
heart of his Kasrielevky world — and that is Stempenyu
the musician, to whom he has devoted an entire novel.

In another setting Stempenyu, the artist, the philan-
derer, the bohemian, is familiar enough in literature.
Against the background of the exclusively Kasrielevkite
townlets and communities which knew him and delighted in him he is not a conventionally unconventional
figure but an oddity and an instructive phenomenon.

Sholom Aleichem was twenty-nine years old when he
wrote this novel, in 1888. It opens with a long and affectionate dedication to " My gentle-hearted Granddad,
Mendelle the Bookseller," concerning whom something
must be said here in the development of our general subject. " Mendelle " (the intimate form of the name Mendel) was the pen-name chosen for himself as a Yiddish
writer by Sholom Jacob Abramovich, who, when he was
barely in his middle age, was already known as the
" Granddaddy." He was the first of the literary masters

of the Haskalah to turn to Yiddish, the language of the poor masses, as his medium. It will be remembered that the Haskalah, or Enlightenment — the Jewish-Russian renaissance of the late 1800's — despised Yiddish and made use only of Hebrew, which was read by the educated middle class. Until Mendelle's time Yiddish had been left to obscure, ungifted scribblers, and to the writers of the ill-printed pamphlets of Chassidic stories. Yiddish was for women, and particularly for servant girls. There was in wide use a Yiddish translation of the Pentateuch prepared for pious women who had no access to the original Hebrew. A scholar or an intellectual would not stoop to the vernacular, which was known — it is still known, in fact — as " jargon," a description which has passed into popular usage even among the masses. " Mendelle the Bookseller " wrote originally in Hebrew; and Sholom Aleichem himself thought of Hebrew as his medium when in his earliest years he entertained vague notions of a literary career. It was Mendelle's example, set on a high level, which initiated the age of Yiddish literature; and it is possible that we have here an echo of the Russian slogan of those years: " Go to the masses! " This explains why, at the age of fifty, Abramovich was already known as the Granddaddy.

In his introduction to *Stempenyu* Sholom Aleichem quotes a letter he had received some time before from Mendelle:

" I would advise you against writing romantic novels, since your spirit and *genre* belong to a very different field; besides, if there is such a thing as the romantic in the life of our people, it is something other than what is called by that name among other peoples."

Sholom Aleichem comments: " Your words sank deep

into my heart, and I began to understand to what extent a Jewish romantic novel must differ from the general type, for Jewish life, and the setting in which the Jew experiences his love, are totally different from the life and setting of other peoples. Apart from which the Jewish people has its own specific character, its own forms and habits. . . ."

Neither Mendelle nor Sholom Aleichem go into the details of what was for them an instinctive grasp of the realities. We, the outsiders, must recall, however, that love among the Jews was not a romance and a passion, but a deep, earnest, and steadfast emotional accompaniment of life's practicalities. Love for its own sake, unharnessed to the solemn business of Judaism, was not simply a sin; it was a revolting frivolity. Jews were too busy having children to bother with sex. The home, with its function as a religious-cultural centre, was the foundation of Jewish survival. It was more than an economic product, though it was that among the Jews as it was everywhere else; it was the stage upon which Jews and Judaism lived themselves out. This is not the kind of folk-setting which makes for romantic love; it makes for something more abiding, and perhaps even more passionate.

Another circumstance turned Stempenyu into an oddity rather than into a familiar variant. Bohemianism was unknown to the Jews. There were no bohemian groups. There were no *Quartiers Latins,* no Grub Streets, no Greenwich Villages. There were no actors, painters, adventurers, professional writers or writers by career, no loose ends in the social web. Above all, there was no popular literature of the *affaire amoureuse.*

Stempenyu was a village fiddler rather than what we

call magniloquently an " artist." Granted that he was unusually gifted, and that he, with his orchestra, gave out
something more than the regulation merry din which
was a necessary accompaniment of weddings, betrothals,
and other joyous occasions. But there was no one to recognize that he had " the privileges of genius." Had he
broken away from the Jewish world and established himself among the gentiles, he would have acquired another
status. For one reason or another, perhaps accident, perhaps because he himself felt at home only among Jews,
perhaps because he was just not good enough to make
a furore among strangers, he remained in the setting of
his birth. His father had been a Jewish musician; so had
his grandfather. It may also be that he had acquired a
peculiar style, perfect in itself, which was attuned only
to the ears of his Jews. In any case, Stempenyu was above
all a wedding and betrothal musician. His father had
been not only a musician but a *badchan* — a wedding
jester, a rhymester and buffoon — as well. Stempenyu
was therefore a product of family and Jewish tradition.

It is doubtful whether any of his love-affairs ever cul-
minated in adultery. Always it was a flirtation with marriage as its presumable end. He led on, and jilted, one
young woman after another; but that is not the same
thing as an *" affaire."* When he fell desperately in love
with Rachel, the beautiful young wife of a " kept " son-
in-law, he was already a married man, for he had played
with one young woman too many and had tangled himself in a net from which there was no escape. What could
be the issue of such an involvement, even if Rachel was
swept off her feet? Elopement meant something else for
these Jews than for gentiles in a great world of their own.
It meant breaking with a civilization, the only civiliza-

tion they had known or could adjust themselves to. There was no " broad-minded " circle of acquaintances for them to flee to, no group to take them up. The Malkin groups in St. Petersburg were not yet in existence. They could, of course, have carried on a furtive relationship — but not for long. The little town in which Rachel lived was not the place for assignations. Besides, she did not think of love as anything but an accompaniment to an earnest common enterprise in life.

Stempenyu is significant as a freak — made so by the impossibility of his surroundings rather than by the singularity of his temperament. Rachel, who almost yielded to him, fled from him at the last moment, to discover that the only conceivable happiness for her was with her young husband. In the transitional world of the early twentieth century it might have ended differently, though whether Rachel and Stempenyu would have been " happy " — I place the word in quotes because it has a special connotation in such situations — is a question (not a very interesting one, to be sure) which has been discussed interminably in stories of this kind. For by the beginning of the early twentieth century the web had been broken; exit was possible; contacts had been established; new ideas had prepared young Jews for transition to another civilization. But Sholom Aleichem was right in choosing this ending for the story. He would have had to make a freak of Rachel, the good, the simple, the beautiful, to choose any other.

CHAPTER XXIX

The Children's World

❀

W̲ E are about through with the grown-up people of Sholom Aleichem's world, with old Kasrielevky and new Kasrielevky, their saints and sinners and snobs and *schlimihls,* their pietists and free-thinkers, their workers and pedlars and merchants and revolutionaries; and now, for complete coverage, we should have to start all over again. For we have been by-passing another world of his, probably his dearer and more intimate world, that of the children. Sholom Aleichem practically began his career with a child's story, *The Penknife,* perhaps his best, certainly his most famous; and toward the end, a middle-aged and ailing exile in America, he was writing about his own childhood, and about Mottel, the cantor's little boy. Throughout his thirty years of creation he kept reverting, in the midst of his preoccupation with the comedy of adult life, to the much more serious business of children. It was not a side-line with him, an occasional digression and relaxation. It was his first and most abiding love. His childhood never died in him, and much of his humour is only the disconcerting common sense of a child intruding suddenly into the grotesque obsessions of its elders.

The child world of Sholom Aleichem is as peculiarly itself, as true to the quality of a special civilization, as his adult world. We can speak interchangeably about his children's stories and about the realities of the old Russian-Jewish life just as we did in the case of his adult studies. It does not matter whether he writes for children, or about children, or both — he is always utterly honest. It was thus that children dreamed, suffered, and laughed in old Kasrielevky; these were their problems and escapes; this was how they talked. You will not find here the priggishness of Samuel Smiles or Horatio Alger, or the falsity and sentimentalism of *A Christmas Carol,* or the carefree whimsicality of *Alice in Wonderland,* or the young Samurai self-consciousness of *Stalky and Co.,* or even the pure fantasy of Grimm and Andersen. Something of *Oliver Twist,* yes. But it is *sui generis.*

Sholom Aleichem's child world has in common with his adult world a dolorous note of extrusion and privation. If the fields and forests and hills are not for the grown-ups of old Kasrielevky, they are not for the children, either; but whereas the grown-ups are broken in, and have a relevant prison philosophy, the little ones can only resort to an imitation of an imitation; it is escape within escape, level beneath level of refuge.

Jewish children do not go bird's-nesting, or fishing, or snaring. They do not run about in the woods. They do not cut pan-pipes from reeds. There are no Tom Sawyers and Huckleberry Finns among them. Jewish children learn, at the age of six or seven, that life is real, life is earnest, and a good time is not its goal. A Jewish child must not even learn to whistle (" Don't whistle! You're not a peasant! ") . Over and over again the child hears, in Sholom Aleichem's stories, as he heard in real life:

287

" What? Eight years old and you still want to play around? Are you a heathen? A lad like you should be deep in the Talmud. A lad like you should be studying, not day-dreaming, not skipping about like a goat, as if he hadn't a care in the world! Why, when I was your age I had two Tractates of the Talmud mastered! When I was your age. . . ."

In the account of the rise of modern anti-Semitism in Russia, we came across Fedka and Feitel, a little gentile boy and the little Jewish boy, in the village of Verebivky. They had been separated, as we recall, a whole winter, and when they found each other at last, on the day before Passover, they had a million things to tell.

Feitel, the Jewish boy, boasted that during the winter he had learned the Aleph Bet from beginning to end. Fedka boasted that he had a new whip. Feitel tells how his father took him to town, where he saw the great and wonderful synagogue. Fedka tells how he tried to get at a bird's nest, and couldn't; so he threw stones at it and killed the baby birds.

" Did you *kill* them? " cried Feitel, horrified.

" They were little ones," Fedka excuses himself.

" But *killed* them? "

" They didn't even have feathers; only yellow beaks and fat bellies."

" But *killed* them? "

There is another story, *The Fiddle,* written in the first person, in which the youngster — who is to all intents and purposes Sholom Aleichem himself — makes friends with a certain gentile, Chechek, the local military bandmaster. Chechek invites little Sholom to his cottage outside the town — a cottage with a garden, with trees, with flowers! And Sholom cries out: " It's so open here! So light, so free, so warm! None of the smell and noise of the town! None of the crowding and yelling of the *cheder*. You want to run, jump, sing, shout; you want to throw yourself down on the earth, stick your nose in the grass — but suddenly you remember — all that isn't for you, Jewish children! Not for you the fresh air, and the open world, and the clear sky! "

No, the joy of high animal spirits, the pagan delight in life, the unreflecting pleasure of the instincts, were from earliest childhood denounced as sin. In this sense the children of old Kasrielevky were never children, or only furtively so. And yet they were not robbed of their childhood. We, with our notions of pedagogy, are at a loss to reconcile cause and effect in this picture. The constant repression, the ludicrous emphasis on " learning " and on life's essential solemnity, with children not yet ten years old, should have crippled the spirit; just as the omnipresence of the religious theme should have produced nothing but hypocrites. Yet Sholom Aleichem's child world has its own naturalness. We must only attune ourselves to it. The key lies in the whole civilization of old Kasrielevky. It seems there were strange pedagogic skills in the folk material of Jewish life which overcame the handicaps of parental clumsiness. The forefathers had provided against the stupidity of the fathers. The fact is that the Jewish child learned to build a fantasy life in the spirit of his people. Flight took the form of sublimation, not of rebellion or of imbecility. If the Sabbaths and festivals were the citadels of the grown-ups, they were also the playgrounds of the children. Rebellion came only with the breaking in of modernity. Certainly children chafed under discipline, here as elsewhere; but the castles they fled to were built out of the

substance of their parents' world. To go like a grown-up
to synagogue! To be able to fast through the whole day
on Yom Kippur! To be known as a good student! To
resemble some famous rabbi!

There was, of course, a certain permissible amount of
play, though it was regarded as a concession, not a right.
On Passover you had games of chance with Brazil nuts;
on Channukah you could play cards, or a game resem-
bling "put and take," with little, four-sided spinning
tops, on which were inscribed letters recalling the miracle of the unspent oil in the Temple in the days of the
Maccabees; on the Thirty-third Day of the Omer (*Lag
b'Omer,* between Passover and Pentecost) there was
actually an outing into the fields! On Purim, as we have
seen, there was a play — to be exact, one of two plays, and
perhaps even both: the drama of Esther and *The Sale
of Joseph.*

But it was undoubtedly the vividness and tangibility
of the symbolism of the ritual that sank deep into the
minds of the youngsters. The Passover was a regular,
annual revolutionary experience, with its house-clean-
ing, its rigid change of food, its brilliant *seder* ceremonial
on the first two nights. The building of a booth for
Sukkos was a family enterprise; no youngster, whatever
world he belongs to, fails to be captivated by the putting
up of a house. The citron and the palm branch of the
festival were centres of fantasy. Even the routine ritual
had a powerful appeal to a child's imagination; the
prayer-shawl and phylacteries, the *mezuzzah* hammered
into the lintel of the door, the recurrent miracle of the
Sabbath peace, the blessing of the new moon in the
open air.

Carried by these play-symbols, the intellectual and

spiritual quality of adult life penetrated the souls of the youngsters. In the children's stories of Sholom Aleichem the day-dreams of the little protagonists move among ancient, treasured images; urchins of six and seven, they are already carriers of immemorial traditions! Their fairy tales have to do with the Talmud, Kabbalah, and the Bible. They tell one another about Akibah and Bar Kochba and the rebellion against Hadrian the Wicked. They are familiar with Pharaoh, with Haman, with Og and Magog, with Asmodeus, the favourite demon of King Solomon. They talk of the hundred and twenty-seven provinces of the empire of Ahasuerus, of Egypt, of Kush, of the Tigris and Euphrates. They are at home among witches and magicians, rabbis and popes and great Chassidic wonder-workers. They do not imagine themselves leading armies and slaying giants. They have not been familiarized with such exploits. Instead, they dream of performing miracles by the power of sanctity and learning; a Kabbalistic talisman is their sword, a verse from the Talmud their buckler. They will not venture across uncharted seas on great ships; they will fly across them on the backs of eagles commanded by an incantation. And even when they poke fun at one another, it is in the sing-song of Talmudic study.

Because we are outside that world of theirs, we imagine that there is a queer, gnome-like quality about their minds, even though we recognize in them the freshness of childhood. Sholom Aleichem's childhood friend Shmulik tells him about a buried treasure, going back to the days of Chmelnitzky. Somewhere under the hill above Kasrielevky the great robber and murderer of old had hidden away his blood-stained accumulation of gold and jewels.

" And is it lost for ever? " asks little Sholom, wonder
ingly.

" Silly! Of course not! " answers his seven-year-old
companion. " What do you think God created the Kabbalah for? The masters of the Kabbalah know exactly
what has to be done to discover a lost treasure. There's a
magic verse from the Psalms, which you have to repeat
forty times . . ."

" What verse? "

" If I only knew! But even if I knew it wouldn't be so
easy. Because first of all you have to fast for forty days,
repeating a certain chapter of the Psalms each day; then,
at the end of the forty-first day, when it's dark night, a
little fire will come out to meet you. . . ."

The dreams of all children, everywhere in the world,
glitter with secret treasures, and are haunted by witches,
magicians, and pixies. But elsewhere than in old Kasrielevky little boys associate the uncovering of the treasure with deeds of derring-do, pirates, battles, and storms.
And in old Kasrielevky the children's talk of magic is altogether more serious and more detailed than elsewhere.
It is learned talk; it could compete with the professional
conversation of practising mediæval magicians.

Little Shimik, in love with little Esther, boasts to her,
not of the strength of his good right arm, or of the sword
he will wield, or of the lands he will conquer when he
grows up, but of his knowledge of the secrets of the
Kabbalah:

" Kabbalah," he tells her, seriously, " is a very useful
thing. With Kabbalah I can make myself invisible; I can
see you but you can't see me. Kabbalah can draw wine
out of a stone — as much as you want; or gold out of the
walls of a house. Kabbalah can lift us both up, as high

as the clouds, and higher. . . ." And when little Esther laughs, he says, compassionately: " The trouble is, you don't know Kabbalah." How can she? She is a girl and does not go to *cheder*. The infinite mysteries are closed to her. " With Kabbalah," he continues, " I can fly across the twelve big mountains which shoot fire. When I get to the top of the twelfth mountain I walk seven miles on foot and come to a river. I swim across the river and count seven times seven. Then an old man with a big, long beard appears in front of me and asks me: ' What is your desire? ' And I answer: ' Lead me to the Queen's daughter! . . .' "

Kabbalah and the Ineffable Name of God, which only the elect may utter, for it gives them command of the world, the River Sambattyon, whose fiery waves and glowing stones rest only on the Sabbath, the Lost Ten Tribes who dwell beyond the Sambattyon, transmigrations of souls, Elijah the Prophet in a myriad guises, mighty scholars who perform prodigies of prayer and fasting, Leviathan, who shall be eaten by the saints in paradise, the " guarded wine " which shall be drunk by them, the Master of the Good Name and other wonder-workers, whose greatest miracles were wrought for the frustration of anti-Jewish decrees — these are the staples of childhood dreams in old Kasrielevky. It is a mixture of Oriental fantasies, of awareness of persecution, of religious dedication, and of otherworldliness in the second degree; for these children begin their flights of fancy out of a world which is already fanciful enough.

Religion was as organic and tacit a part of child life as of adult life. Writing in middle age about himself in childhood, Sholom Aleichem recalls, in a letter to a friend, the earnestness of the religious motif. " I remember till this day the sweet taste of the tears which we shed so copiously when our Rebbi, our teacher, used to read to us out of the moralistic books. Afterwards, when we stood at prayer, we would confess our sins and beat our bosoms. For in the midst of all our piety we young-sters were a sinful lot. We used to lie! We used to skip passages in the prayers! We didn't obey our parents! We stole goodies from the cupboard and even money from the charity box! And we had dreadful, wicked, sin-ful thoughts, too — there was an older boy who told us all kinds of obscene things. . . . And after one of our Rebbi's lectures we would weep passionately, we would promise ourselves to be good, to say all the long prayers without skipping a word, to sin no more. . . ."

Just like their parents, these youngsters could not understand how a Jew could be other than pious, or could live outside the framework of the ritual. In *The Pen-knife* there is a German Jew living at the house of the young hero, a German Jew who shaves, like a heathen, wears a short coat instead of the full-length gaberdine, walks about bare-headed and never says his prayers, morning or evening or afternoon. " When I got to know him better, and became very fond of him," the youngster tells, " I didn't care any more that he didn't pray like the rest of us, and didn't wash his hands and bless the Lord before sitting down to a meal. But at first I just couldn't understand how he *lived!* How was it that God *permitted* him to live? How was it that he didn't choke to death on the food he sat down to with unwashed hands? From my own Rebbi I heard that this German Jew was a transmigration: the soul of a Jew in a German body, you understand, and this same soul could afterwards pass into a wolf, or a cow, or even a duck! Yes, even a duck! "

The term " transmigration " is very grown-up for us; not so with the children of old Kasrielevky. Everyone knows what a *gilgul* is. It is equally natural for them to talk of the " good inclination " and the " bad inclination " in man, and to debate a moral issue in terms of the struggle between Ormuzd and Ahriman. Philosophic dualists at the age of nine! One youngster collects on a certain Purim, by way of gifts and earnings for the delivery of *shalachmonus,* the sum of one rouble and forty kopecks. At once he becomes the battlefield between the " good inclination " and the " evil inclination."

Says the good spirit: " What's the sense of keeping all that money, you big fool? Buy yourself lots of things, cakes, frozen apples, cookies — they're wonderful! "

" To which I replied," the lad tells us, " ' What? Give way like that to the call of the belly? Spend all my money in one day? No, not I! '

" ' Good for you! ' says the good spirit to me. ' Look how much nicer it would be if you lent that money to mother. She could use it.'

" ' Clever! ' answers the evil spirit. ' And when would you get it back, eh? Where will she get it from? '

" ' She has such a hard time,' says the good spirit. ' Look, she has to pay for your schooling.'

" ' What's it got to do with your schooling? ' asks the evil spirit. ' You better buy yourself a whistle, or a penknife. Or I'll tell you what — a purse! A purse! '

" ' And what'll you keep in the purse? ' answers the good spirit. ' Your poverty? '

" ' No, buttons! ' says the evil spirit.

" ' What good'll that do you? ' asks the good spirit. ' You listen to me. Take that money and give it to the poor.'

" ' The poor! ' says the evil spirit. ' You're one of the poor yourself.' "

All of the children of old Kasrielevky are religious, and practically all of them are poor. Like Mottel, the son of the cantor, they may not take their poverty to heart; but they are aware of it; it fills the house, it is the continuous undertone in their lives, it lurks in all the conversations of the grown-ups. It is a presence and a personality — *dallus,* poverty — referred to with a sort of affection, born of long familiarity. Poverty and exile are part of the world order. Poverty and exile and the Jews — a threefold cord that shall not be broken!

Because they were poor, and numerous, these children did not get much attention from their parents. That which we call nowadays " understanding " between father and son simply did not exist, not even as a concept. Children were loved, but they were nuisances; childhood was a disorder which time and discipline cured. The discipline was not scientific. It was the random result of pressures. Fathers and mothers do not have cosy conversations with their children — who ever heard of such nonsense! Children must not even listen in on the talk of grown-ups. A box on the ear, a slap, an angry word, a moralistic admonition — of these we hear, not of caresses. That is, as long as the child is well. Nowhere do we find traces of resentment. Children knew themselves to be nuisances and did not expect any other kind of treatment. They would have been alarmed by any attempts at intimacy. The net results of this rough-and-tumble relationship were, as I have said, all out of kilter with our modern concepts of upbringing. Love was taken for granted; the difficulties of life were understood early; little egos were not pampered. And we are tempted to

296

odd reflections. Is it possible that our mania for " understanding " is a self-indulgence and a sentimentality? Is it possible that a child does not want grown-ups to be on a level with him, that he resents this intrusion on his privacy? Does he feel it to be a fake, a subtle form of tyranny which is all the more irritating because it is accompanied by such obvious moral superiority? However this may be, it is certain that young individualities were not crushed, spirits were not broken, love was not destroyed. We do not encounter twisted and stunted children in the world of Sholom Aleichem, either as he describes them or as we find them in other records, including those of our memory. We remember them to have been healthy, active, and imaginative. The authentic magic of childhood was there, too, the innocence, the trust, and the affection.

Still, it is true that the best-beloved children's stories of Sholom Aleichem are predominantly sad. He writes about Methusaleh, the broken-down old horse that belonged to the water-carrier of Kasrielevky; about Rabchek, the homeless dog; about the grandfather-clock which died a painful and lingering death after many generations of service; about a stolen penknife, and about the sickness into which the little thief declined under the pressure of his conscience; of the little boy (he who debated the moral issue a few pages back) who bought himself a flag for the festival of Simchas Torah, only to have it burned on the day of his triumph; about another youngster, an older one this time, probably fourteen or so, already engaged to be married, who passionately wanted to learn to play the fiddle, and got himself slapped by his father and jilted by his bride.

These little ones had to get their laughter — and they

did get it, just like their parents — out of what seems to us to have been a sad world. It was a good training for the life they would have to face; for they were not simply human beings growing up; they were, throughout, Jews, Kasrielevkites, in the making.

CHAPTER XXX

The Cheder

❈

THE *cheder*, the one-room Hebrew school of old Kasrielevky, emerges out of the descriptions copiously furnished by Sholom Aleichem — and for that matter out of the recollection of hundreds of thousands of Jews still living — as a unique juvenile madhouse. Twenty or thirty children are jammed into a space of something like fifteen by fifteen feet. Except in the hot summer days, the windows are kept closed. The ceiling is low, the walls suppurate. The air in the room is indescribably foul. The youngest of the children may be four or five years old, the oldest are in their early teens. From morning till night — the older ones ten or even twelve hours a day — they sit at primitive benches and they study, audibly; for audible study is meritorious, according to the sages of old, and in the *cheder* it is an accepted corollary that the greater the audibility, the higher the degree of merit. Naturally not all of them are studying the same thing. While some — the beginners — are chanting the alphabet, others are translating the week's portion of the Pentateuch into Yiddish, together with the penetrating commentaries of Rashi, perhaps the greatest of the mediæval scholars; older ones — from nine up, that is —

are engaged on Talmudic argumentation, or conning the pages of *The Prepared Table,* a digest of the Jewish ritual code. The Rebbi moves from group to group, chanting now with this one, now with that one. Three languages mingle in chorus: the Hebrew of the Bible and the prayers, the Aramaic of the Talmud, and the Yiddish into which both are translated. The general effect is a pedagogue's nightmare.

It happens frequently that the *cheder* is not even reserved exclusively for Rebbi and pupils. It may be a bedroom, or a living-room, or a kitchen. The Rebbi's wife may be in and out all day, her brood of little ones rolling about on the floor. The pupils breathe in, together with each other's breath and steam, the odour of cooking and baking. It is not unusual for a poorer pupil, whose father pays only two or three roubles a season for his tuition, to be detached for an hour or two from his Bible or Talmud and detailed to rock the baby, or bring in water from the yard, or chop up a few logs of wood. Of course the sons of richer householders — " sons of fathers " — are never forced to submit to such indignities.

The children bring their lunches along; or else, since the townlet is not more than twenty minutes' walk from any outskirt to the centre, mother sends it with a boy, who gets a kopeck for the errand, or maybe a slice of bread. Twice in the day — assuming that the children have said their *Shachris* at home, in the early morning — there are prayers, from which only the tiniest tots are exempt. But even they must say the benediction over a glass of water or over a mouthful of food.

In the midst of this pious pandemonium the Rebbi

will also have his special pupils to instruct. This one is about to be confirmed and has his confirmation address to learn by heart, besides which he must be letter-perfect in certain Biblical readings which he will have to perform in public, out of the Scroll in the Synagogue, in which no vowels are printed. He must also be adept in the laying on of the phylacteries, a vivid and complicated ritual with a high charge of symbolism. Another one may be preparing an address for his wedding day. A third may be the star pupil, who must receive special attention from the Rebbi. A fourth may be unusually stupid, but the son of a rich man; he will need attention of another kind.

The method of tuition is based largely on sheer memorization; the Rebbi reads forth, the children repeat. They repeat again and again until they have it by heart. Wherever possible, auditory memory is supported by visual memory. The Talmud is always printed with the same pagination so that the pupil can always refer a certain text to the same page. Where the popular Vilna edition of the Talmud is used, both the pagination and the position of the words are constant, and virtuosi among students show off with the needle test. A needle is stuck into a certain word on a certain page of the Talmud, and pressed through for ten or fifteen pages; the student being told the word pierced on the first page, he will read off the words pierced on all the other pages. As a rule, however, such prodigies are to be found not in the *cheder*, but in the *yeshivos*, the higher institutions of learning. In any case, this sort of memory work is peculiarly of the ancient East; it goes back to the time before writing was in common use, and records of all kinds,

history, laws, genealogical tables, cosmology, were entrusted to official memorizers and formed part of the
cultural equipment of every superior person.

According to the accepted notion, the *cheder* was a
second home, the Rebbi a person to be loved and honoured on the same level, at least, as one's father. Actually
there is scarcely a Rebbi mentioned in Sholom Aleichem,
or in other writers, who seems to have commanded any
degree of affection. The idea that there was an *art* of
pedagogy in general, or a special approach for the individual child, had hardly begun to dawn on anybody.
The use of the *kantchik* (the cat-o'-three-tails) was
sanctified by age. Teaching without flogging was simply
unthinkable, and Rebbis were known to their pupils,
usually, as " the Murderer " or " the Death-Angel."
Punishments were handed out on general principle, even
when not earned. It was good for a child to be punished,
whether for having a poor memory, or being inatten-
tive, or getting in the Rebbi's way, or simply as a safe-
guard against spiritual pride because he had none of the
usual defects and committed none of the regular sins.

The little hero of *The Penknife* tells us: " I had only
just begun the study of Talmud with Motte, the Death-
Angel. The text was: ' An ox having gored a cow ' —
and the first deduction I learned to make was that if an
ox gored a cow I had to get slapped." And if he was not
slapped because an ox gored a cow, it might be because
the cow had upset a pail of milk, or a goat had snatched
some straw from a barrel and had upset the barrel. The
legal consequences of the possession of an unruly ox or
cow or goat in ancient Palestine were of passionate interest to the older folks in Kasrielevky, and the children
had to acquire the same taste. These youngsters had to

know a vast number of strange things: the laws of the
Red Heifer for the Temple offerings, the exact manner
in which the High Priest sprinkled the blood of the sacrifice on the walls of the Holy of Holies, the laws of civic
damages, the laws of separation between husband and
wife during the wife's menstrual periods. At any rate,
they had to be able to repeat the laws, even when they
had not the remotest notion of their meaning.

From this responsibility there was no flight. The boy
in *The Penknife* goes on to tell: " When I came home
evenings from the *cheder,* with swollen cheeks and ears
red and raw from the twistings they got — all because an
ox had gored a cow — what was I to turn to for comfort
if not my little penknife? " But when his father caught
him wasting his time with such nonsense, he cried out in
genuine despair: " Penknives! Look at him, the baby!
Playthings he wants! The hooligan! Eight years old if a
day, and doesn't know enough to sit down quietly with
a holy book! You empty-headed little loafer! Penknives! "

What would the shades of Pestalozzi and Froebel —
they had been shades for many years when the old-style
cheder was still flourishing in Kasrielevky — have said
could they have witnessed this scene from one of the
children's stories:

Yudel, " the Death-Angel," is the name of the Rebbi
in question. The time is the day before Lag b'Omer, an
unusual type of semi-festival. It commemorates the cessa-
tion of the pestilence which raged among the pupils of
Rabbi Akiba in the days of Bar Kochba's rebellion
against Hadrian. It is, in part, a children's military festival — something altogether incongruous in Jewish life.
On Lag b'Omer the *cheder* boys go out into the fields
and woods to play at soldiers. They carry bows made of

303

barrel staves, or cast-off crinoline ribs, wooden swords, and shields consisting of old dish-covers. By way of uniform they wear paper helmets. First there is a feast in the *cheder*, then the contingent marches off, with weapons and lunches, out of the town. There are no lessons on that day. If the Rebbi is in an exceptionally good humour, he will spoil things by coming along. On this particular pre-Lag b'Omer day Yudel " the Death-Angel " thus apostrophizes his pupils:

" So! Tomorrow is a holiday! You all know it! No *cheder*! The very mention of it makes you forget the sacred books, and sets you dancing like wild nanny-goats. Well, children, let me tell you in advance, if one of you comes back from the woods with his clothes torn, or his face scratched, or any other signs of misbehaviour — well, I don't have to tell you. . . ." Then, probably bethinking himself that this is hardly fair to the young soldiers, or remembering the experience of past years, he changes his tone to one of sweet reasonableness: " Come, boys, what's the good of lecturing you? What's the use of wasting words? You *know* you're going to misbehave, and you *know* I'll have to let you taste the *kantchik*. Don't you think it's better for you to get it over with, take your little lashings the day before, and have it off your minds? " And Yudel " the Death-Angel " looks meditatively at his *kantchik*, which he has drawn forth from the pages of a Talmud, strokes the thongs with loving fingers, and walks over to the whipping bench.

" Well, little Joey, you'll take it first, won't you? " And little Joey, being a quiet, willing victim, gets off with a few mild strokes. " So, there you are, for being a good boy. And now you, Mottele — I like my Joeys and Motteles, they don't let themselves be coaxed: you tell them to lie down across the bench, and down they lie. And next it's little Shmulik, of course, and he's going to be followed by Leibel. . . ." Thus it goes, down the line, for no reason whatsoever except that little boys ought to get whipped from time to time. And then there is only one boy left, Lippe, the oldest, and he already a bridegroom. Him the Rebbi treats with mock deference, calls him up to the thrashing in the traditional Sabbath chant of the cantor calling up a householder to the " Reading of the Law " in the presence of the worshipping congregation.

" Yes, yes, my good friend Reb Lippe — I know, you're already confirmed, and you've got a bride, and a bridegroom's presents, a watch and chain, and a phylactery bag, but we won't let that stand in the way, will we? And we may be sure it'll all heal up before the wedding. There, now, confess that you feel a different man, and a better man, after a thrashing. . . ."

To be sure, this was half in playfulness, except, perhaps, for the oldest boy, who had to let his trousers down like the rest and lay himself across the bench. He trembled much less for the thrashing than with the thought that it might be reported to his bride. For that matter, neither he nor the others took even a serious thrashing very much to heart. It was all in the day's work; a *cheder* was a *cheder*, a Rebbi was there to hand out thrashings, with or without reason. Would God have made *kantchiks* if they were not meant to be used? Besides, they may have felt that however guiltless they were in this or that particular respect, they were, as a group, no blessing to their Rebbi. And if we are inclined to feel sorry for the youngsters, let us save some of our compassion for the Rebbi, for God knows that of all tormented, overworked, conscientious, underpaid public servants, none carried so heavy a burden for so little a reward as he.

In *The Penknife* there is a report of the more vicious, the almost sadistic side of the discipline, the savagery which in the end brought about the decline of the old-fashioned *cheder* and gave rise to the " modern " or " improved " *cheder*.

Little Berele has been caught stealing from the charity box which hangs in nearly every Jewish home, including the poorest — the box into which even professional mendicants drop tiny contributions for the upkeep of the old scholars who have gone to spend their last days on the holy soil of Palestine. Berele is put in the centre of a circle of children, and his *cheder* mates are led by the Rebbi in a chant, consisting of the repetition of " Berele the thief — Berele the thief." Sholom, hero of the story — who has himself just broken the eighth commandment, having been unable to resist the altogether wonderful penknife which he saw in the possession of the German Jew living in the house — is ice-cold with horror and cannot contribute more than a choked whisper to the chorus.

" Louder, you little heathen," the Rebbi yells at him, sensing in his lack of enthusiasm an alarming indifference to the crime of theft. " Louder! "

When this public demonstration is over, every pupil is invited to state what he thinks should be done to a boy who steals kopecks from a charity box. Called on in turn, Sholom looks at little Berele, standing stark naked, pale as death, in the ring of pupils, and faints away.

Of another Rebbi, one Boaz, his pupil tells:

" The method of Boaz could be summed up in a single **word**: the *kantchik*. But why the *kantchik*? Boaz ex-

plained it very simply. A child, he would say, may be likened to a horse. What makes a horse go? The whip! He
is afraid of the whip. And children must be afraid, too.
They must be afraid of God, afraid of their Rebbi, afraid
of their parents, afraid of sin, afraid of an evil thought.
Ah, there isn't a finer thing in the world than a good
whipping! ''

In none of Sholom Aleichem's many children's stories
is there a single instance of a boy who likes his Rebbi. As
for the idolization with which modern youngsters sometimes regard their teachers, the suggestion of it would
have sounded unbalanced to those youngsters. On the
other hand, though children were willing to play tricks
on the Rebbi now and again, we never meet with genuine rancour. A Rebbi was looked upon as a natural calamity; it was in the nature of things that he should
be impatient, unsympathetic, handy with the *kantchik*.
Children learned to accept his cruelties with something
like good humour, and in this they were training themselves for life as Jews. They would have much to put
up with from a surrounding world more impatient, more
unsympathetic, and handier with the whip than even
their Rebbi.

Once, and only once, do we read of a genuine, con-
certed act of revenge, carried out against a Rebbi, whose
nickname, for a change, was not '' Death-Angel,'' but
Mazeppa (in pious and precocious tribute to a murderous anti-Semitic Cossack hetman of the seventeenth century) . This Mazeppa, like every other tyrant, had de-
luded himself into the belief that he meant well by his
charges, that he loved them, that he whipped and
whacked and walloped them entirely for their own good.
And of course he believed similarly that his pupils like-

wise loved him; probably he could not conceive that pupils of his were so sinful that they did not love their
Rebbi. Dislike of a Rebbi was tantamount to *lèse-majesté*
— what am I saying? to *blasphemy*. On the other hand,
it may just have been the utter incapacity of the average
human being to conceive that he may be essentially un-
likable — a limitation touchingly shared by a divinity
whose ways are incomprehensible. At any rate, it did not
occur to Mazeppa that the gifts his pupils brought him
on Channukah and Purim and Lag b'Omer were not
spontaneous expressions of affection; and he could not
believe that when, in a burst of generosity, he decided to
become young again and accompany his pupils into the
woods for the festival, it would be greeted with anything
but incredulous gratitude.

Berel Yossel, whose father kept a wine-shop (we know
what a " wine-shop " was in a Kasrielevky townlet, both
from our knowledge of the drinking habits of Kasrielevkites, and from our recollection of the moonshine activities of Berel the lame, of Teplik) , Berel Yossel brought
along for the Lag b'Omer feast two bottles of wine freely
and willingly contributed by his father, and a bottle of
whisky, also contributed by his father, but not so freely,
since he was unconscious of the contribution. As Berel
Yossel explained to his companions, he had " swiped "
it (Kasrielevkite youngsters too had their euphemisms
for unpleasant words) from the cellar. And it was a grand
feast, marred only by Mazeppa's unseasonable graciousness. But this very graciousness turned out to be his un-
doing. For Mazeppa tasted of the wine, and then of the
whisky, and then of the wine, and again of the whisky;
and his soul expanded, his heart warmed, his childhood
memories broke through the crust of the years, and after

the feast he invited himself to the traditional excursion into the woods: an outrageous breach of the unwritten constitution, for on that one day the children had the right to throw off their Rebbi's jurisdiction.

Ginger Ellie, the oldest lad in the *cheder*, past thirteen and already betrothed, had a score to settle with Mazeppa; not because he had been less considerately treated than the others, but because he had more spirit. Others of his age, laid across the bench with their trousers down, to have the fear of God driven in at one end because they had denied it voluntary entrance at the other, had swallowed the humiliation and forgotten it. Not so Ginger Ellie, who probably grew up to participate in the first " expropriation " of Kasrielevky. Ginger Ellie had a plan.

When the gay company reached the woods Mazeppa, half drunk, lay down to snatch a nap. Then Ginger Ellie unwound the Rebbi's belt, tied him to a tree, and suddenly yelled into his ear, in a voice that was not human: " Rebbi! Rebbi! Help! Murder! Thieves! Bandits! Rebbi! " — and with that he and his companions, who were more terrified than if they had really been attacked by a band of the original Mazeppa's slaughterers, fled to the city to give the " alarm."

Six weeks Mazeppa lay sick in bed with the fright of his experience, and during those six weeks the revenge turned sour in the stomachs of his victims. When Mazeppa returned to his duties he was no longer the same man — and his pupils were no longer the same boys. No more *kantchik*. No more " Berele, down with your little trousers, a whipping is a great remedy for wickedness." Quiet, broken, gentle, Mazeppa only asked every now and again for a detailed description of what had happened on that afternoon, and with every repetition he

309

would shake his head, and a queer smile would appear on his lips. But, for all the change in the spirit of Mazeppa, the youngsters regretted everything! They could not accustom themselves to this unnatural softness. If only he would be the old Mazeppa again! If only he would reach for his *kantchik*, or for a pupil's tender ear, if only he would say a harsh word! This was not a Rebbi at all!

They had too much conscience, those youngsters; they began too early in life to see too well the other man's case. It is from the same story that I quote a typical conversation between children whose ages range from eight to thirteen. It has all the overtones of irony which belong to sophisticated adults, and through it sound the oddest echoes of esoteric learning.

Berel, having " swiped " the bottle of whisky from his father's store, offers it triumphantly to his companions. One of them, a simpleton, can't get over it.

" ' Swiped '? " he asks. " ' Swiped '? You mean *stole!* "

" Why, you sage in Israel," says Berel, grinning, " and suppose we say *stole?* "

" But it's written in the eighth commandment: ' Thou shalt not steal '! "

" Idiot! This is for a festival banquet."

" Oh, I see. You mean that for a festival banquet it's permitted? It's a good deed? "

" Of course! " Berel turns to the others in despair. " What do you think of this ignoramus! "

But the young scholar is not satisfied. He must have chapter and verse.

" What book is it in? Who are the rabbis who hold this view? "

" It's in the Book of Bimbom."

" What Tractate? "

" The Tractate on green cheese. And the view is supported by Rabbi Veverik of Veveronko, who had it from his master, Rabbi Ocherik of Pocherik."

Speaking of the superficial relations between parents and children, we asked ourselves how it was that the latter suffered no ill effects from the wholly unscientific attitude of the older to the younger generation. The question recurs in startling form in connection with the *cheder*. How was it that this institution, continuing generation after generation, did not leave incurable stigmata on the minds of the children? How is it that they did not become idiots, but on the contrary maintained an astonishingly high level of intelligence and, what is more, actually learned what they were taught?

Granting that the accounts are biased, that not all Rebbis were " Death-Angels " and not all *cheders* Black Holes of Calcutta, the general picture leaves us appalled, and by any standard acceptable to moderns the system should have destroyed the mind and body of the Jewish people in the course of fifty or sixty years.

We can only conclude that we moderns are prone to exaggerate the sensitivity of the young, and to underestimate the resilience of the human animal at all ages. To borrow an analogy from quite another field: we hear of primitive peoples among whom the women make almost as little fuss about giving birth to a child as we do about begetting one. The expectant mother retires to the shadow of a bush, gives birth, picks up the new-comer, and goes about her regular business. The original constitution of these women, their equipment at birth, that is, differs in no wise from those of our own — so much at least we learn (with certain allowances) from the the-

311

ory of the non-transmissibility of acquired characteristics. It may even be that the physical training through
which these women pass does not produce a hardihood
commensurate with the difference in reaction to this test.
It cannot be doubted that most of the capacity to endure
derives from a simple acceptance of the situation; the
readiness to endure is half the trick of enduring, and
those who have not known the better do not lose half
their strength whimpering over the worse.

Samuel Butler, who had an enlightened view on the
education of children, and remembered with detesta-
tion the brutalities and repressions visited upon his childhood contemporaries, wrote, nevertheless: " The want
of fresh air does not seem much to affect the happiness of
children in a London alley: the greater part of them sing
and play as though they were on a moor in Scotland. So
the absence of a genial mental atmosphere is not commonly recognized by children who have never known it.
Young people have a marvellous faculty of either dying
or adapting themselves to circumstances. Even if they
are unhappy — very unhappy — it is astonishing how
easily they can be prevented from finding it out, or at
any rate from attributing it to any other cause than their
own sinfulness."

The inherited power of resistance of Kasrielevky's
children was neither superior nor inferior to that of modern children. But because they took for granted what
they had to face in the way of training, they were im-
mune from most of the negative effects. Thirty children
bawling five or six different choruses simultaneously in
a crowded room managed to keep their minds on their
lessons. They simply had the trick of ignoring irrelevant
noises. The thrashings of the Rebbi did not hurt very

much, largely because there was not, usually, the sense of outrage. It is astonishing what physical pain a child can endure without a whimper if it is " all in fun " or if the child has not been encouraged to whimper. The long hours in the *cheder* did not cripple the intelligence largely because there was no chafing against them — at any rate, not more than, with easier standards, other children experience because of higher expectations. It is more a question of psychological adjustment than of original physical or mental equipment. It is clear that too little attention was paid in the *cheder* to pedagogy, and too much to the mechanical acquisition of information (whether the information was useful or not is irrelevant in this connection) ; but it is also possible that we pay too much attention to pedagogy and too little to the acquisition of information. Those had much to teach and did not know how; we know how to teach and do not know what.

There are other reasons for the astonishingly good results of the *cheder*. One of them was the congruity of outlook between children and adults in the matter of the material of study. Boys were learning in *cheder* that which their fathers knew and cherished. They were treated as children but they were challenged as adults. You did not have, on the father's part, an attitude compounded of indulgence, amusement, unjustified superiority, and uncomfortable ignorance with regard to the substance of the *cheder* curriculum. Father *never* said, or felt: " Oh, well, that's what you learn in school; when you grow up you'll discover life is different." Or, on the other hand: " Of course you know that particular passage, that quotation. You're still at school, you're in the midst of your studies. When you've been out of school as

313

long as I have, when you've had more important things
to occupy your mind, you'll forget, too." It was a shame-
ful thing to have forgotten what you had learned in *cheder*, and there was nothing in adult life more important
than the things children were learning. If the youngsters
did not like *cheder*, at least they saw their fathers, at
home, taking time out from the business of earning a
living to dip into a page of Talmud, or at least to re-
hearse the week's lesson from the Pentateuch. The atmosphere of adult life was impregnated with a universal
respect for book-knowledge. A youngster was really dis-
tressed when his father said: " Do you want to grow up
an ignoramus, like so-and-so? " How many of us adults
today are humiliated because we cannot do a quadratic
equation, like any schoolboy of thirteen or fourteen, or
because we cannot remember the central dates in history?

Something else we must take into account if we are to
understand how the children of old Kasrielevky actually
flourished in a world which we in retrospect contem-
plate with bewildered horror. Much that the Rebbi
thumped or whipped into the minds of his little charges
was, or seems to us in our setting, quite meaningless:
the debates of scholars dead two thousand years, the
complicated legal code of a social and economic world
which we cannot reconstruct, the details of a ritual which
conveys nothing to our free minds. But embedded in
this material were stories and legends of extraordinary
beauty. The Talmud swarms with fascinating characters, who did and said extraordinary things. There are
martyrs, warriors, and saints; there are penetrating
aphorisms, illuminating anecdotes, stories of heroism,
examples of sweet, unaffected humility, legends and par-

ables which leave ineradicable traces on the young mind. It is as wrong to judge the Talmud solely by its dry-as-dust legalism as to judge the Bible by its genealogical tables and ritualistic instructions.

It is not easy to get into the intellectual and spiritual moods of the children of old Kasrielevky. All of us are snobs in the sense that we are inclined to regard as unnatural other forms of self-expression than our own, just as we cannot help feeling that a person who lisps does not have the same sincerity behind his words as we do, or that the stilted English of Jane Austen's heroines was evidence of shallower emotions than ours.

The young boys of Kasrielevky dreamed as passionately as any other young boys; they fell in love, and they suffered in love; and we must not be misled by what strikes us as the impossible pedantry of their utterances.

A certain boy called Mottele, still in his teens, loved a certain little girl called Esther, the daughter of his former Rebbi. When he sent her a proposal, it was in the form of a playful scholarly commentary on the book of Esther.

" And it came to pass," he wrote, " that a Jew by the name of Mordecai, who is Mottele, dwelt in the capital city of the Kingdom of Ahasuerus, called Shushan, which is none other than our own city . . . and the maiden was fair and beautiful, and she found favour in the eyes of Mordecai. But Mordecai instructed Esther to reveal no word thereof to any man. . . ." And what shall we say of a boy of ten who applies to his little playmate, in all innocence and delight, verses from the Song of Songs: " Come, my beloved, let us go forth into the field, let us lodge in the vineyards, let us see if the vine flourish, whether the tender grape appear and the pomegranates bud forth. . . ." And when the little girl says that she wishes she were his sister, there spring to his lips the words: " Would that thou wert as my brother. . . ." Or " My beloved is mine and I am my beloved's." When he has offended her and she will not speak to him, he thinks of the verses: " Let me see thy countenance, let me hear thy voice. For sweet is thy voice, and thy countenance is comely."

No, this is not pedantry or insincerity. It is as direct, as immediate to the emotions, as the inarticulateness which we have been taught to associate with sincerity. The children of Kasrielevky acquired the equipment of adults at an earlier age than we; but the peculiar irrecoverable beauty of childhood was not denied them; and it may be that because they learned to reconcile it at a very early age with the bitterness of manhood, they managed to retain its flavour into later years than we.

CHAPTER XXXI

Aurora Americana

❈

IF this pilgrimage of ours, recorded in words, had used music as its medium instead, we should have got something like Tchaikovsky's *1812*. Very faintly, at the beginning of the record, there would have crept in the note of a strange Western world, the beginning of a melody utterly alien to the mournful reflectiveness of Chassidic chants: namely, the cheerful, festive trumpet-call of *The Star-Spangled Banner*. Before the reversal of Russia's liberal policy in 1881, only a trickle of humanity, comparatively speaking, flowed from Kasrielevky to Columbia. *Anacreon in Heaven,* snatched (no doubt to his bibulous astonishment) from the banqueting table to the solemn destiny of a national anthem, is barely heard behind the doleful strings and woodwinds of Stempenyu's orchestra. Then, with the May Laws and the pogroms, the American theme takes a sudden leap into the middle ground. When Sholom Aleichem was a little boy, dreaming of Chmelnitzky's buried treasure, one talked little of America, even in the Pale. When he was a lad in student's uniform, the first fever of the stampede was in the air. As the years passed, and pogroms and expulsions succeeded one another in Russia, while in America there developed an almost insatiable hunger for human material to fill empty spaces and develop potential treasures, the American melody moved ever more strongly into the foreground. By the time Sholom Aleichem was an elderly man, himself a bubble in the turbulent westward torrent, America dominated the mind of Kasrielevky. American words became familiar in the ears of Kasrielevkites; American freedom and American opportunity dominated their hopes. For we must remember that between the failure of the 1904 revolution and the opening of the First World War, Russian tyranny and reaction took on an illusive but disheartening appearance of stability. To all but a handful of brilliant and fanatical rebels it looked as though the Romanovs were entrenched for another three hundred years. Russia, then, was hopeless; the gates of America were open. The murmur just audible at the opening of the symphony now thundered from the brasses and drums.

Writing in prose instead of in music, I have had to compartmentalize my material; and I chose to leave the great migration to the end because in another sense, too, it belongs to the end of Sholom Aleichem's world, and was one of its solvents. There were others, as we have seen; there was a purely natural and worldly assimilation within Russia; and there was a conscious and directed revolutionary program. America alone, though it became the home of nearly two million Russian Jews in the course of nearly thirty-five years of immigration, nowhere near exhausted the original source. For when the First World War broke out, there were still some six million Jews in Czarist Russia. Migration, massive though it was, took away little more than the natural increase, if that.

Sholom Aleichem's records cover not only the parting in Russia, but the first stages of the resettlement in America. Mottel the cantor's son (he was the irrepressible little *Kasriel* who, we remember, had such a grand time when his father was dying and the house was being dismantled for the purchase of food) migrated with his older brother Ellie and the rest of the family. We meet them on the streets of New York; we have a full report, in the inimitable Sholom Aleichem style, of their early struggles. We encounter other Kasrielevkites or Kozodoievkites. And very pathetic they look to us in the promising pandemonium of the West. But this is not Sholom Aleichem's world and is not part of our pilgrimage. I add some observations only as an envoi; also because the pain of the readjustment had its repercussions in the heart of Kasrielevky.

Most of the accounts of immigrants, and of their integration with American life, have been written by such as have been in America a long time and have largely forgotten the spiritual struggles of the transition. There is little in the books about the trauma of the uprooting, and the general impression is that of human beings in weird, cruel, impossible foreign countries, whose single, exclusive impulse was to escape to the freedom of the West, and whose single, exclusive emotion was that of relief when they set foot on the blessed soil of their future.

It was not so simple.

People with no hope show a queer reluctance to die; men whose childhood was unhappy recall it, across the mist of the years, as something invested with magic. The Prisoner of Chillon left his dungeon willingly, we are sure, but " with a sigh." What is this? Sentimentality? Perversity? No; we shall, I think, see that it is something deeper, and of the very stuff of life. Our friend Tevyeh the dairyman, grown old, widowed, bereft of his children, living in a Russia which is doing its utmost to make itself intolerable to its Jewish subjects, prepares to pull up stakes and migrate to the Holy Land, for which, as for so many other Jews, there has always been a longing in his heart. He has been dreaming since his childhood of the streets of Jerusalem, sanctified by the memory of Isaiah and Jeremiah, of the grave of Mother Rachel, and of the ruined wall of Solomon's Temple. And as he tells Sholom Aleichem of his resolve, and of the dispositions he is taking, tears well into his eyes at the thought of leaving Russia.

He tells him first how Goldie, his wife, Goldie, the simple, the railing, warm-hearted, much-suffering mother, died, in that cottage emptied of all the youngsters. " Tevyeh," she said, weeping, " what have I to live for, without child or chick? They're gone, all of them. And even a cow, God forgive me, weeps when you take away her calf." But Tevyeh, never at a loss for words from Holy Script, answers: " Come, come, Goldie dear. God in heaven is our Father. He is a great God, and a good God, and a wise God, though, to be sure, He has a way of playing tricks on us that make our hair stand on end." " Tevyeh," says Goldie, in a weak voice, " Tevyeh, I'm dying. Who'll cook supper for you? " " Goldie! " cries Tevyeh, frantically. " You've been a good and faithful wife for me all these years. You're not going to let me down in my old age, are you? " But let him down

320

she did, and his last bond with the village by the forest was snapped. Whereupon he sets about preparing for his last journey but one. There are others going to Palestine: young people whose ears are closed to the siren call of America. For them the only hope is the Jewish homeland to be. *They* are going to live there, to lay the foundations; Tevyeh is going to die there. And still the parting from stepmother Russia is a hard one.

When it came to the selling of his pitiful household goods, every little article took with it a piece of his heart. Worst of all was the farewell to his ancient nag. " I sold him to a water-carrier," he says, " because the draymen are a tough lot. When I showed them my horse they laughed. ' Reb Tevyeh,' they asked, ' is that a horse? ' ' What else? ' I answered; ' maybe you think it's a sideboard.' ' That isn't a horse, and it isn't a sideboard,' they tell me. ' It's one of the thirty-six hidden saints who save the world by starving in caves.' That's the kind of answer I got from them. So I sold him to a water-carrier. And believe me, when I'd shaken hands on the bargain, the old nag turns his sorrowful face round toward me, as much as to say: ' Is this my portion, Tevyeh? Is this my reward for the years of faithful service? ' God help me, I was ashamed to meet his eyes! Reb Sholom Aleichem! You're laughing at me, aren't you, because my heart is sore for my old horse? Man! Don't you think my heart is sore for everything I'm leaving behind? Don't you think I'll be longing for the village, and for the house, and for the peasants, and even for Ephraim the marriage broker, may his bones be broken! "

Very odd indeed this is! Very few, if any, were the happy memories that Tevyeh had to carry away with him from Anatevka. One daughter lost to the revolu-

tion — perhaps, like Masha Bashkevich, in *The Storm,*
she had killed herself in a Russian prison; another married to a gentile, and divided from him for ever; a third
the wife of a wretched swindler; a fourth a suicide because of a hopeless love-affair. And all around him Russian Jewry in the grip of the Romanov persecutions.
What did this mournfulness at the parting refer to? It
referred to the years, unhappy as they were, that he had
invested in the dolorous past. It was his life that he was
leaving behind, and life is precious and beautiful in and
for itself. The years make us what we are; and whatever
we are, we love ourselves; therefore, in retrospect, we
love the years which were the artificers, kind or cruel,
of our being.

Hundreds of thousands of Jews streamed westward
out of Russia toward America, leaving behind them
some fragment, great or small, of their lives, leaving behind them the streets and alleys of their childhood, the
memory of the *cheder,* the Sabbaths and festivals, the
" Eternal Home," the resting-place of the bones of their
forefathers. They were going to a new land which shone
from afar with the radiance of freedom and opportunity,
but it was a land which, they forefelt, would not understand them.

And did America understand them? Hardly. The typical attitude toward the immigrant was and is, at its best,
generous but devoid of insight: it is philanthropic and
not charitable. The immigrant is looked upon — I am
speaking of the attitude at its best — as welcome human material, but it must be *raw* material. An immigrant is supposed, as it were, to come out of nowhere, as
far as his future is concerned. The associations he brings
with him, the good and the bad alike, must be dis-

carded as soon as he lands, or as soon after as possible. Ideally he should be a sort of faceless and malleable accretion to the population, a spermatozoon flung up by the sea for America's increase. And yet many immigrants brought with them deep and powerful cultures, the product of centuries. They were not, they could not become, blank human forms with nothing more than potentialities; they were filled with realized values, the discarding of which was difficult and painful and — in the last analysis — detrimental to America. They did not come only to take; they had something besides willing arms and latent spiritual development to give. They were not wholly beggars; and they were not quaint characters needing to be reformed, and re-educated, in the human sense, from their beginnings. And the foreknowledge that all their sanctities would, in the land of their new destiny, be looked upon at best as amusing oddities, best forgotten in the least possible time, touched their eagerness and gratitude with sadness and foreboding.

The physical transit itself was an ordeal. In those days of the great migration American and English shipping companies made vast fortunes out of the importing of future American citizens. The accommodations for the poor were vile. The reception at Castle Garden and Ellis Island, which could, with little effort and no expense, have been gracious and radiant, as was fitting for the first lesson in the spirit of America, was, instead, grim and impersonal. That was a pity. And there were also unavoidable tragedies — separations of parents from children, breaking up of families, because of sickness, chiefly of the eyes. Behind it all, in the mind of the immigrants, was the recollection of the world they had known, disintegrating, fading away; and everything that had once been precious in the midst of suffering becoming less than a memory.

The habit which immigrants have of holding together in groups we commonly attribute to their helplessness, their desire to be among those who speak their language and share their habits. This is only partly true. Deep in the common consciousness of immigrants there is a feeling of piety for old values. It is not only for convenience and rest that they come together; it is also for the observance of a kind of ritual. The Kasrielevkites created many Kasrielevkys in America, large ones and small ones, all of them doomed of course to extinction as new generations came up without the recollection of the original Kasrielevkys: synagogues, meeting halls, newspapers, cafés, Chassidic circles (we encountered one of them a few chapters back), cemeteries, ceremonials, echoes of the life that was gone. They re-created also their old rivalries and snobberies. They did it in part automatically, and in part because they felt deeply that the tradition of so many centuries was not a thing to be tossed away lightly.

It is not all gone, by any means. The last American census reveals that one and three quarter million American Jews still give their mother tongue as Yiddish. There are influential Yiddish newspapers, theatres, organizations of all kinds. But beyond this there has passed into the "assimilated" section of American Jewry, and through it into American life generally, a number of social impulses originating in Kasrielevky. But Kasrielevky, the centre of Sholom Aleichem's world, is not to be equated with all of European or even Russian Jewry as transplanted to America. It is impossible now to dis-

324

entangle the various threads that have gone into the American pattern; but quite certainly some of the strongest, no longer identifiable in relation to their origin, were spun by the Tevyehs and Goldies and Reb Yozifels in ancient Yiddish settlements not far from the banks of Grandfather Dnieper. Identifiable, and affirmative among the world's movements, are the labour organizations of the American Jews, Yiddish- or English-speaking, their social-welfare agencies, their religious institutions, their powerful contribution toward the rebuilding of a Jewish homeland in Palestine. But these are not part of our pilgrimage, which has now come to an end.

CHAPTER XXXII

Death in Exile

❀

F OR Sholom Aleichem the pilgrimage was permanently broken off on Saturday, May 13, 1916. The way
station where he died was an apartment house at 968
Kelly Street, the Bronx, and the time was the middle of
the First World War.

Those were dark, bitter years to die in, for a Jew sen-
sitive to the fate of his people. The Yiddish-speaking
world of Europe was the battlefield in the vast war of
movement between Russia and Germany. Nicholas I
was still on the throne — what hopes could the Jews repose on a Russian victory? But Germany was the cradle
of modern anti-Semitism. The greatest Jewish historian
of our time has pointed repeatedly to this fact. His *History of the Jews of Poland and Russia,* published thirty
years ago, made the dilemma clear even before the First
World War began. What hope, then, was there for the
Jews in a German victory? No wonder Sholom Aleichem
himself said, in his *New Arabian Nights* — the record
of the Jewish agony in the First World War: " Of course
this is a Jewish war — its purpose is the annihilation of
the Jewish people." The spirit of the time, and his own
share in the flight from Europe, helped undermine the

resistance which he had put up for nearly a decade against tuberculosis and diabetes; and the death of a son came to him as a solemn forewarning of his own impending departure.

He did not foresee that worse was to follow for the Jews; the Polish pogroms and the mass slaughters organized under the Ukrainian hetman Petlura (one cannot speak of them simply as pogroms) were yet to come. And in the not too remote future, after a breathing-spell in Poland and a liberation in Russia, there was to follow the total eclipse of Hitler's advance over the remnants of the Yiddish world. But what he lived to witness was bad enough — and he closed his eyes to it, defeated at last.

There he lay, used up and burned out, in the little apartment in the Bronx. Three bearded old Jews of Pereyeslav, the townlet of his birth, had performed the last rites for him, washed his body, wrapped it in cerements, swathed him in his praying-shawl. For thirty-six hours — two nights and a day — a permanent guard of Yiddish writers stood over him, while an interminable line of mourners wound through the adjoining streets to take a last look at the tired, clever, puckish face, relaxed in death. They tiptoed in, stood for a few moments staring down at the waxen features under the candlelight, and passed on. Fifteen thousand of them managed to get a last glimpse of Sholom Aleichem in the flesh, and thousands more came too late on the morning of Monday. A hundred and fifty thousand lined the streets at the stopping-places of the cortege, at the Ohav Tzedek synagogue at One Hundred and Sixteenth Street and Fifth Avenue, at the Jewish community centre at Second Avenue and Twenty-first Street, at the offices of the Hebrew Immigrant Aid Society, and at the building of the Educational Alliance on East Broadway.

In a sense it might be said that his pilgrimage was not broken off — it had come to its end. Those who believe that the tempo of a man's work is dictated unconsciously by the number of years placed at his disposal, may add Sholom Aleichem to the evidence. It was in 1908, the forty-ninth year of his life, that he was first struck down by sickness. But that same year was marked, all over the Jewish world, by an extraordinary celebration of Sholom Aleichem's completion of a quarter of a century of literary activity. It was a demonstration which probably has not its like in the exilic history of Jewry. In hundreds of towns in Russia, Poland, England, the Americas, South Africa — wherever Yiddish was read — in the Kasrielevkys of the Pale, Kasrielevky on the Hudson, Kasrielevky on the Pampas, Kasrielevky in the Transvaal, there were meetings at which his works were read forth, and the *Kasriels* in exile laughed with Sholom Aleichem and at themselves, wept with him and over themselves. He had by then achieved a place in the folk which was final and unchangeable. He wrote much that was great in his last eight years; when he died he was engaged on great work, and had great works in mind. They would have added to the delight of his readers, not to his name.

In another sense, too, he had completed his pilgrimage. He had known all the vicissitudes of a Jew, he had tasted all the experiences which were peculiar to the history of his people. He had been a *cheder* boy in old Kasrielevky, and a Russian Gymnasium student; he had passed from the mediæval to the modern; he had been a

tutor, a Crown Rabbi, a businessman; he had dealt in
sugar, had gambled on the Yehupetz stock exchange, had
turned insurance agent; he had been very rich, and very
poor. He had been a Mæcenas of literature, and he had
known what it was to need a Mæcenas and not to find
one. He had published lavishly the works of lesser writers, and had been unable to find publishers for his own.
He had been adored and ignored. He had had his plays
turned down by producers, he had been bullied by New
York newspaper editors who told him they knew better
than he what the public wanted. And always he had written. He wrote in health and sickness; he wrote on trains,
in droshkies, on the kitchen table, at his business desk,
in the midst of ledgers, balance sheets and I O U's. He
wrote even on his deathbed. He was driven by an intolerable creative strength. The excessive imagination, the
gifts of observation and of memory, and the irresistible
impulse to mimicry which had made him a portent in
his *cheder* days stayed with him to the end. But never
was he the less a man, living with his fellow men, because he was the writer; and as a man he had lived
through all that his people had suffered.

It is not a formality to speak of the thousands who
poured out into the streets of New York on that day as
" mourners." It was not formality that caused hundreds
of unions, brotherhoods, societies, Zionist clubs, benevolent orders, and Socialist organizations to call hasty
meetings on the Sunday of May 14, and to send their
representatives to the cemetery on the morning of the
15th. It was not formality that brought delegations to
New York from every town in America within overnight
distance. Nor was it Sholom Aleichem himself that they

mourned. It was a part of their life which had been torn
away from them. They were attending the rehearsal of
their own obsequies, saying the *Kaddish* in advance over
their way of life, for they knew that none would say it
afterwards. Brighter days might indeed come for the
Jewish people, but the savor of their world would not
be tasted by their children, and they would be a mystery
to their own posterity.

This " they " felt. And who were " they "? None other
than the people he had written of. Tevyeh himself left
his milk-cart at the corner of Intervale Avenue, and
came with Goldie to say farewell to Sholom Aleichem.
Menachem Mendel the *schlimihl* came with them. Not
far off was Sholom Ber of Teplik, no longer the *nogid,*
but a rag-pedlar; and behind him limped along Berel
the Lame, who had gone to Heissin in his company on a
memorable day. Mottel the cantor's son, and Ellie the
tailor, and Leizer Wolf the butcher, and old Reb Yozifel, the pietists and the revolutionaries, the skullcaps
and the bowler hats — they filed through the living-
room where he lay in state, they darkened the streets of
the lower East Side, they waited for him at the cemetery.
They heard the singing of the requiem — " God, full of
mercy " — and it was as though a people were being con-
signed to the grave. Why, then, should they not mourn?
Who was to speak for them now that Sholom Aleichem
was dead, and who was to remember them if he was
forgotten?

Sholom Aleichem lies buried in Mount Nebo Cemetery in Cypress Hills, Brooklyn. He had asked that his
body be transferred, after the war, to the cemetery of his
beloved Yehupetz; but this could not be done, and it is

330

better so. In other respects the provisions of his testament were carried out. His grave is simple, and only his epitaph distinguishes it from those that surround it. He had said: " Let me be buried among the poor, that their graves may shine on mine, and mine on theirs."

A NOTE ABOUT THE AUTHOR

MAURICE SAMUEL *was born in Rumania in 1895 and was educated in England. He came to the United States in 1914. He served from 1917 to 1919 in the American army in France. Immediately after the war he served as interpreter at the Peace Conference and with the Reparations Commissions in Berlin and Vienna, returning to America in 1921. He traveled extensively in this country and abroad, partly as lecturer and partly to acquire information. Mr. Samuel died in 1972.*

His major interest for nearly fifty years was the position of the Jewish people in the Western world; of his twenty books, fifteen are concerned with the exposition of Jewish values or examinations of the relations between the Jewish and Christian worlds. He occupied himself particularly with the problem of anti-Semitism as a feature of Christian civilization, and with its effects on Christendom and Jewry.

28

Due 14 Days From Latest Date

JAN 1 6 1987			
FEB 3 1987			
MAR 2 7 1987			
APR 2 5 1987			
JUN 1 1 1987			
AUG 2 2 1987			
SEP 1 9 1987	WITHDRAWN		